WITHDRAWN
UTSA LIBRARIES

Tierra y Libertad

CITIZENSHIP AND MIGRATION IN THE AMERICAS
General Editor: Ediberto Román

Tierra y Libertad: Land, Liberty, and Latino Housing
Steven W. Bender

Tierra y Libertad

Land, Liberty, and Latino Housing

Steven W. Bender

NEW YORK UNIVERSITY PRESS
New York and London

NEW YORK UNIVERSITY PRESS
New York and London
www.nyupress.org

© 2010 by New York University
All rights reserved

Library of Congress Cataloging-in-Publication Data
Bender, Steven.
Tierra y libertad : land, liberty, and Latino housing / Steven W. Bender.
p. cm. — (Citizenship and migration in the americas)
Includes bibliographical references and index.
ISBN-13: 978-0-8147-9125-7 (alk. paper)
ISBN-10: 0-8147-9125-5 (alk. paper)
ISBN-13: 978-0-8147-8722-9 (ebk.)
ISBN-10: 0-8147-8722-3 (ebk.)
1. Hispanic Americans—Housing. 2. American Dream.
3. Immigrants—United States. I. Title.
HD7288.72.U5B46   2010
363.5'9868073—dc22   2010011989

New York University Press books are printed on acid-free paper,
and their binding materials are chosen for strength and durability.
We strive to use environmentally responsible suppliers and materials
to the greatest extent possible in publishing our books.

Manufactured in the United States of America
10 9 8 7 6 5 4 3 2 1

Library
University of Texas
at San Antonio

To my son, Dominic Luis, and my niece, Tren, hoping someday they will each own a house "clean as paper before the poem."*

*Sandra Cisneros, *The House on Mango Street* (New York: Vintage Books, 1984), 108

Contents

Acknowledgments   ix

Introduction   1

PART I   Loss   11

1   Loss and Lettuce: The César Chávez Legacy   13
2   Southwest Ranchos: Land Grants and Land Loss   17
3   Fields of Dreams: Farm Worker Housing   29
4   Loss in the Tortilla Flats   37
5   Lenders and Loss: The Destructive Legacy of Subprime Mortgages in Latino/a Communities   45

PART II   Exclusion   57

6   Exclusion of Undocumented Immigrants   59
7   Exclusion by Public Law: Zoning Laws   73
8   Exclusion by Private Law: Restrictive Covenants   85

PART III   Geographic Examples of Loss and Exclusion   95

9   Born in East L.A.: The Legacy of Loss and Exclusion in Southern California   97
10   Little Havana   107
11   Spanish Harlem   113

PART IV Reclamation and Reform	119
12 Tierra y Libertad: Reclaiming Individual and Collective Space	121
13 Policy Considerations in Formulating Housing Reform	141
14 Lowering the Cost of Housing and Credit	155
15 Equity for Latino/as and the Poor	175
Conclusion	189
Notes	193
Index	239
About the Author	243

Acknowledgments

I am indebted to those who read drafts of my manuscript or contributed ideas through conversations that helped shape it, especially Keith Aoki, Joaquin Avila, Gil Carrasco, Jo Carrillo, Richard Delgado, Mechele Dickerson, Ernesto Hernandez, Berta Esperanza Hernandez-Truyol, Kevin Johnson, Guadalupe Luna, Pedro Malavet, George Martinez, Michael Olivas, Lupe Salinas, Randy Shaw, and Jean Stefancic. The project was further enhanced by presentations to law faculties at the University of Oregon and Seattle University, and to law students at the University of Washington.

My research assistants who helped bring this project to fruition include Tracy Frazier, Will Macke, Abigail Molina, Jesus Palomares, Matt Snell, Hsiu-Ming Tom, and especially Daniel Prince. Stefanie Herrington, former editor of the *Oregon Law Review*, contributed her editorial expertise.

At the University of Oregon School of Law, secretary Debby Warren and research librarian Angus Nesbit performed their usual tireless work. Dean Margie Paris supported this project with a summer research award.

It was my pleasure to work again with the editors at New York University Press, particularly Deborah Gershenowitz and Despina Papazoglou Gimbel.

Finally I owe much to my wife, Ana, for adding color to the walls of our house and my heart.

Introduction

> We have come to a clear realization of the fact that true individual freedom cannot exist without economic security and independence.... We have accepted, so to speak, a second Bill of Rights under which a new basis of security and prosperity can be established for all—regardless of station, race, or creed. Among these are ... the right of every family to a decent home.
> —Franklin Delano Roosevelt, 1944 State of the Union Address

> Housing is never merely shelter. However inadequate and temporary, one's shelter becomes the ground floor for meeting basic needs, a foundation for job search and education, and a piece of one's identity—a "home" of sorts. For those who have always been adequately housed and take it for granted, a full appreciation for the importance of adequate, decent and affordable housing can probably only be gained by experiencing its loss.
> —Tim Iglesias, "Housing Impact Assessments: Opening New Doors for State Housing Regulation While Localism Persists," *Oregon Law Review* 82 (2003): 433, 442

¡Tierra y Libertad!—land and liberty—was the slogan of the Mexican Revolution of the early 1900s. With charismatic revolutionaries such as Emiliano Zapata at the helm, that epic struggle sought to reclaim vast agricultural lands in Mexico held by the government and elites and disburse them for individual and collective agrarian uses. Although hundreds of thousands of landless peasants gained the liberty of land ownership, reform was incomplete. Hunger for land continues in Mexico and Latin America today, under the banner carried most prominently by the Zapatista movement in the southernmost Mexican state of Chiapas.

In the United States, Latino/as' loss of land and their hopes for reform have taken the different path detailed in this book. Latino/as throughout the

Americas share a deeply rooted passion for land and home ownership. The fervor of efforts in the U.S. Southwest to reclaim property once subject to community-based land grants from the Spanish and Mexican governments, as well as other recurring protests and occupations of disputed lands by Latino/as, evidence the cultural, even spiritual, connection between Latino/as and land, whether owned by individuals or collectively.[1] Like most cultures and groups, particularly those from backgrounds of scarcity, Latino/as cherish the land and aspire to home ownership, and they are passionate in their pursuit of these ideals.

Given Latino/a culture's grounding in the love of family, the core of the Latino/a affinity for land is the family home. Whether living in rural surroundings or in crowded urban terrain, family is the organizing force and glue for the Latino/a experience. One of the few authentic media productions depicting Latino/a life, the PBS drama *American Family*, illustrated the preeminence of the home in the opening and closing episodes of its first season in 2002. The pilot episode found the aging patriarch Jess Gonzalez (played by Edward James Olmos) and matriarch Berta (played by Sonia Braga) leaving their brightly colored but deteriorating home in East Los Angeles for a condominium complex designed as an Italian hill town. But when Berta dies suddenly during their move, Jess and his children reclaim their old residence because it embodies her life and memory. As Jess puts it, "That house is everything to me. . . . It's your mother. . . . I guess she'll never leave there." Echoing a similar theme of the vibrancy and sentiment of the past as channeled by the family home, the season finale, titled "La Casa" (The House), brings the family together to repaint their home, replacing its bright but flaking interior green, blue, and peach walls with lighter tones. Reminded that "every time something happens, it's all stored in the house," the family decides to restore the original colors to the white-washed walls and thereby retain their connection to the legacy of the home that tracked their own familial history.

As prompted by their rural roots and other motivations, most Latino/as aspire to own and reside in single-family detached dwellings—the American dream of comfortable family living. Despite their desire to become homeowners, disproportionate poverty leaves many Latino/as as bystanders in the American landscape. The unsettled immigration status of millions of Latino/as further challenges their presence on these American streets of dreams. Past and present discrimination also plays a significant role in shaping U.S. residential landscapes. Impeded by these constraints, Latino/as lag well behind Anglos in homeownership, and, whether they rent or own, their residences are often small, overcrowded, and deteriorating.[2]

A study of Mexican Americans in three major U.S. metropolitan areas found that despite the relatively low number of Latino/a homeowners, more than 86 percent declared homeownership a household goal.[3] Contributing to this imperative is the fact that Latino/as in the United States are more likely (38 percent) than other groups (23 percent) to be married with children.[4] A 2002 study confirms the primacy of family in motivating Latino/as to become homeowners, finding that nearly 40 percent of Latino/a homeowners identified "more room for a growing family" as their top reason for purchasing a home, followed by only 22 percent who were motivated to purchase their home as a financial investment. Moreover, 90 percent strongly agreed that "owning a home is better [than renting] for raising a family."[5]

Although culture and family protection are at the core of the affinity between Latino/as and homeownership, ownership for Latino/as is important for other reasons. Wealth accumulation by Latino/as is just one casualty of their lack of homeownership. The housing gap drives the wealth gap, and the converse is also true. Spurred by tax incentives for homeowners that include deduction of mortgage interest and exclusion of capital gain on resale, some 44 percent of U.S. wealth takes the form of home equity.[6] A 2004 Pew Hispanic Center report revealed that although the median income of Latino/a households is two-thirds that of White households, this disparity is dwarfed by the wealth gap. Due in part to barriers to homeownership, the wealth of Latino/a (and Black) households is only one-tenth that of White households.[7] The report found a strong positive relationship between homeownership and household net worth, concluding that the "single most important asset for all races and ethnicities is a house."[8] For example, in 2002 the median net worth of Latino/a renters was only $762, while Latino/a homeowners had a median net worth of $62,839, about eighty-two times that of renters. Overall, more than one in three Latino/as (36 percent) had a zero or negative net worth.[9] Upwards of two-thirds (71 percent) of the net worth of Latino/a households is comprised of home equity,[10] and the home is likely the only potentially appreciating asset the Latino/a family owns.[11] Of course, homeownership is not always an engine of wealth acquisition, as the current collapse of housing markets and widespread reverses in home values demonstrate.[12] But real estate values are cyclical and tend to recover after downturns, so that the long-term prognosis for home values is steady, albeit less strident, growth.

Low homeownership among Latino/as injures them beyond this impact on acquisition of wealth. Research also suggests a correlation between homeownership and higher child achievement rates, as well as lower high-school drop-out and teen pregnancy rates.[13] Studies also point to a correlation between homeownership and voting, as well as to greater participation in local affairs, such as schools, churches, and neighborhood groups.[14] Homeownership, then, is the recipe for community stability, upkeep, commitment, and prosperity—each hallmarks of assimilation that could help silence xenophobic voices questioning the assimilative abilities and desires of Latino/as.

History shows how local officials have used lack of homeownership to diminish the rights of Latino/as in the United States. For example, Crystal City, Texas, invoked its city charter in 1970 to disqualify a Latino candidate for the local school board because he did not own property in the city.[15] Neighborhood elections sometimes limit eligibility to property owners. In 2002, for example, a water district in central California's Tulare County restricted a vote on price increases to property owners in a county with an extensive population of low-income Latino/a farm workers, few of them homeowners.[16]

The U.S. legal system favors homeowners over renters in many settings. As noted, the federal tax code offers mortgage interest and real estate tax deductions to homeowners. Additional examples include foreclosure laws that supply greater protection to borrowers in default than do laws governing delinquent tenants under leases, and homestead laws that shield some of the owner's home equity from judgment creditors.[17]

Studies link homeownership to higher rates of self-esteem, self-efficacy, and even to physical health and overall happiness.[18] Self-efficacy presumably flows from the homeowner's freedom from potential rent increases, as well as the ability to decide who enters and shares the dwelling and greater autonomy to modify or improve the home to one's personal taste.[19] Owned housing is also better protected from urban renewal and gentrification; today's rental apartment may become tomorrow's high-end condominium dwelling. Consistent with their desire for freedom on the home front, Latino/as have a history of building their own homes that continues today with large numbers employed in the construction trade and others engaged in do-it-yourself home improvement. Increasing Latino/a homeownership, then, is a modern-day formula for achieving the Tierra y Libertad rallying cry of 1900s Mexico, with a home constituting the *tierra* and homeownership supplying the *libertad* of self-determination.

Related to the psychological detriment that an absence of homeownership triggers, land loss in the Southwest, particularly among collective owners in northern New Mexico, continues to plague and incite Latino/a residents there. Some activists in a northern New Mexico county even attribute the county's staggering death rate from illicit drugs to collective grief over that loss of land.[20]

The deleterious effects of lack of homeownership are augmented by the impact of living in overcrowded, dilapidated, or unaffordable housing that characterizes the Latino/a experience in the United States. Obvious health and safety problems associated with substandard housing include lead poisoning, rat bites, fires, and respiratory disorders. Overcrowding has been shown to produce stress and family tension, to the detriment of education and marital stability.[21] Affordability gaps between housing and wages strain household budgets and force hard decisions in cutting other necessities such as food, utilities, and health care.[22]

Latino/as are among the poorest U.S. residents, with some 22 percent earning below the federal poverty level, in contrast to only 9 percent of Anglos.[23] Their wages reflect low educational attainment; 40 percent of Latino/a householders lack a high school diploma, and Latino/a immigrants are handicapped by even less education.[24] Hampered by disproportionately low income and wealth accumulation, Latino/as fall far short of Anglos in homeownership. Over the last few decades, the homeownership gap between Latino/as and Anglos exceeded 20 percent; in 1980, the Latino/a rate was 43.3 percent, compared to 68.5 percent for Anglos. Buoyed briefly in recent years by subprime lending, homeownership rose among Latino/as to a peak of 50 percent in late 2005. However, Anglo ownership also soared, peaking at 76 percent in 2004, to maintain a 26 percent gap with Latino/as.[25] In California, the top five surnames of homebuyers in 2005 were Latino/a, but the overall Latino/a household ownership rate was 47 percent, compared to 66.7 percent for Anglos.[26] Moreover, the ownership gap is more than a mere percentage gap. Impeded by their dismal economic station, Latino/as purchase homes mostly in the lower-price housing brackets. When compared to Anglo home values in the United States, the median home value among Latino/a owners is only 75 percent as high.[27]

Reverses in national homeownership accompanied the mortgage crisis beginning in 2007. As detailed in chapter 5, that crisis is stripping Latino/as of their homes by foreclosure of subprime loans. By the end of 2007, the national homeownership rate for all groups had slipped from a record high in 2004 of 69.2 percent to 67.8 percent, with more losses expected, particularly among minority groups.[28] From 2007 to 2008 alone, Latino/a homeownership dropped from 49.8 percent to 48.9 percent.[29]

In addition to low educational attainment and incomes, Latino/as as a group share other characteristics that suppress homeownership. Although Latino/as are a diverse population, and not all of these characteristics hold for all Latino/a subgroups, nevertheless sufficient negative factors exist to dampen their participation in housing markets. These include the relative youth of the Latino/a population, with more than one-third (34.3 percent) under age eighteen and a median age of only twenty-eight.[30] Critics of broad-scale reform to boost Latino/a housing opportunities might contend that the low rate of Latino/a homeownership simply reflects this youthful demographic, and that as Latino/as age they will become homeowners at rates rivaling Anglos. Yet, we cannot assume the Anglo model will carry over to Latino/as. As detailed in chapter 15, Latino/as suffer an educational gap that affects their long-term wealth and income. Given alarming drop-out rates and the lack of education of older Latino/a immigrants, the traditional model of home acquisition in later adult years is less likely for Latino/as. Moreover, Latino/as disproportionately hold jobs in unskilled or low-skilled industries that do not reward long-term experience. Rather, they favor youthful energy and hold little opportunity for wage gains and employee retention that will foster savings and income growth toward homeownership. These jobs are also often dangerous; the life expectancy of migrant farm workers, for example, is only forty-nine years, suggesting many will not even reach the age at which their Anglo counterparts move up to comfortable houses. Moreover, it is cold comfort to suggest that the Latino/a housing crisis will have a happy ending over time through aging, while the short-term brings housing in overcrowded, dilapidated conditions, if one is fortunate to have steady shelter.

Other impediments to Latino/a homeownership include the noncitizen (and often undocumented) status of millions of Latino/a immigrants. Further, both immigrant and native-born Latino/as reside disproportionately in high-cost housing markets such as Los Angeles and New York City.[31] Of the ten million residents of Los Angeles County, almost half (47.3 percent) are Latino/a.[32] Reflecting its costly urban real estate, New York State is tied with Massachusetts for the lowest rate of Latino/a homeownership at 26 percent.[33] Ironically, arrivals of new immigrants streaming to these segregated areas heat up housing markets, exacerbating obstacles to obtaining affordable housing and purchasing homes. Latino/as increasingly are an immigrant population, with some 40 percent of the population foreign born. At the homeownership peak just before reverses began in 2007, ownership among Latino/as ranged from a high of 62 percent for U.S.-born Latino/as to a low of 34 percent for foreign-born, noncitizen Latino/as (undocumented as well as documented). Puerto Rico–born Latino/as share the lower end of the homeownership spectrum, with a rate of only 38 percent.[34]

An appreciation of the challenges of housing and land reform for Latino/as demands study of their history of loss, exclusion, and hardship in real estate. Once beneficiaries of huge landholdings in the Southwest conferred by the Spanish and then Mexican governments, Latino/as now find themselves a mostly urban, landless population of renters that resides primarily in overcrowded and dilapidated housing. Latino/as in the United States have transformed from a mostly land-rich but cash-poor population in the mid-1800s to the dominant model in the 1900s and 2000s, a laboring class that is both land- and cash-poor and prone to discriminatory exclusion and even exploitation, most recently by subprime lenders.[35] Evident in this historical review of pernicious forces that have undermined Latino/a housing opportunities is the sustained campaign of government and private actors to keep their feet on the backs of Latino/as in the housing market. Redlined from receiving mortgage loans until civil rights legislation imposed imperatives of equal opportunity in the housing market, Latino/as recently became targets of a different brand of discrimination, singling them out to exploit their language barriers, nontraditional credit histories, and lack of familiarity with mortgage lending. Neighborhood restrictive covenants were overtly racist until the Supreme Court refused to enforce them. But communities responded to this judicial imperative by curtailing affordable housing through zoning, by attacking crowded Latino/a households indirectly through density regulations, and by directly prohibiting housing of undocumented immigrants. Developers excluded Latino/as by restrictive covenants designed to inhibit the poor and thus to better survive judicial scrutiny, but which affect predominantly Latino/as and other minority buyers. Overall, Latino/a housing has always faced challenges from a diverse group of actors implementing a wide array of discriminatory strategies that operate outside or just inside the law.

The loss and exclusions of the past and present set the tone for the reforms articulated below, which aim to construct an agenda of equal housing opportunity for Latino/as and to establish the family home as the centerpiece for dignity among diverse Latino/a populations in the United States. The premise for this review of history and hope for Latino/a housing is that today's working class, including Latino/a immigrants, should have the same opportunities to achieve the American dream as past groups. Latino/as should enjoy the liberty of housing proximate to their employment without barriers of discrimination or affordability that have plagued them in the past. They deserve the reward of decent, uncrowded housing for their hard work and contributions to America's cultural and economic growth, as many past immigrant groups have enjoyed. Immigrants to the United States historically have tended to pursue homeownership with vigor. For example, a 1900 study in Detroit revealed high percentages of homeownership by immigrant groups of German, Irish, and Polish background, rates one commentator stated would "have been virtually inconceivable in Europe at the time."[36] The door should not be shut now that Latino/as are the group at its threshold.

As demographics in the United States shift toward a model of aging Anglo homeowners[37] and youthful Latino/a renters, the urgency of removing longstanding barriers of discrimination and affordability is apparent. If the American dream of a comfortable home as a reward for hard work and initiative is to survive as a cultural marker, the torch of homeownership must be passed willingly to Latino/as and especially to Latino/a newcomers to the United States.

The first chapters detail this history of land loss and housing exclusion, as well as the current techniques employed against the Latino/a population. Chapter 1 recounts César Chávez's childhood loss of his family homestead as it fell victim to the Great Depression and the forces of lawyers, foreclosure, and economic struggle. The Chávez family's misfortune reprised some of the same factors that shifted millions of acres of land in the Southwest from Mexican to Anglo hands in the second half of the nineteenth century. Chapter 2 examines the role of law, lawyers, squatters, and nature in this monumental loss of land, which displaced the once land-rich Latino/as and reconstituted them as a migratory, land-poor working class. Chapter 3 completes the transformation in rural settings by surveying the miserable state of housing today for farm workers, a group disproportionately comprised of Latino/as and especially of Latino/a immigrants. Chapter 4 visits the first geographical stop on this national housing survey, examining the wrenching economics for farm workers and other manual laborers in California's affluent Monterey and Santa Cruz counties. That chapter also offers literary examples of the popular conception of Latino/as as poor stewards of their houses and the land, which resonates in society's shabby treatment of Latino/as in the arena of housing policy. Chapter 5 concludes the discussion of loss with an overview of the current subprime mortgage crisis, whereby after decades of exclusion Latino/as flirted briefly with artificial jumps in lending approvals and consequent homeownership that gave way to the tragedy of foreclosure and loans more prone to abuse than to improve the health and wealth of the Latino/a community.

Chapter 6 opens the discussion of exclusion by addressing public and private efforts to exclude undocumented Latino/a immigrants from local housing and from crossing ranchland in the southwestern border states. Public efforts include those of several cities to prohibit rentals to undocumented immigrants, as well as to restrict the presence in the community of Latino/a day laborers. Private efforts include those of southwestern ranchers and their supporters who wield the legal doctrine of trespass to exclude transitory immigrant crossings. Chapter 7 surveys historical and current efforts to exclude impoverished residents and Latino/as from urban terrain by means of zoning laws directed at the circumstances of impoverished Latino/a housing, whether owned or rented—overcrowding and extended-family living arrangements, as well as the externalities of overcrowded housing such as residential street and lawn parking. Chapter 8 confronts the history of private means to exclude Latino/as and other unwelcome groups from residential neighborhoods by use of restrictive covenants among homeowners, as well as covert techniques employed after the Supreme Court invalidated racially discriminatory contracts.

Chapters 9 through 11 explore the urban geographies of Mexican American, Cuban American, and Puerto Rican residents in their U.S. mainland urban hubs of Los Angeles, Miami, and New York City. The history of loss and exclusion in these geographies infuses the agenda for reform in later chapters. Moreover, the diversity of the Latino/a population presents challenges for reform strategies that propose one-size-fits-all solutions, as the needs of rural Mexican farm workers in California may differ from those of immigrant communities in New York City. Among other grounds for difference, Latino/as vary in their ethnic and racial background, their citizenship status, and their residence in urban, suburban, and rural landscapes. The reform strategies that follow are mindful of these potential divides.

Chapters 12 through 15 detail strategies for giving Latino/as equal opportunities for homeownership and for resolving the ongoing land disputes in the Southwest. First addressed is the historically and culturally based strategy of protest by land occupation. Recognizing shortcomings of this strategy, the remainder of the book articulates proposals for reform that are micro- and macro-based. Some confront and respond to the immediacy of the subprime-fueled housing meltdown. But most offer broader strategies for change, mindful that concentrating too much on the subprime debacle might only restore the already miserable conditions prevailing before that crisis. Therefore, chapter 15 suggests long-term structural and institutional measures that encompass education, employment, and immigration and are designed to stabilize and move the Latino/a community toward fair and equal housing opportunity.

While articulating these reforms, these chapters also tackle contentious policy issues that must be resolved before Americans find the political will to enact and implement these vital proposals. Preeminent among them is why Americans should care about the dismal state of housing for Latino/as, and whether undocumented and documented immigrants deserve the same treatment as Latino/a citizens. Chapter 13 addresses these and other policy conundrums, such as the dilemma of whether regulation of overcrowding, housing quality, and loan eligibility will hurt more than help by pricing or otherwise driving Latino/as out of purchase, rental, and housing finance markets.

Part I

Loss

Over the past two centuries, Latino/as in the United States have undergone a transformation of ownership that embodies the theme of loss. Once owners of vast lands in the Southwest, Mexicans through a variety of catalysts lost much of their U.S. lands to Anglos in the second half of the nineteenth century. As illustrated in chapter 1 with the story of César Chávez's childhood, the loss of ranch and farmland continued at least into the Great Depression era. Latino/as had once forged an identity as ranchers and farmers in the Southwest. Indeed, the history of the West could not be written without dozens of words derived from Spanish that reflect the identity of Mexicans as the original cowboys—words such as rodeo, corral, chaparral, desperado, bonanza, bronco, and even ranch (from the Spanish *rancho*).[1] Because of these losses, both the reality and perception of Latino/as shifted to that of migrant laborers adrift and struggling for a foothold in the American dream of home and land ownership. The current assessment of farm worker housing in chapter 3 reveals the extent of the transformation those of Mexican descent have undergone in the United States, from landowners to a renting class coping with overcrowded and dilapidated housing, for those fortunate enough to afford steady shelter. Given the transitory nature of the farm worker population and the significant numbers of undocumented laborers within its ranks, farm workers today experience loss of a different kind. Vulnerable as undocumented persons, many farm laborers tolerate the miserable housing provided by their employers or third-party landlords, knowing that if they complain they will lose their housing, either through termination of their employment or, worse, by being reported to immigration authorities.

In recent years, the experience of Latino/a housing shifted again when liberal mortgage lending policies in the 1990s and early 2000s opened the door to homeownership. By 2006, however, the predatory side of many of these loans emerged, as Latino/a borrowers faced foreclosure of loans that were misrepresented to them or otherwise designed for failure through teaser introductory rates or other artifices. During the last two centuries of Latino/a settlement in the United States, then, an overarching theme of home and land ownership has been loss and the fleeting chances of Latino/as to grasp the American dream.

1

Loss and Lettuce

The César Chávez Legacy

The history of loss of land and housing by U.S. Latino/as stretches from the broadscale usurpation of ranch and farmland in the 1800s to the heartbreak of the subprime lending implosion in the early 2000s, which cost thousands of Latino/as their fledgling piece of the American dream. This survey of recurrent loss, however, begins at the midpoint of the Latino/a experience in the United States—with the Depression-era loss by César Chávez of his family homestead in southern Arizona.

César Chávez (1927–1993), an inspirational union leader, is best remembered for his efforts centered in Delano, California, to organize the national grape boycott in the 1960s, as well as for co-founding, with Dolores Huerta, the union that became the United Farm Workers in 1972. But Arizona, lettuce, and land have a place in Chávez's legacy too. Although some of the story's intermediate details are unclear and contradicted by varying accounts, the beginning and end are clearly marked. In the late 1800s, Chávez's grandfather acquired rural acreage near Yuma, Arizona, under federal homestead laws. After the Chávez family lost this farm during the harrowing economy of the 1930s, Chávez put down roots in California but was back in Arizona in 1993 defending a lawsuit brought against the United Farm Workers by Bruce Church, Inc. In a compelling bit of irony, the agri-giant Church company owned the land the Chávez family had lost in the 1930s. Here in Arizona, a few miles from where Chávez was born, he died in his sleep at age sixty-six while the lawsuit raged around him. The story of Chávez's homestead is one of loss and pain, but as this book's conclusion will reveal, there is hope for reclamation.

Congress awarded millions of acres of U.S. land to soldiers who fought wars such as the American Revolution, the War of 1812, and the Mexican-American War.[1] Moreover, pursuant to the federal Homestead Act of 1862, U.S. citizens and immigrants eligible for naturalization were entitled to acquire up to 160 acres on the condition they reside on and cultivate the land for five years. Before Arizona became a state, and a retirement haven for the wealthy, it lured Chávez's grandfather, Cesario, for whom César was named. The elder Cesario came to the Arizona Territory from Chihuahua, Mexico, in 1888, obtaining citizenship and the rural homestead in pursuit of his American dream. In the early 1900s, Chávez's father, Librado, and his mother, Juana, raised César on that same family homestead. Its terrain included a spacious adobe farmhouse built by the elder Cesario, his wife, Dorotea, and their children.[2] Among the crops grown on the farm were grapes, melons, squash, beans, tomatoes, chiles, and lettuce.[3] While cultivating the family farm, the ambitious Librado purchased nearby land and operated a grocery store, garage, and pool hall that prospered until the Great Depression arrived and forced their sale.[4]

Librado had an early brush with loss when he purchased the forty acres surrounding his businesses in exchange for clearing eighty acres of stumps from the seller's remaining property. When the seller refused to honor the bargain, Librado, on the advice of a lawyer, borrowed money and purchased the land. When Librado was unable to pay the loan, the same lawyer bought the land and eventually sold it back to the original seller.[5]

The Chávez family still had their agricultural homestead. But in the throes of the Depression and a crop-snuffing drought, unpaid property taxes mounted.[6] Librado was entitled to a farm loan under a New Deal federal loan program, but the loan was blocked by a local bank president, who happened to own the land adjoining the Chávez property.[7] United Farm Workers cofounder Dolores Huerta remarked more generally that "during the Great Depression, banks would lend to Anglos but not to Mexicans."[8] Hoping to save the family farm, the Chávezes headed west to California in 1938 to find work in the fields as migrant laborers. Trading the comfort of their own land and a thick-walled adobe home, they resided in a rickety shack while harvesting the fields of others. In the winter of 1939, they made camp in a waterlogged tent or worse, living at times in the family's Studebaker automobile or under a tree with a piece of canvas overhead.[9]

Unable to raise the money to save their Arizona farm, the Chávez family suffered its sale by public auction in 1939 to this same local banker. While the Chávezes packed up as many of their belongings as would fit in and on their car, the new owner bulldozed a corral. César Chávez lamented:

> Our farm was good land. My father had worked it well. It was close to the Colorado River, and the new Imperial Dam was being built just north of us, which would make the surrounding land very valuable in the years to come.[10]

We were pushed off the land.... When we left the farm, our whole life was upset, turned upside down. We had been part of a very stable community, and we were about to become migratory workers. We had been uprooted.[11]

Chávez remarked that his father, now cast adrift as a migrant laborer, never forgot the love of land: "He would get down and look at the ground, taking some dirt in his huge hands. 'You could really raise things here!' he would say."[12] Chávez suggested later that his own memories of land ownership helped guide his efforts on behalf of migrant laborers in a campaign to restore land, liberty, and dignity to those who cultivated the land: "Some had been born into the migrant stream. But we had been on the land, and I knew a different way of life. We were poor [on the family farm], but we had liberty. The migrant is poor, but he has no freedom."[13]

Years later, the former Chávez family homestead came into ownership of Bruce Church, Inc., a giant lettuce producer. In the 1980s, César Chávez and the farm union tried to alert the public to the dangers of pesticides in the lettuce fields. The Church company countered by suing the union in Arizona, seeking monetary damages for the union's pickets and mailings to consumers and grocers that accused Church of using toxic pesticides and child labor. Although the judicial trial resulted in an annihilating jury verdict of $5.4 million against the union, the Arizona Court of Appeals overturned the verdict in 1991. The appeals court determined that the trial court had improperly applied Arizona state law prohibiting secondary boycotts (for example, striking a supermarket selling Church lettuce) to reach union activities outside Arizona, particularly campaigns in California, where labor laws were less tilted toward growers. Chávez returned to Arizona to attend the retrial of Church's separate legal claim alleging wrongful interference with its business, and died there in his sleep at a friend's house near Yuma.

Although the Chávez family lost their home and farm during the Great Depression, their story mirrors the systematic loss of expansive rancho properties in the Southwest in the second half of the nineteenth century. Then, holders of Spanish and Mexican land grants lost their lands and their liberty through a variety of perils that included greedy lawyers and foreclosure for unpaid real estate taxes. In a process repeated for the Chávez family in Arizona, proud Latino/a land and homeowners gave way to migrant, landless workers toiling outside the American dream.

2

Southwest Ranchos

Land Grants and Land Loss

The beneficiary of several land grants in 1800s California, Don Julio Verdugo saw his land fortunes collapse, along with those of most other Mexican land holders there, after California came into U.S. hands. In 1861 he mortgaged his sprawling Rancho San Rafael (which encompassed the entire present-day Southern California city of Glendale and part of Burbank) in order to pay real estate taxes (required in California after 1850) and make improvements to his home. Accruing interest at 3 percent monthly, the $3,445 loan eventually swelled beyond reach, prompting a foreclosure sale of the rancho by public auction at which Don Julio's lawyers purchased the property. Don Julio traded his remaining lands for the 6,600-acre Rancho Los Feliz, but sold off parcels to pay debts until twenty Anglos and lawyers owned that rancho and he was left in 1871 with just 200 acres from his previous land fortune.[1]

In the present-day U.S. Southwest, Mexicans once held vast lands granted to them by the Spanish and later the Mexican government. The annexation of Texas and the Mexican-American War together brought more than half of Mexico's territory into U.S. control during the mid-nineteenth century, and within fifty years Mexican landholders lost most of their extensive *tierra* to Anglos. Although all or part of the Western states of Arizona, California, Colorado, Kansas, Nevada, New Mexico, Oklahoma, Texas, Utah, and Wyoming once fell under Spanish and then Mexican control, the discussion below centers on California, New Mexico, and Texas. These states were home to the most significant population of Mexicans, and thus to the largest land grants, and they ultimately experienced the biggest shift in ownership away from Mexican hands. Although some areas conquered by the United States had few or no Mexican settlements of consequence, California was then home to about 7,500 so-called Californios (Mexicans residing in California), and Texas to about the same number of Mexicans. New Mexico had the largest number of Mexicans, with about 60,000.[2]

Varying somewhat by region, diverse forces accomplished the divestment of Spanish/Mexican land grants from Mexicans to Anglo settlers and the U.S. government. Explanations differ as to the root causes of divestment. Although most historians and legal commentators decry the abusive role of law and lawyers, among other causes, in the divestment, others attribute the transfer to potentially legitimate factors such as voluntary sale, loss of land in foreclosure of debts incurred through improvidence, or judicial denial of land claims that were procured by fraud. These possibilities are explored below. Regardless of its cause, however, the experience of Latino/as in the Southwest has been one of a dramatic loss of land that still today evokes a rallying cry for Tierra y Libertad among some.

Land grants from Spain and then Mexico took two primary forms—individual and community. In New Mexico, for example, land grants to individuals were customary in the eighteenth century, but in the first half of the nineteenth century community grants became more prevalent. These community grants usually conferred individual plots for construction of homes and maintenance of vegetable gardens and orchards, which could be sold as private property, as well as substantial community (*ejido*) land, not subject to individual sale, for grazing, hunting, fishing, firewood, logs for building, drinking water, and other uses.[3] Surrounding the individual plots of land, which were often situated along rivers, the community land constituted the major share of these grants, typically 90 percent of the total area.[4] Land grants were awarded for military service as well as to help populate these northern territories controlled by Spain and then Mexico, and thereby to protect them from colonization by others. Large land grants were common. Some rancho grantees in California acquired several hundred thousand acres.[5] Only thirty-four grants were awarded to Californios during Spanish rule, but the brief period (1821–48) of Mexico's control of California witnessed the award of several hundred land grants, some to the same owner.[6] According to an 1849 estimate, two hundred Californio families owned fourteen million acres.[7] About 295 land grants were issued in what is now New Mexico, of which 141 went to individuals, with the rest made as community land grants.[8]

The Treaty of Guadalupe Hidalgo, ratified by the United States and Mexico at the conclusion of the Mexican-American War in 1848, ostensibly protected these land grants in the territory ceded to the United States. As originally drafted, the treaty explicitly honored the land grants, providing in Article X, "All grants of land made by the Mexican government or by the competent authorities, in territories previously appertaining to Mexico, and remaining for the future within the limits of the United States, shall be respected as valid, to the same extent that the same grants would be valid, if the said territories had remained within the limits of Mexico." But the U.S. Senate struck Article X from the treaty, leaving the less resolute assurance to land grant holders under Article VIII:

> Mexicans now established in territories previously belonging to Mexico . . . shall be free to continue where they now reside, or to remove at any time to the Mexican Republic, retaining the property which they possess in the said territories, or disposing thereof and removing the proceeds wherever they please. . . .
>
> Those who shall prefer to remain in the said territories, may either retain the title and rights of Mexican citizens, or acquire those of citizens of the United States. But they shall be under the obligation to make their election within one year from the date of the exchange of ratifications of this treaty; and those who shall remain in the said territories, after the expiration of that year, without having declared their intention to retain the character of Mexicans, shall be considered to have elected to become citizens of the United States.
>
> In the said territories, property of every kind, now belonging to Mexicans not established here, shall be inviolably respected. The present owners, the heirs of these, and all Mexicans who may hereafter acquire said property by contract, shall enjoy with respect to it, guaranties equally ample as if the same belonged to citizens of the United States.

At the time, millions of acres stood in Spanish or Mexican land grant ownership, constituting an area "nearly as big as Vermont and New Hampshire combined."[9] But most of this land was lost within a few decades. Among the tools of divestment and loss that Mexican landowners faced in the Southwest once under U.S. control were the confirmation procedures Congress established for land grant holders. Running contrary to the spirit of deleted Article X, these procedures required grant holders to initiate official proceedings to legally confirm their land titles. To resolve the validity of land grants in California, Congress created the California Land Claims Commission in 1851. For New Mexico, Congress established the Office of the Surveyor General in 1854 to investigate land grants and recommend their approval or rejection to Congress.[10] But Congress considered few titles for certification,[11] and in 1891 the unwieldy Surveyor General procedure was replaced with a judicial mechanism, the Court of Private Land Claims, to resolve remaining land grant claims.[12]

These claim confirmation procedures proved disastrous to many landowners. Sometimes the necessary documentation had been destroyed in the

Mexican-American War or otherwise.[13] In other cases the war disrupted completion of the granting process from the Mexican government. Contradicting Spanish and Mexican law, the Court of Private Land Claims ruled invalid those grants not issued by governors, such as those by *alcaldes* (Spanish municipal magistrates) and lieutenant governors.[14] Land descriptions under Mexican law (and previously Spanish law) sometimes used ephemeral reference points such as rocks, cow skulls, tree stumps, and natural landmarks that U.S. authorities found too imprecise.[15] Even owners with perfect titles faced the burden of initiating complicated, lengthy, and costly certification proceedings with U.S. officials. Most cases were appealed to the courts, many to the U.S. Supreme Court, with the average time for resolution of claims in California a staggering seventeen years.[16] To navigate these English-language proceedings rife with legalese, the land grant holder was forced to hire an attorney, leading to abuses considered below.

Many Mexican landowners failed to file claims to confirm their land grants. Perhaps these rancho owners did not have money to hire a lawyer or were concerned their land documents would be lost or destroyed if they turned them over to U.S. officials. Some may have known of deficiencies in their title that would have derailed confirmation. Others may have been unaware of the confirmation procedure. Likely, too, some landowners assumed that the confirmation procedure only applied to titles in doubt. But the Supreme Court concluded in 1889 that owners in California with perfect grants nonetheless had to file a claim with the California Land Claims Commission within a statutory two-year deadline or lose their land.[17] In so ruling, the Court characterized the burden of confirmation as a fair one: "Nor can it be said that there is anything unjust or oppressive in requiring the owner of a valid claim, in that vast wilderness of lands unclaimed and unjustly claimed, to present his demand to a tribunal possessing all the elements of judicial functions, with a guaranty of judicial proceedings, so that his title could be established if it was found to be valid, or rejected if it was found invalid."[18]

Even those who possessed a valid title and filed on time weren't always successful. Stripping Mexican claimants of vast acreage, the Supreme Court in 1897 ruled that the common lands in a community land grant were owned not by the collective of landowners, but by the sovereign, thereby passing ownership to the United States under the Treaty of Guadalupe Hidalgo.[19] This decision awarded the common lands of the more than ninety-year-old San Miguel del Vado land grant, amounting to more than 300,000 acres, to the United States. These and other collective lands, once the subject of Mexican ejido ownership, now encompass most of the Carson and Santa Fe National Forests controlled by the U.S. Forest Service.[20]

Surviving the certification process was no assurance of retaining title, as Mexican landowners faced considerable pressures of divestment from multiple sources. Most landowners were land rich but cash-poor, and many had insufficient liquid assets to pay the lawyers retained for their confirmation procedures. Lawyers offered fee arrangements whereby for successful claims they received from one-fourth to one-half or even more of the entire confirmed acreage outright or as a fractional undivided interest in the whole parcel.[21] Arguably this arrangement differs little in substance from today's standard contingency fee agreement struck by lawyers representing personal injury victims. But lawyers today are governed by ethical and judicial constraints on the reasonableness of their fees, as well as prohibitions on acquiring a proprietary interest in the subject matter of any lawsuit.[22] These constraints were often absent in the frontier days of free enterprise that found some lawyers overreaching in their quest for land. Moreover, some lawyers receiving a share of the land in exchange for their services in the certification process found other tools to overreach. Lawyers taking a fractional interest in the whole confirmed property (say, a one-third interest) could readily subvert an individual or a community grant by seeking judicial partition of the entire property based on the lawyer's percentage ownership interest. In awarding partition, the court might either carve the larger parcel into separate ownership portions, thus awarding the lawyer one-third of the acreage, or sell the entire parcel at a partition sale at which the lawyer, with ready financial ability, might bid on the entire acreage and acquire it for an unconscionably small sum.[23] One observer remarked contemporaneously on the role of lawyers in stripping land from Mexican owners in California:

> Between the poor ignorant native [Mexican] and the lordly Land Commission, in too many cases the medium of communication was the lawyer, often crafty and dishonest, who in securing the approval of title took half of the land as his fee, or even more when the pretext of appeals could be used to advantage. In countless other ways have their simplicity and ignorance been taken advantage of to the impoverishment of their estates.[24]

The cost, then, of the federal confirmation procedure after the United States gained control of the Southwest was that even victorious land grant holders emerged stripped by their lawyers of a substantial portion of their land.

Other sources of divestment were without question outrageous. Some settlers defrauded Mexican landowners, taking advantage of language barriers: "When the men from the states came out west to dispossess the poor natives of their lands they used many subterfuges. One was to offer the owner of the land a handful of silver for the small service of making a mark on a paper. The mark was a cross which was accepted as a signature and by which the unsuspecting natives deeded away their lands."[25] Sometimes the Spanish-speaking landowner intended to sign a mere lease of the land to the pioneer for grazing or other purposes, but ended up signing a deed written in English.[26]

Other times the pioneers dispensed with trickery and simply killed or terrorized the Mexican landowners in order to steal their land.[27] In the frenzied atmosphere of the 1850s gold rush in northern California, and especially in Napa Valley and the San Francisco Bay area, squatters overwhelmed the Mexican rancho properties. Following the discovery of gold, 100,000 people poured into California in 1849 alone.[28] Mexicans, who a few years earlier constituted a majority in California, by 1850 accounted for only 15 percent of its population; by 1870, the number had decreased to 4 percent.[29] Squatting pioneers coveted the vast acreage of the Mexican ranchos and moved onto the land, building shanty housing, erecting fencing, stealing cattle, burning crops, and harassing the Mexican owners, sometimes purchasing the property at cut-rate prices from the frustrated owners.[30] Violence was commonplace:

> During the period of title indeterminacy [when Mexican owners were compelled to prove their titles], there was almost constant warfare between the squatters and the rancheros. Murders, mob violence, lynchings, and intimidations of all sorts on the part of the Anglo-American squatters were common occurrences throughout California, especially in the north where land was more valuable and Anglos more numerous.[31]

By 1853, as one historian suggested, "every rancho within a day's march of San Francisco Bay had its contingent of uninhibited nonpaying guests."[32] The squatters even formed leagues to strategize their usurpation of the rancho properties. Their influence helped spur the 1851 law establishing the California Land Claims Commission, which rendered all rancho land titles in doubt until proven and certified.[33]

Needing cash to file land claims, pay surveyors (essential in the certification process), hire lawyers, fight squatters, and pay real estate taxes, rancho owners faced the dismal prospect of borrowing. Financiers of the time, predominantly Anglos, obliged Mexican landowners at exorbitant rates, taking as collateral their properties. The uncertain title status of rancho properties prompted even higher interest rates, ranging from 3 to 10 percent per month,[34] for an annual rate that could exceed 100 percent! Thomas Catron, a lawyer and leader of the Santa Fe ring, a group of New Mexico lawyers and businessmen avidly acquiring land grant property, authored a law that allowed bank loans to exact up to 240 percent annual interest.[35] Even subprime housing loans of recent vintage typically were in the high single-digits or low teens, a bargain compared to these outrageous rates of the frontier 1800s. To avoid foreclosure of high-interest loans, Mexican landowners sometimes sold their properties at cut-rate prices. Failing that, they suffered a foreclosure sale at which lawyers, local officials, and land developers gathered to bid at bargain prices.

Complementing the financial pressure of usurious financiers, the burden of real property taxes was a constant threat to ownership in the newly instituted cash economy. In contrast to the Mexican system, which taxed production on the land, rancho owners now faced taxation based on the assessed value of their extensive land holdings. Many of these owners, who grazed cattle and raised crops for subsistence rather than profit, lost their land in tax delinquency auctions after property tax assessments were instituted in California in 1850 and New Mexico in the 1870s.[36] Because gold mines in northern California weren't taxed, the tax burden fell on the rancho owners, especially those in Southern California, who paid for the infrastructure of government in the rollicking north.[37] Taxation rates were excessive and discriminatory, with one commentator revealing that taxation at $1.50 an acre for Mexican owners became only twenty cents per acre for new Anglo owners of the same property.[38]

Marriage played a role in the transfer of rancho properties from Mexican to Anglo hands. Whether for love in a terrain with few women or by pernicious design, Anglo men frequently married into Mexican rancho families and thus acquired a share of the land by marriage. One sociologist concluded: "These marriages provided strategic access to lands held by the old elite. Thousands of acres passed into the hands of Anglo men as part of the inheritances some Californio women brought to marriage. Moreover, Anglo sons-in-law were often the first ones given access to land sold by rancheros desperately needing cash."[39]

The impact of nature on cattle and crops also contributed to the dispossession of Mexican landowners in the latter half of the nineteenth century. Disastrous floods in 1861 slogged homes, destroyed fencing, uprooted orchards, and drowned cattle. In the water's wake came three years of terrible drought that parched the grasslands and decimated the surviving cows—killing an estimated 70 percent of the livestock in Los Angeles County.[40] Between January 1862 and March 1864 Southern California received only four inches of rain.[41] One writer described the great rancho lands during this drought as "littered with thousands of cattle carcasses."[42]

Class played some role in the dispossession of rancho land, helping to determine the tools of loss. A Texas historian addressed the role of class in the loss of Mexican lands in that state:

> Lower-class Mexicans in Texas probably lost their lands through force and intimidation, while the upper-class hacendados saw their lands disappear legally through circumstances similar to those in California and New Mexico: expensive and interminable litigation, chicanery of lawyers, overlapping claims [to the land filed by both Anglo squatters and Mexican rancho owners], and high taxes based on the alien concept of assessed value of land rather than on what the land produced.[43]

Geography was a factor too. In northern California, where the water supply was suited to raising crops, squatters drawn to the region by the gold rush posed the biggest threat to Latino/a landowners. Divestment pressures mounted in Southern California and New Mexico as well, as the railroads that crisscrossed the landscape in the 1870s and 1880s prompted a rise in land values and the loss of land due to the factors detailed above.[44]

In addition to that gauntlet of perils stripping rancho owners of their lands and homes, some land changed hands to Anglos by more legitimate means. In order to protect its newly drawn boundary with the United States, Mexico's government offered land and compensation to those Mexicans willing to relocate south of the border. But given the favorable climate of California and the gold rush there, few Californios sold or abandoned their land to return to Mexico.[45] Others who stayed in the United States voluntarily sold some of their extensive holdings to the new Anglo settlers or to developers of residential subdivisions, particularly during Southern California's population boom in the 1880s after the railroads arrived.[46] Some Mexican landowners fell victim to their own improvidence by living extravagantly or by gambling, which forced them into the hands of usurious financiers and ultimately off their land. As one unsympathetic historian portrayed the land loss:

Historians who have so uniformly blamed the Act of 1851 [creating the California Land Claims Commission] and the prolonged litigation over claims for the losses suffered by old Californians provide no evidence for their assertions. Studies of individual ranchos show that other factors, particularly the drought years, litigation over division of the ranchos among the many heirs, high living, taxes, and inability to compete with shrewder Yankee businessm[e]n were more important.[47]

As evidenced by these sentiments, scholars and officials disagree over the number of claims that survived the cumbersome certification process. A 2004 Report to Congressional Requestors by the U.S. General Accounting Office pointed out that land grant scholars typically maintain that only 24 percent of the acreage claimed in New Mexico was ultimately confirmed, with a higher percentage (73 percent) confirmed in California.[48] That federal report argued that New Mexico actually experienced a higher confirmation rate (55 percent), when counting just acreage within the present state boundaries of New Mexico.[49] But the acreage failing confirmation nonetheless was extensive by any measure. For community land grants alone, some 3.42 million acres of rejected claims came under U.S. control for disbursal to newly arriving settlers or retention as parkland.[50] Of the 5.3 million acres in New Mexico confirmed to community grants (other than to Pueblo Indians) before the Supreme Court appropriated these grants to the U.S. government in 1897, the report noted that all except 322,000 acres were lost post-confirmation.[51] The report thus concludes that, at least in the case of community land grants in New Mexico, more acreage was lost after the confirmation process.[52] In light of the historical experience detailed above, however, looking simply at the substantial acreage confirmed is misleading. Among other things, lawyers acquired a significant percentage of the acreage confirmed as the contingent fee for their services. What land remained was subjected to the clutches of tax collectors, usurious lenders, squatters, and others, with a result that belongs with the regrettable legacies of theft of Native American land and internment of Japanese Americans as defining episodes in American history of loss of property, wealth, dignity, and *libertad*.

Texas provides a good example of the ravages, distinct from the land grant confirmation process, that stripped Tejanos of their landholdings. In contrast to the rest of the conquered territory of the Southwest, the validity of Spanish-Mexican land grants in Texas was determined through submission to a state commission (the Bourland-Miller Commission) and ultimately by confirmation of the state legislature.[53] While in New Mexico a significant number of claims were denied, the Texas legislature confirmed the vast majority of land grant claims.[54] Still, although Tejanos hung tenaciously to their land, the outcome by the end of the nineteenth century was the same. Many of the factors operating elsewhere chiseled away the Texas land grants. A few Mexicans fled Texas after the Texas Revolution, leaving their land behind.[55] Others were divested through fraud, theft, intimidation, or force. Lawyers took their share in the confirmation process. Livestock prices fell in the late 1800s, and ranchos were sold for delinquent taxes and by lenders in foreclosure. Partition suits and intermarriage took their toll on the leftovers, with the result that by 1900 in Texas "the Mexican upper class would become nonexistent except in a few border enclaves."[56]

Land divestment in the Southwest continues into the twenty-first century, with developers chipping away at the vestiges of the Spanish and Mexican land grants. Most notably, heirs of the Atrisco Land Grant in 2006 sold their landholdings—57,000 acres west of Albuquerque (roughly twice the size of Boston)—to a California developer of master planned residential communities. Although the multimillion-dollar proceeds of the sale funded the creation of a heritage foundation and initiation of a scholarship program to help finance higher education for land grant descendants, the approval of the sale by the ejido owners was contentious, and lawsuits have been filed challenging that approval procedure.

By any account, although some dispute the means of divestment, the fact of land loss by Latino/as in the Southwest in the 1800s was real and staggering. Millions of acres of land grant property owned by Mexicans were lost in the burdensome confirmation process after the United States took control, and most of the acreage that survived confirmation in Mexican hands was soon lost by other means, both legitimate and illegitimate. Although some of the Mexican residents in the early 1800s were already a landless lower class that labored on the ranchos of the Mexican landed class, no doubt the developments of the second half of the 1800s impeded the opportunities for adequate representation today of Latino/as among the class of home- and landowners. As one commentator summed up the sorry state of affairs for Latino/as prevailing in the United States by the early 1900s and continuing today: "Mexican-Americans, through legal defeat, fraud, or financial exhaustion, had been all but wiped out as a landholding class in the southwestern United States. Their transformation from masters into servants had been completed, and set the stage for a new chapter in U.S.-Mexico relations: the exploitation of low-wage, migratory Mexican and Mexican-American labor."[57] Other commentators have compared the current dichotomy to plantation society in the South: "the Anglo farm family lives in the big house, the Mexican workers in shacks on the far side of the spread."[58] This transformation of ownership launched the housing crisis this book confronts next—that of migrant farm workers in the United States, predominantly Latino/as, who are unable to purchase homes or land and face substandard and overcrowded housing, if they are fortunate enough to be housed at all.

3

Fields of Dreams

Farm Worker Housing

> When we arrive I'll see if I can find a good bed for my wife; her kidneys are really bothering her. I hope we don't wind up in a chicken coop with a cement floor as we did last year. Even covering the floor with straw didn't help because as soon as the cold weather settled in it became unbearable. I'm sure that's why my rheumatism hit me hard.
> —Lament of fictional migrant farm worker in Tomas Rivera, . . . *Y no se lo tragó la tierra/. . . And the Earth Did Not Part* (1971), 160

Farm workers today face near-insurmountable challenges in attaining the American dream of comfortable housing and living as a reward for their hard work. Many are young, with little or no savings toward a down payment for purchasing a home, or even the security deposit and initial payment required for renting one in their own name. Dismal wages, stagnant for years, offer little hope for savings, and tend to lure Latino/a undocumented workers with scant bargaining leverage or organizing potential. A 1997–98 study found that half of all farm worker families earned less than $10,000 a year.[1] Migrant workers earned a median income of $6,250 in 2000.[2] Recently, an economist lamented that "twenty-five years ago, a worker made 12, 13, 14 cents for [picking] a bin of oranges. Today that same bin pays maybe 15 or 16 cents—in spite of 250 percent inflation."[3] Such work is typically seasonal, which contributes to the low annual wages of farm workers. Traditionally, farm workers from Mexico and Central America would migrate north for harvest time and return to their families and the cheaper cost of living south of the border for the remainder of the year. But with border enforcement mandates raising the cost and peril of migration for undocumented workers, these migrants must stay through the down season. Farm work is often situated in rural areas that lack sufficient infrastructure for housing laborers. Some of these rural agricultural settings, particularly in Napa Valley and elsewhere in northern California, are in desirable and therefore pricey areas with no inexpensive residential options within a reasonable commute. Long harvest-season workdays leave little time to enjoy the sanctity of the home, so that housing becomes a functional space for eating and sleeping rather than an aesthetic nucleus for life, growth, and celebration of family. Indeed, the immigrant farm worker's family may have stayed outside the United States.

As one would expect with this economic and practical gauntlet, farm worker housing is a national crisis. Sadly, the problem has persisted for decades despite federal, state, local, and private efforts to confront the crisis in affordability and habitability. Mexican farm workers in the government's Bracero labor program of the 1940s, 1950s, and early 1960s often faced miserable housing conditions, living in decrepit trailers, train cars, and chicken coops that sometimes gave way to government-sponsored housing that was overpriced and substandard.[4] A photographer in 1956 captured the despair of *bracero* housing in Texas, with a single building sheltering two hundred Mexican workers in continuous bunks of stretched canvas.[5] Surveying more recent conditions reveals the tragedy in housing still faced by America's farm workers, a predominantly Latino/a population. One study of California farm worker housing found severe overcrowding, with significant numbers of occupants in structures not meant for residential use—such as garages and tool sheds. Worse, many migrants and their families lived in fields, in cars, and in caves.[6] Another study discovered migrant workers who had spent four years living inside a hole they had dug in the ground, using cardboard for a sleeping mat.[7] An Oregon farmer housed seventy migrant workers together on a floor on thin pieces of carpet or cardboard, with bathroom facilities consisting of one working shower and four outdoor port-a-potties.[8] A Latino activist reported in 2000 that many Washington state farm laborers were homeless, using cardboard and plastic to cover themselves and bathing in cold rivers.[9] A Mexican immigrant ranch hand in California found shelter in his employer's discarded metal horse trailer, without heat or water, requiring him to bathe with an outdoor hose.[10] Mexican workers harvesting peppers and cucumbers in Southern California crowded into huts built of tree branches, scrap lumber, cardboard, and black plastic, effective to keep out the rain but not the rattlesnakes.[11] In 2006, the United Farm Workers union described the miserable housing conditions accompanying grape harvest season in California's Coachella Valley near Palm Springs, with pickers sleeping in cars or on the ground in parking lots—aside from the lucky ones who secured housing in a garage or a dwelling jammed with twelve to fifteen other farm workers.[12] A 2006 study of Coachella Valley farm workers found one-third living in places not meant for human habitation, and a *Los Angeles Times* reporter in 2009 found similar conditions still prevailing—notably a "camp of last resort" behind a Coachella Valley market with dozens of Latino/a grape pickers sleeping in pickup truck beds, in cars, and on flattened cardboard in the dirt.[13] The *San Francisco Gate* reported in 2004 that sleeping al fresco by the Napa River or in cars on rural back roads had become the norm for wealthy Napa Valley's farm worker community.[14] Nationally, the housing picture was no less gloomy. A study released in 2001 found that more than half of U.S. farm worker housing (excluding dormitory and barracks housing) was overcrowded, especially substandard housing and housing occupied by children.[15] By comparison, only 3 percent of all U.S. households lived in overcrowded conditions.[16]

Both choice and circumstance consign farm workers to these miserable conditions, posing a challenge to reform strategies. Even where habitable alternatives exist, many farm workers choose the cheapest option. In Napa Valley, for example, a campsite costing only ten dollars a day proved too much for many migrant workers, who opted instead for the hard ground:

> To almost any U.S. citizen, that's a helluva bargain. But if you're from a little mountain village in southern Mexico, $10 is real money. If you're only in Napa for a few months, saving every penny you can send home, you are anxious about spending $10 a day on room and board. Down there [in Mexico], that's a month worth of corn and beans, or a few hundred pounds of charcoal, or a down payment on an irrigation pump. . . . [So sleeping by] the river is a reasonable alternative.[17]

Overcrowding within motel rooms, apartments, single-family homes, and other structures is prompted as much by the dismal economics the farm worker faces as by housing shortages, real or artificial. Squeezing ten farm workers into a two-bedroom apartment, renting for $1,000 a month, is an alternative to the street, but landlords are hesitant to rent to migrants both because of their tendency to overcrowd rental units and the likelihood they will leave or be unable to afford to stay after the harvest season ends. These risks shrink the supply of available units, driving up rents and prompting a vicious cycle in which even more workers must crowd into the rental unit to afford its inflated price.

In addition to being overcrowded, farm worker housing units are often substandard. A 2001 national study of farm worker housing found that more than 9 percent of housing units lacked working toilets, 8 percent were without a working bathtub or shower, and more than half had no access to a laundry machine.[18] Laundry and bath or shower facilities are particularly crucial for the health of the farm worker family, as many workers own insufficient changes of clothing, potentially exposing children and other family members to field pesticides. Many units in the 2001 study had structural issues such as rodent or insect infestation, evidence of water leakage, or frayed wiring.[19] Although these shortcomings might be remedied by complaining to the landlord or, failing repair, to local housing officials, these options are not practically available. In some jurisdictions, state residential landlord and tenant laws that provide self-help and other remedies for substandard housing exclude transient farm worker housing from their scope. Housing shortages plague rural agricultural districts, meaning that the tenant who complains might be evicted and replaced with a more desperate renter. Rehabbing rental properties is likely to result in higher rents that could price the farm worker out of the unit. Farm worker tenants may be undocumented and fearful that complaining to housing officials would reveal their immigration status in any ensuing investigation. Some farm workers obtain housing in farmer-owned barracks or other structures as part of their employment compensation. Given the prevalence of at-will employment in agriculture, a worker in employer-provided housing understands that complaints may result in both termination of his employment and loss of his dwelling unit, without legal protection.[20] Live-in domestic workers, who are often Latina, hold a similarly tenuous grip on their housing, knowing that typically the law will regard them as having a mere revocable license to remain in the employer's home after termination of their at-will employment, rather than as possessing independent rights in their servant's quarters as tenants under a lease once their job is gone.[21] Retaliatory discharges are common, as reflected in the following account of farm workers in northern California's Sutter County, who lived in structures

> that included a burned out two-story building where about 20 to 25 single men slept on the floor every night. . . . The septic system was overflowing and there was raw sewage all over the place. There was no potable water supply. The gray water from the shower and washing machine was next to the well and that was the only source of drinking water. As soon as [the workers] complained they lost their jobs.[22]

The same economics that drive Latino/a farm workers in Napa Valley to sleep by the river to save on housing costs inhibit farm workers from complaining about substandard housing. In many cases, the farm worker has chosen to suffer such conditions on the assumption—true in theory and sometimes in practice—that substandard housing is a cheaper alternative to habitable housing. Similarly, the landlord of substandard housing may be less inclined to charge steep initial housing deposits or to police the number of residents sharing the unit. Tragedy sometimes ensues in these dangerous conditions—on New Year's Eve 2003 near Cincinnati, a Latino tobacco farm worker's wife and two young children died in a fire caused by an extension cord running a portable heater in an old mobile home without central heating.[23]

The troubling economics of reform are exemplified by *colonia* housing, found primarily along or near the U.S./Mexico border and also scattered in agricultural counties of central California and elsewhere.[24] Colonias are self-built communities lacking basic utilities and services such as clean water, sewage systems, paved streets, and street lights. Texas has upwards of 2,000 such communities, their more than 400,000 residents comprised almost entirely of Mexican Americans and other Latino/as. Some colonia residents are farm workers, while others commute to low-wage industrial jobs in nearby cities. In one commentator's view of the "decrepit trailers, shacks made of wood slats, tin, or cardboard nailed onto scavenged pallets, and condemned homes moved from the city," colonia housing is bared in its disturbing state:

> The best built homes in the colonias are small bungalows of two to four rooms, constructed of concrete block. Although such houses look neat from the outside, inside it is not unusual to find no floors, walls, or ceilings. In addition, only half of colonia homes in one . . . [1990] study had indoor toilet facilities. In one-room shacks, walls are frequently built of cardboard or of wood slats covered with plastic sheeting.
>
> Families typically build a colonia home slowly over the course of years, often beginning with a trailer or camper and then adding rooms or constructing a separate building as time and money become available.[25]

These mostly self-built neighborhoods arose in rural areas with few or no land development regulations. Reformists often call for heightened community standards to ensure basic utility services and housing safety, or they demand construction of cheap multifamily rental housing in the closest

Fields of Dreams: Farm Worker Housing

urban areas. But these strategies overlook the economic roots of the colonias—impoverished residents who seek a foothold in the American dream of homeownership in a rural setting, which they prefer over an urban multifamily rental unit. Indeed, homeownership rates in the colonias far exceed those of Latino/as elsewhere, and even of U.S. residents generally, with one study finding that 85 percent of homes in colonias were owner-occupied.[26] Yet 80 percent of the colonia residents earn incomes at or below the poverty level.[27] As one commentator suggested:

> Texas' response to the colonia issue [by regulating border subdivision infrastructure at the local level] has effectively shut down all future colonia development. Texas' approach, however, solves the symptom of the miserable conditions in the Texas colonias, without addressing the disease of lack of adequate housing along the border. . . . I wonder whether the outlawing of all colonia construction on the Texas-Mexico border is somewhat like the laws prohibiting the poor from sleeping under bridges.[28]

Similar regulatory dynamics have imperiled farmer-provided housing. Barracks and other employer-provided housing offer workers the opportunity to overcome transportation costs or local housing shortages. But increasing regulatory and watchgroup scrutiny leads some farmers to abandon these options rather than rehabilitate their housing.[29] At the same time, the history of barracks housing reveals often miserable conditions of overcrowding, posing challenges to reformers.

In areas where regulation of housing quality is more vigilant, farm workers and day laborers sometimes resort to camping outdoors or in their cars. For example, San Diego County has a significant population of Latino/a immigrants who camp in its canyons and ravines. Stringent housing regulation does them little good when scraping to make a living in one of the least affordable areas of the country.

Apart from colonia housing, most farm worker housing is rental property that reflects the transient nature and inadequate pay of farm work. Since the demise of the ranchos in the southwestern United States, Mexican American farm workers have shifted from a significant landowning class to a transient population living in substandard rental housing, if in any structure at all. But in recent years Latino/a-owned farms have gained steadily in number, increasing in acreage from 16.8 million to 20.8 million between 1997 and 2002.[30] During the same time period, as measured by the 2002 Census of Agriculture, the number of Latino/as acting as principal operators of a farm in the United States rose by 51 percent.[31] Many of these farmers began as migrant workers, and many Latino/a-owned farms are family and extended-family operations, thus helping to replant the family farm as a sustainable local alternative in an agricultural sector now dominated by mega-industrial ownership with ready access to capital and production efficiencies that squeeze small farms out of existence.

One example of this Latino/a agricultural resurgence is the Robledo Family Winery in Napa Valley, founded by Reynaldo Robledo. Reynaldo came to the United States in 1968 from Michoacán, Mexico, at age sixteen with his relatives to work in the grape fields. Now his family business owns 220 acres in California's wine country, with parcels named for family members, such as Rancho Maria for Reynaldo's wife, Rancho La Familia for his children, and Rancho Emiliano for his youngest son.[32] Reynaldo and Maria's nine children each help run the winery business, signaling the resurgence of the family farm in California and beyond.

Another example is Javier Lopez, who grows organic rhubarb and raspberries on leased land in Washington state. Javier originally planned to save enough money to buy a home in Mexico by working in the United States, but he soon dreamed of owning a farming operation and eventually the land he farms. As with many of the new crop of Latino/a farmers, Javier started as a field worker, earned a promotion to foreman, and then bought the farming operation through hard work and savings.[33] Too few migrant farm workers achieve this goal, however, as little margin for error exists when America's poorest group aspires to a dream of Tierra y Libertad.

4

Loss in the Tortilla Flats

Farm workers in Salinas, California, survive the nation's least affordable housing market by crowding together. One Mexican American family houses as many as ten people in their deteriorating unit with less than 400 square feet of living space. Another Mexican American couple in Salinas shares a four-bedroom apartment with eight children, three of them married, who each occupy a bedroom with their own families. Their apartment, which shelters as many as twenty-six people, has an extra refrigerator in the living room and a freezer on the front patio. Another Mexican American couple resides in a 300-square-foot unit consisting of a living room, kitchen, and tiny sleeping area. They share the sleeping area while their three daughters use a hide-a-bed in the living room.[1]

The Salinas Valley in northern California's Monterey County is the top vegetable-producing region in the United States, earning the city of Salinas the nickname "Salad Bowl of the World." Salinas holds another distinction: in 2005 the *New York Times* labeled it the least affordable place in the country to live.[2] Using as a measuring rod the percentage of household income devoted to mortgage payments, California that year was home to the nation's eleven least affordable metropolitan areas, with Santa Cruz–Watsonville coming in second to Salinas. The Pajaro Valley produces 90 percent of Santa Cruz County's agricultural income, and together with the nearby Salinas Valley forms one of the world's most productive agricultural regions. With its proximity to the affluent coastline areas of Carmel and Monterey to the west, and the lucrative Silicon Valley technology sector to the north, this agricultural district is ringed by wealth, and yet it is home to a crisis in affordable housing for farm workers. Adding to these woes, solutions that call for construction of additional low-income housing for farm workers are routinely opposed by environmentalists from the affluent coastal areas, where some of the most expensive homes in the world are located.[3] Environmental arguments center on preserving open space in Monterey County, where three-quarters of the land is sheltered from development, but the brunt of this stance is borne by later-arriving farm workers not fortunate enough to own or to have inherited land or homes.

A 2001 study of farm worker housing in the Salinas and Parajo valleys found that 99 percent of the workers were Mexican or Mexican-American, with the vast majority (79 percent) between the ages of 18 and 44, and with 61 percent of them men.[4] Three-quarters had less than a seventh-grade education. Their earnings fell into the lowest occupational category in the two counties, with an average combined family income of only $12,825 for Monterey County farm worker families and $15,006 for Santa Cruz families. As can be expected with these numbers, only a tenth of those surveyed owned their own home.[5] Rents are no bargain, either. In 2005, a two-bedroom apartment rented for $825 to $1,600 a month in Monterey County, and $1,000 to $1,775 in Santa Cruz County.[6] Farm worker rental properties in these two counties tend to be overcrowded, with an average of 5.3 people per household, forcing some workers to sleep in living rooms, hallways, garages, or sheds. In contrast, the average household size of the population generally in the study areas was 3.6 occupants; statewide the average was only 2.8 per household. Two-thirds of the farm workers lived in residences with more than two people per bedroom. About one-fifth of single-bedroom residences had more than five people sleeping in them. One-third of the workers shared their home with nonrelatives. Many of the farm worker residences (41 percent) were multifamily structures; by comparison, only 31 percent of the general population in the study areas lived in multifamily residences. Many of the farm worker dwellings were substandard, with 17 percent lacking plumbing, 18 percent harboring rodents, and 15 percent with leaking ceilings.

Such overcrowded, substandard housing feeds a familiar derogatory stereotype of Latino/as, particularly of Mexican Americans, as dirty, reflected in the common image of the "dirty Mexican."[7] This longstanding construction paints Mexicans as content with filthy, otherwise intolerable living conditions. In 1920, one U.S. magazine wrote, "Having few standards to begin with, it is not surprising that the poor Mexican immigrant is content in the tenements with one toilet and one hydrant for fifteen families, four or five of these families living in one or two rooms."[8] The *San Antonio Express* editorialized in 1871 that "the hogs lived as much in the [Mexicans'] houses [as the Mexicans did] . . . and from the similarity it was hard to tell where the hogs left off and inhabitants began."[9] Another familiar stereotype, that of the fertile Latina, helps justify the view that overcrowded conditions are natural for Latino/a families. Already invoked in campaigns to deny social welfare programs and benefits for Latino/as, such as California's Proposition 187 in the mid-1990s, this image of the fertile Latina might also be employed to dampen housing reforms for Latino/as. Another powerful conception that intersects with the themes of this book is the media and social construction of Latino/as, particularly of Mexican Americans, as irresponsible owners and users of land.

These derogatory images color two popular American novels centered on the dwellings of Mexican Americans: John Steinbeck's 1935 novel *Tortilla Flat* follows the owner of two houses above Monterey Bay; T. C. Boyle's *Tortilla Curtain*, set some sixty years later, portrays trespassing immigrant campers living in a shanty (or worse) of sticks in the urban canyon of a Southern California state park. These literary images complement the history of literal loss of Latino/a land and homes, as well as their historic and current exclusion from the American dream. Steeped in these stereotypes, U.S. policymakers might question initiatives to help Latino/as to acquire or rent property, when the recipients might squander the opportunity through their supposed irresponsibility and lack of stewardship. These perceptions of the shiftless Latino/a landowner even helped reinforce the nineteenth-century land grab of rancho properties in the Southwest, accomplished through hostile laws, squatters, intimidation, and the like. As one scholar explained: "[T]he early Anglos wanted land. Primarily the rich lands of California and the Southwest, but a little later, the island of Puerto Rico. For this purpose, they coined the stereotype of the lazy Mexican [or Puerto Rican]. This myth suited the Anglos' purposes because it justified taking a rich land away from people who were not making good use of it."[10] Rather than exposing the real structural, institutional, and discrimination-based culprits for the miserable housing of Latino/as, these stereotypes help justify the notion that Latino/a culture prompts and promotes substandard housing. Housing reform proposals that invite structural change must buck this longstanding perception that Latino/a culture drives overcrowded and substandard housing choices.[11]

Steinbeck paints a dreary picture of irresponsibility and missed opportunity in coastal Monterey, some seventeen miles west of his birthplace in Salinas, California. When Danny, a "paisano" mixture of "Spanish, Indian, Mexican and assorted Caucasian bloods,"[12] inherits two small wooden houses with weedy yards in "Tortilla Flat," he is immediately elevated in status yet weighted "with the responsibility of ownership."[13] Preferring to spend days sleeping and reveling in wine and song rather than attending to the upkeep of his inheritance, Danny measures his currency in wine gallons. The water company's demand of a three-dollar deposit for Danny represents three gallons of wine, each more precious than water. His three drunken *paisano* tenants, with the help of an unattended candle, burn down one of the houses and must move, with an older man and his five dogs, into Danny's small adjoining home, which survives the inferno. In this crowded house, hands are raised, not toward care of the home, but with fruit jars full of wine. The roof leaks, but not in places under which anyone cares to sit. Its curtainless windows are obscured by cobwebs and husks of flies. Danny's companions convince him against cleaning them, explaining that "[m]ore light would get in. We would not spend so much time out in the air if it were light in here."[14] Eventually the responsibility of homeownership, even of a single home without utilities, is too much for Danny, who reminisces about his days of careless freedom, when he "slept in the woods in summer, and in the warm hay of barns when the winter cold was in. The weight of property was not upon him. . . . Since his inheritance had lifted him, he had not fought often. He had been drunk, but not adventurously so. Always the weight of the house was upon him."[15] Infused with three gallons of wine, Danny finds his adventure but is killed in a fray in the gulch behind his house. The night of Danny's burial, his friends refrain from dousing the flame of a discarded match, lest some stranger, some "joyless relative" of Danny's, inherit the house. At the novel's conclusion, they leave the smoldering pile of cinders behind, with no two men walking together. For them, apparently, libertad comes from homelessness and wanderlust rather than from the stability of ownership and the responsibility it carries.

Danny's housing fortunes were brighter than those of the undocumented Mexican couple in *Tortilla Curtain*. Cándido and América inhabit Topanga State Park, living in a makeshift camp with a firepit for cooking and a shelter of sticks. They dream of their own house with a yard—"nothing fancy, no palaces like the gringos built—just four walls and a roof."[16] But in the short-term their American dream is even less lofty—an apartment with a single room, a hot shower, and a toilet.[17] Still, the requirement of first and last months' rent plus a security deposit makes their modest dream elusive. So the couple endures life in the urban wild and tries to improve their surroundings with more enterprise than Danny showed—adding a veranda to their shelter of sticks with a cut willow, and damming the trickle of a creek to supply water. But while roasting a Thanksgiving turkey they have lucked into, their roaring campfire sparks an inferno that destroys the camp and incinerates their buried stash of rent savings. Fire and Mexicans apparently are a poor mix, whether in Tortilla Flat or inside the Tortilla Curtain.

Cast away from their campsite, Cándido and América take shelter in the hills above an exclusive gated community, Arroyo Blanco Estates, in a lean-to of scavenged wood pallets with a sheet of plastic for a roof—a place "hardly bigger than the king-size beds the gringos slept in."[18] This humble haven proves fleeting, however, as a mudslide brings down the mountain and their shack with it. Cándido and América survive, perhaps to dream again of a fruit jar filled with savings for rent rather than Danny's sweet wine.

Lyrical Latino/as fare as poorly as their literary counterparts in taking care of their abodes. The residents in the 1948 number one hit song "Mañana (Is Soon Enough for Me)" by Peggy Lee and Dave Barbour care little that their faucet is dripping, their fence is falling down, and that rain is coming through a broken window—why not wait until *mañana* to fix them? Perhaps taking a cue from *Tortilla Flat*, the singer reveals that she even burned down the family home with her hot chili stove pot. And the cartoon Mexican mouse in Pat Boone's 1962 novelty hit "Speedy Gonzales" lives in a roach-infested adobe with a leaking roof that goes neglected while he prioritizes his thirst for booze and *señoritas*.

It often takes a Latino/a voice to break a stereotype—here the unbelievable notion that Latino/as cannot steward their own homes, much less keep from incinerating them through their carelessness.[19] Mexican American novelist Sandra Cisneros strikes a different match in her acclaimed coming-of-age novel *The House on Mango Street*. A Latina in a poor Chicago neighborhood moves with her family into the Mango Street residence. Although this starter home frees the family from the binds of paying rent, young Esperanza (Spanish for hope) is alight with dreams of owning her own house someday, a place with a porch and purple petunias, a house "clean as paper before the poem."[20]

Steinbeck's unflattering depiction of Mexican Americans in *Tortilla Flat* drew some contemporary criticism, and he responded by writing a foreword, found only in the 1937 Random House edition, that explained:

> When this book was written, it did not occur to me that paisanos were curious or quaint, dispossessed or underdoggish. . . . I wrote these stories because they were true stories and because I liked them. But literary slummers have taken these people up with the vulgarity of duchesses who are amused and sorry for a peasantry. These stories are out, and I cannot recall them. But I shall never again subject to the vulgar touch of the *decent* these good people of laughter and kindness, of honest lusts and direct eyes, of courtesy beyond politeness. If I have done them harm by telling a few of their stories, I am sorry. It will not happen again.[21]

The setting of *Tortilla Flat*, Monterey, was once a Spanish and then a Mexican pueblo. By special concession from the Spanish crown, Monterey received more than the standard four leagues (each league consisting of about 4,428 acres) allotted to pueblos.[22] But through a dilemma reminiscent of the Mexican holders of land grants detailed in chapter 2, in confirming its pueblo grant with the U.S. Board of Land Commissioners, the city of Monterey lost its municipal land to its lawyer, Delos Ashley. Despite obtaining a successful decree of confirmation in the mid-1850s, Monterey had no treasury funds to pay Ashley the $991.50 it owed. Ashley and a local land developer, David Jacks, acquired the entire pueblo tract at public sale for $1,002.50, the amount of the debt plus the costs of the sale. Eventually, Ashley sold his interest to the developer. Monterey later fought to regain its pueblo land in the early 1900s, but California's Supreme Court rejected its argument that the municipal commons could not be alienated, and Monterey thereby lost its entire pueblo lands for the cost of attorneys' fees it could not afford.[23] No doubt some of today's preservationist voices from Monterey reside on this once public open space.

Steinbeck apparently derived the name Tortilla Flat not from the geographical setting of his novel on the hillside overlooking Monterey Bay, but from the name given the real-life settlement of Mexicans and Carmel Valley Indians in nearby Carmel. These residents lived in shacks outside town and labored as domestic help for the well-to-do residents of Carmel.[24] Steinbeck borrowed this colorful name for Monterey's own settlement of "paisanos," who inhabited the hillside above the fabled Cannery Row, which, as Steinbeck admitted, "isn't a flat at all."[25] The illustrations in his book's 1937 hardbound edition depict these houses as small wooden homes with yards overrun by weeds. But in the current, inflated northern California housing market, even two tiny homes in this area might together fetch slightly over $1 million.[26] The Topanga Canyon area in Southern California is equally affluent, which required situating the Mexican immigrants in Boyle's modern-day retelling of *Tortilla Flat* in a squatter's camp of public ownership, rather than in a modest home (or homes) of their own.

In recent times, to purchase homes in these unaffordable areas of California Latino/as often had to resort to unconventional loans offering unsavory terms, such as teaser introductory interest rates. This ushered many Latino/as into foreclosure and branded California as the nation's foreclosure capital. Abusive practices were rampant. In late 2007, for example, Latino/a homebuyers in a Salinas subdivision called Tuscany at Monte Bella sued the developers, alleging they used unfair sales practices to lure Spanish-speaking buyers to purchase homes with subprime loans. These homes are now imperiled not by fire, but by foreclosure in the current subprime mortgage meltdown—described in the next chapter—which threatens to erase the minimal national gains by Latino/a homebuyers in the early 2000s. As their lawyer described the Salinas homebuyers, "These are all hardworking people who were trying to reach their part of the American dream."[27]

──5──

Lenders and Loss

The Destructive Legacy of Subprime Mortgages in Latino/a Communities

After thirty-three years in the United States, a Mexican-born resident of Albuquerque and his Latina wife realized their American dream and purchased a home in March 2006. The couple obtained a thirty-year adjustable-rate mortgage loan for about $194,000. Their broker told them that the starting interest rate was only 4 percent, and would adjust after seven years by 1 or 2 percent. But contrary to these assurances, the teaser rate lasted only a month, and by May 2006 had more than doubled to 8.4 percent—already more than 2 percent above the going rate for prime loans. The borrowers' credit score was 712, good enough for prime credit. Refinancing was out of the question, as a substantial prepayment penalty of $8,000 applied to early repayment.[1]

Extending over 150 years, the history of loss for Latino/as in the United States is mostly a forgotten or ignored tragedy. Although land loss in the 1800s has long defined the inequality of Latino/as in the historical record, the current subprime crisis may rewrite that history given the far greater numbers affected. Just as the losses of the nineteenth century doomed Latino/as to inequality in housing markets and beyond, the current foreclosure crisis may consign them to another century of separation from the American dream.

Mortgage lenders are a vital part of the homeownership equation, and almost three-quarters (71.6 percent) of Latino/as who own homes have an outstanding mortgage loan.[2] As the following chronology demonstrates, however, mortgage lenders and their supporting cast have not always been Good Samaritans for the Latino/a community. Rather, historically they contributed to the exclusion of Latino/as and other minorities from the American dream. As discussed in chapter 2, high-interest loans helped spur the loss of Mexican ranchos in the Southwest during the 1800s. Even the federal government served as a catalyst for discriminatory lending through its

Home Owners Loan Corporation (HOLC), which during the Great Depression made low-interest loans to recover homes from foreclosure but steered clear of Mexican neighborhoods. This practice continued through the Federal Housing Administration (FHA), created in 1934 to supply government mortgage insurance for private lenders and spark development of residential neighborhoods. The FHA boosted home loans and suburban development by insuring 90 percent of the collateral value, thus decreasing typical down payments from at least one-third of the property value to 10 percent, as well as extending the loan repayment period, thereby lowering monthly payments.

FHA policies encouraged construction of new residential subdivisions away from the inner city instead of rehabilitating existing urban residences. As Douglas S. Massey notes:

> This bias toward suburbia was evident in FHA practices and regulations, which favored the construction of single family homes but discouraged the building of multifamily units. . . . In addition, FHA loans for the remodeling of existing structures were small and had a short amortization period, making it easier and cheaper for a family to purchase a new house than to renovate an older one.[3]

In addition to favoring construction in suburban areas where Anglos were congregating, the FHA once routinely promoted racially restrictive neighborhood covenants barring nonwhite buyers. Color-coded appraisal maps specified in red high-risk neighborhoods that both the HOLC and the FHA tried to avoid for their loan programs. Black, Mexican, and Asian neighborhoods were consistently classified as red zones, as were neighborhoods with self-built housing.[4] East Los Angeles and surrounding neighborhoods such as Chávez Ravine and Elysian Park were designated as red zones, as were the African American neighborhoods near downtown Los Angeles.[5] HOLC appraisers filling out worksheets for Los Angeles–area Mexican neighborhoods made remarks such as, "The vast majority of the population, while American-born, are still 'peon' Mexicans, and constitute a distinctly subversive racial influence," and "Infiltration of goats, rabbits, and dark skinned babies indicated."[6] Accordingly, most federally backed loans were made in middle-class suburbs to Anglo borrowers. Discrimination by mortgage lenders flourished in this atmosphere of government complicity and conspiracy until private discrimination in housing was finally outlawed by civil rights laws such as the Fair Housing Act in 1968 and the amendment in 1976 of the Equal Credit Opportunity Act—originally enacted to target gender and marital status discrimination—to specifically prohibit discrimination by lenders on the basis of race, color, national origin, and other protected grounds.

The weight of discrimination on many societal fronts—including housing that deprived Latino/as of generational wealth creation, employers that long discriminated against Latino/a workers, and barriers to an adequate education that serves as the gateway to prosperous employment—contributed to the poor standing of Latino/as in U.S. housing markets. Even with overt discrimination in lending (and in employment and education) ostensibly removed by federal law from the burdens confronted by Latino/a homebuyers (at least for citizens), the deficit of this legacy of discrimination stymied the growth of homeownership. As discussed in the Introduction, by 1980 Latino/as (43.3 percent) remained well behind non-Latino/a Whites (68.5 percent) in homeownership rates.[8] Over the next twenty-five years, and particularly during the Clinton presidency and George W. Bush's first term, Latino/a homeownership rates grew to a peak of 50 percent in late 2005.[9] This period saw the real estate recession in the early 1990s, which deflated home prices to more affordable levels, as well as a modest increase in Latino/a incomes. But Anglo homeownership rates also rose during this period at a near equal pace, peaking at 76 percent in 2004, thus sustaining the huge ownership gap between Latino/as and Anglos.

Proponents of housing equality had little time to celebrate these gains. In 2005, *USA Today* ran a story titled, "Hispanics Prospering under Bush Administration," touting the rise of Latino/as into the middle class through home purchases since 2000. But the underbelly of these gains in Latino/a homeownership was soon exposed, as subprime mortgage lenders helped write another chapter of loss in the history of the Latino/a housing landscape.

"Subprime" describes loans made on less favorable terms than prime mortgage loans—in theory, to borrowers with less-than-stellar credit ratings. In practice, subprime loans control for this greater perceived risk of default by their often onerous terms, which include steep interest rates—typically, 3.5 percent higher than prime loans—as well as higher fees. The impact on monthly payments is substantial. In the case of a thirty-year prime loan of just $100,000 at 6 percent interest, the monthly payment would be $599.55, but a subprime loan at 9.5 percent interest would carry an $840.85 monthly payment, commanding $86,877 in additional interest over the life of the loan.[10] Subprime loans cheated many borrowers out of wealth acquisition, since payments went toward high interest and loan costs rather than principal. Worse, many subprime borrowers lost possession of their homes in widespread foreclosures prompted by unfair or unanticipated loan terms.

In contrast to the traditional mortgage loan with a fixed interest rate for the fifteen- or thirty-year term and a down payment requirement of 10 or 20 percent of the purchase price, subprime loan programs offered piggyback varieties to enable a purchase without any down payment, teaser ARMs (adjustable-rate mortgage loans) with introductory low interest rates followed by a dramatic rate adjustment in later years, and so-called flex loans that gave borrowers flexibility to submit a monthly payment less than the accrued monthly interest, with unpaid interest added to their eventual balloon payment of the principal balance. Adjustable rather than stable, fixed-interest rate loans were the subprime norm, with about 70 percent of subprime loans in 2005 carrying adjustable rates.[11]

Many subprime loans to Latino/as and other borrowers were specifically designed or arranged to abuse the borrower. Mortgage brokers arranging loans for these borrowers sometimes received kickbacks (known as yield spread premiums)[12] from the lender when they succeeded in procuring the borrower's agreement to an interest rate higher than the lender required to qualify the borrower. Because the broker kickback was based on the expected high interest to be earned over the life of the loan, the lender needed to protect against early repayment or refinancing by charging steep penalties for the privilege of prepayment,[13] thus trapping the borrower in an expensive loan. By contrast, few prime loans offering the historically low interest rates of the early 2000s carried prepayment restrictions. Closing costs on subprime loans consisting of points, document preparation fees, broker commissions, and assorted junk charges were often higher than fees for prime loans. Given the lack of down payment savings, closing costs sometimes were wrapped into the loan balance (known as packing) and paid at high interest rates over the loan's duration. Many of the loans were funded without regard to the borrower's annual income and ability to repay; rather, the lender relied on the value of the home to satisfy the loan, as needed, at a foreclosure sale. In 2006, half of subprime loans were made without income verification, an abandonment of traditional loan underwriting requirements.[14] Rather than enabling new home purchases, many subprime loans refinanced existing home loans carrying lower interest rates. Borrowers who enjoyed long-term fixed-rate loans were bombarded with ploys and pitches urging them to refinance for a cheaper initial monthly payment—often accomplished by means of a teaser (temporary) introductory rate that gave way to a rate higher than the original loan.

The mortgage market, once the domain of commercial banks and savings and loan institutions that made and held onto loans for their duration,[15] changed in recent years with the development of Wall Street channels for securitization of home mortgages. Although government-sponsored entities initiated the securitization push by purchasing and reselling home loans in the securities markets, these federally regulated entities tended to purchase only loans made to prime borrowers with traditional down payments and income verification procedures. In the early 2000s, mortgage lenders marketed loan products designed for vulnerable borrowers with damaged credit or inadequate income or savings, and it became the norm to sell these loans to remote investors through securitization markets while bypassing the safeguards of the federal system.[16] Wall Street buyers were hungry for securities comprised of these largely unregulated loans paying returns above those of prime loans, fueling efforts to further expand the pool of subprime borrowers.

Latino/as and African Americans were a natural demographic target. Researchers have demonstrated that where minorities are more geographically concentrated, the incidence of high-cost subprime lending rises, thereby linking subprime lending and neighborhood segregation.[17] As an NAACP lawyer observed, "It's almost as if subprime lenders put a circle around neighborhoods of color and [said], 'This is where we're going to do our thing.'"[18] In 1999 the nation's largest mortgage lender, Countrywide, mounted an extensive Latino/a advertising campaign that included a weekly radio program originating in Miami called "Su Casa, Propia Con Countrywide" (Your house, own it with Countrywide). A Countrywide executive explained that the broadcast sought to "demystify the process of homebuying for the Spanish-speaking audience," and, noting the company's low-down-payment programs, to "dispel myths, such as the 20 percent-down myth."[19] Subprime lender New Century Financial Corporation sponsored a discussion panel to promote Latino/a housing at the 2006 National Latino Congreso, a gathering of thousands of grassroots Latino/a activists and organizers to confront pressing social and economic issues. By 2007, New Century had tumbled into bankruptcy—and the legacy of loss prompted by subprime lenders in Latino/a neighborhoods had reached crisis level.

Lured by these promotions, Latino/a and African American borrowers became the lifeblood of the subprime lender. Lending tactics ostensibly avoided overt discrimination but masked business as usual. Previously rejected by discriminatory lenders who ignored neighborhoods of color, Latino/a borrowers in the 1990s and early 2000s found themselves pursued aggressively by subprime lenders and mortgage brokers wielding predatory terms. In contrast to the days of mortgage lenders overtly "redlining" minority neighborhoods and denying their residents home loans, subprime lenders and brokers engaged in reverse-redlining. They actively targeted minority borrowers perceived as

Lenders and Loss: Subprime Mortgages | 49

susceptible to predatory loans due to lack of credit history, unfamiliarity with home purchasing and borrowing, and potential language barriers. The Federal Reserve reported that almost half (46.6 percent) of Latino/as financing home purchases in 2006 used subprime financing (the rate for African Americans was even higher at 53.7 percent). By contrast, the subprime rate for Anglo home purchasers was 17.7 percent.[20] In 2005, 56 percent of Latino/a homebuyers in California used subprime loans,[21] and in New York City even Latino/a borrowers with annual incomes of $150,000 to $250,000 obtained subprime loans at a rate of 50 percent. By contrast, Anglo borrowers in New York City at the same income level used subprime financing only 20 percent of the time.[22] Although Latino/as tend to have lower incomes than Anglos, this discrepancy does not explain the subprime gap, as illustrated by the New York statistics, and also by a 2009 report that determined high-income Latino/as were about as likely as low-income Latino/as to receive a subprime loan.[23] Some point to differences in credit history to explain the high incidence of subprime lending to Latino/as. Latino/as are more likely than Anglo borrowers to have a credit score below 620 points, which in practice is the cutoff between prime rate and subprime financing. Still, many analysts believe that lower credit scores also fail to account for the entire gap in subprime usage between Latino/a and Anglo borrowers. Moreover, creditors' widespread reliance on credit scoring in gauging risk and pricing loans disadvantages Latino/as, who culturally may tend to avoid incurring debt in smaller purchases that build credit history under traditional models, and whose rent and utility payments may be uncounted toward their credit records.

Discrimination and predatory practices appear to be responsible for at least some of the subprime gap between Latino/a and Anglo borrowers. A federal analysis of lending in 2006 revealed that Latino/as were turned down by lenders (presumably many of them prime lenders) at a rate (25 percent) twice that of Anglo borrowers (13 percent).[24] The National Council of La Raza suggested that although some of this disparity was caused by demographic factors such as age, income, and immigration status, "fair lending research has demonstrated consistently that demographic factors alone do not entirely explain the inconsistent approval and denial rates."[25] For example, research findings suggest that as many as one-third to one-half of subprime borrowers of all backgrounds could have qualified for a cheaper conventional prime mortgage.[26] Similar findings by the New York Attorney General spurred the state's fair lending law enforcement action and settlement with Countrywide Home Loans in late 2006, based on pricing discrepancies between loans given to Black and Latino/a customers and those given to Anglo customers.

Employing expert statistical analysis, the Attorney General concluded that although demographic factors accounted for much of the disparity, they did not explain all of it, thus signaling impermissible influences at work, particularly on loans generated by mortgage brokers.²⁷

A 2004–6 study by the National Community Reinvestment Coalition (NCRC) reveals the prevailing discriminatory lending market in which mortgage brokers (and lenders) lured Latino/as into unfairly priced loans. This study supplied Latino/a and Black test shoppers with more attractive credit profiles than Anglo testers, which should have resulted in their somewhat better treatment at the hands of the mortgage brokers. Rather, the results demonstrated compelling tactics of discrimination against Latino/as and Blacks—for example, loan pricing discrimination was practiced against them in 25 percent of the tests. Mortgage brokers more often discussed fixed interest rate products with the Anglo borrowers (77 percent) than with Black and Latino/a testers (50 percent). Further, Anglo testers received two specific rate quotes for every one quote given to Black and Latino/a testers, and Black and Latino/a testers were more often discouraged in their efforts to meet with the mortgage brokers. As the NCRC reported to Congress, these results "document the fact, controlling for the credit and individual applicant qualification factors, [that] African Americans and Latino/as are being discriminated against in the marketplace and being forced to pay a 'race tax' due to unequal access to credit."²⁸ As real estate brokers once (and some perhaps still) famously steered minority buyers away from Anglo neighborhoods, today's mortgage brokers often steered minority homeowners and buyers away from prime loans to the dangerous terrain of the subprime loan.

> Dealing with a mortgage broker, a fifty-four-year-old Mexican immigrant and resident of Santa Ana, California, borrowed money for his first home purchase. The lender funded the entire purchase price of $615,000 with a high-interest-rate loan. The borrower counted on his wife and three of his daughters to contribute toward the payments, as he made only $9 an hour as a glass blower. Although the family's annual income was only $60,000, the mortgage broker falsely listed their income as $157,000 on the loan application. Not able to read or speak English, the borrower relied on the broker's representation that the mortgage payment would be $3,600 monthly. Upon learning after the closing that the payment was actually $4,800, the borrower was forced to sleep with his wife on the couch and rent out the bedrooms, garage, and the enclosed porch. Desperately ill and unable to work, the borrower is in default and headed for foreclosure.²⁹

Preying on the non–English-speaking borrower's language barrier is increasingly common in mortgage lending. For example, in a 2007 Oregon court case, the Spanish-speaking borrowers claimed they were promised a refinance loan at 7.8 percent interest, but they ended up signing loan documents in English providing for a 13 percent loan.[30] The borrowers came to the United States from Mexico in the late 1980s and worked together at a factory earning low wages. With help from friends and family they purchased a home in 1996 using prime financing. In fall 2000, Beneficial Oregon lent them $17,948 for a new roof and to consolidate other debts, at a staggering interest rate of 23 percent. A second mortgage on the house secured that loan, but just months later, in January 2001, Beneficial through its Spanish-speaking agent convinced the immigrant borrowers to refinance and consolidate both their low-interest (7 percent) first mortgage from another lender and the smaller second mortgage in favor of Beneficial. They understood the combined interest rate to be 7.8 percent, and they were led to believe that their monthly payments included property taxes and insurance. But the loan documents, written in English, specified a much higher interest rate of 13 percent, and a monthly payment that failed to include annual taxes and insurance. When the borrowers discovered the scheme months later, they refinanced the entire loan at only 7 percent with another lender, and brought a successful lawsuit for fraud. Still, these lawsuits are a gauntlet for borrowers, as lenders and brokers may insist they explained the true loan terms to the borrowers, and in any event will argue for the sanctity of enforcing the written deal.

Most loan disclosure laws fail to require translations for non–English-speaking borrowers. For example, the federal Truth in Lending Act that mandates disclosure of interest and other loan charges before consummation of the loan does not require a Spanish-language translation.[31] Even where state law mandates translation, or the lender or mortgage broker voluntarily provides one, problems can arise from difficult concepts in mortgage lending. For example, the English marketing phrase "no out-of-pocket expenses" means that the lender will finance the loan closing costs into the loan, but the Spanish translation sometimes used, "no te va a costar nada," suggests the closing costs are free.[32] Consumer education programs proposed in chapter 14 would help address misunderstandings in the loan process, but the subprime loan experience also signals the need for translations of crucial loan documents both through legislative mandate and by private initiative in the lending markets.

Subprime mortgage loans aren't the only catalyst for Latino/as to overpay in the housing credit market. Given their youth and lack of income relative to the general population, Latino/as disproportionately purchase manufactured housing, which is not always the bargain it appears to be. In Texas, for example, Latino/as constitute almost half of the manufactured home population, with nearly one in ten Latino/a homeowners residing in manufactured housing.[33] Because manufactured housing appeals to impoverished groups, restrictive covenants and local zoning ordinances often exclude such housing from U.S. neighborhoods, relegating these structures to mobile home parks.[34] Mainstream mortgage lenders disdain manufactured housing, and about half such homes are situated on rented land, leading many purchasers to finance them through vehicle financers. These lenders charge interest rates two to five percentage points higher than prime home loans.[35] Abuses lurk in the purchase transaction. A National Council of La Raza publication reported abuses of Latino/a buyers such as bait-and-switch scams where buyers received mobile homes different from what they ordered. Some mobile home sellers also exploited language barriers with written terms in English that differed from verbal promises made in Spanish.[36] Because manufactured homes tend to be situated on leased land in rental parks, the resident faces multiple threats of ouster—from the home should the owner default on the purchase financing, and from the trailer park should the resident default on the monthly space rental or should the park owner default on its own financing. Trailer park rents can fluctuate at the whim of the landlord, and developers view the park as potentially vacant land convertible into other, more lucrative uses. Manufactured homes often depreciate in value over time, in contrast to the underlying land that a landlord might own. Manufactured homes often are in disrepair; if not, the trailer park itself might have substandard conditions that rival those of colonia neighborhoods, with decrepit water and sewer systems, unsafe electrical service, and unpaved and unmaintained roads.[37] In sum, although cheap manufactured homes may lower housing costs, their specter of affordability masks these opportunities for abuse on the fringes of the American dream.

> A single mother and Mexican native, immigrating to the United States in 1978, acquired her home in the late 1990s, after twenty years of work. She bought the home with a thirty-year fixed-interest-rate loan and converted the backyard into a garden for fruits and vegetables. In 2001, she refinanced with another fixed-rate loan to pay off other debts and to begin sending money to her ninety-year-old father in Mexico. She refinanced again in 2005 to help put her son through college, but this time with a subprime loan carrying an adjustable interest rate that started at 7.5 percent but

two years later had nearly doubled. Although fluent in English, she didn't understand the subprime terms her lender used to sell the loan. While the value of her home drops in the tempest of the current mortgage crisis, her payments are applied solely to interest rather than to principal and augment that value decline. She struggles to make her loan payments and fears losing her home, lamenting, "If I lose my home, it will break my heart."[38]

Particularly in the early 2000s, subprime lenders made it possible for many Latino/as to join the ranks of homeowners. On balance, however, they did far more damage than good. From 1998 to 2006, subprime lending enabled 1.44 million borrowers from all backgrounds to become first-time homeowners. But during the same time period, subprime loans resulted in 2.37 million foreclosures, a net loss of almost one million homes even before the foreclosure explosion that began around 2007.[39] Subprime loans fueled home price increases by expanding the pool of homebuyers,[40] leading to higher loan amounts and ultimately to the collapse of housing values when these loans failed and subprime loan products disappeared. Subprime loans proved particularly harmful because many borrowers refinanced and traded relatively stable, fixed-rate loans used to purchase their homes for adjustable-rate subprime loans obtained to pay off ancillary debts such as credit cards, hospital bills, car loans, or home-improvement expenses. Alternatively, some subprime borrowers refinanced purchase loans not to consolidate other debt, but with the impression created by teaser introductory rates that they would thereby lower their monthly payments. As these teaser introductory rates continue to explode, the number of home losses attributable to subprime lending will no doubt increase in the coming years.

With little or no savings, many Latino/a households are vulnerable to default. A 2009 report revealed that more than one-third (36 percent) of Latino/a homeowners—and more than half (53 percent) of those foreign-born—feared that their home might go into foreclosure.[41] The impending loss of homes to foreclosure of subprime loans has already been called the "greatest loss of wealth for communities and individuals of color in modern U.S. history,"[42] with losses estimated at between $164 billion and $213 billion.[43]

Embedded residential segregation, together with the disproportionate marketing of subprime loans to borrowers of color, combined to plague Latino/a landscapes with the virus of foreclosure. Four states with burgeoning Latino/a populations—Arizona, California, Florida, and Nevada—lead the way in defaulted loans, with communities such as Las Vegas and California's Stockton, Fresno, Bakersfield, and Riverside–San Bernardino vying for the inglorious title of the nation's foreclosure capital. A 2009 Harvard study concluded that lower-income households have borne the brunt of collapsing prices thus far because of their proximity to neighborhoods with widespread foreclosures.[44] These are predominantly the geographies of residents of color.

The perils of foreclosure are far-reaching. Foreclosure harms the individual borrowers; their children, who often move to different schools in the upheaval; and their struggling neighbors in America's segregated neighborhoods:

> Foreclosures can and do have a devastating impact on individual families, which lose their homes and are left with damaged credit records. This not only undermines their ability to secure a home loan in the future but also raises the cost of borrowing for other purposes, such as purchasing a car to get to work. In distressed neighborhoods, foreclosed properties can remain vacant for prolonged periods of time, depressing property values and becoming a magnet for crime. By discouraging families or new businesses from moving into a neighborhood, high foreclosure rates contribute to neighborhood instability and stigmatization.[45]

As described in chapter 2, during the second half of the nineteenth century, Latino/a landowners in the Southwest were systematically deprived of their extensive landholdings through a variety of tactics. One of the methods of divestment was through high-interest loans that led to default and foreclosure sales whereby an assortment of moneyed developers, local officials, and lawyers would acquire title. Few, if any, of these loans were obtained to acquire the rancho properties. Rather, they were equivalent to today's home equity loans that enabled owners to improve the property, to run their ranching or farming business in times of drought or flood, or in some cases to purchase life necessities or even extravagances. Because the Mexican and Spanish land grant holders lived on their ranchos, foreclosure meant they lost their homes too and were forced to rent or live a transient existence. Similarly, today's subprime borrowers are losing their homes to foreclosure in significant numbers. Some of these loans were obtained to acquire a home. Although some might argue a lack of emotional attachment by those subprime borrowers, who had lived in their new home for only a few months or years before foreclosure drove them out, the devastating loss can also be stated in practical terms. Having saved for years in low-income jobs and borrowed from friends and family, Latino/a borrowers may only have one

Lenders and Loss: Subprime Mortgages | 55

chance at the American dream of homeownership.[46] A subprime foreclosure will extinguish that dream for too many.

Ironically, those subprime borrowers who cling to their properties may face deleterious consequences of their own. Families straining to make payments on loans priced above prime loans, or on those with rates that adjust upward while wages remain stagnant, may divert monies from education, health care, and other familial needs.[47] High-cost subprime loans might also strip opportunities for wealth acquisition. One study found that homeowners in four subject cities paying just two percentage points' interest over prime rates generally would have fared better renting and investing their monthly savings.[48] As mentioned earlier, subprime loans typically are 3.5 percentage points over prime rates. If Latino/as aren't paying excessive rent as tenants occupying overcrowded, dilapidated units, then they might be throwing money at expensive mortgages in a sometimes desperate grasp at the American dream.

Part II

Exclusion

The 1800s were marked by tactics that separated Latino/as from their land in the United States. By contrast, as the country shifted from scattered rural to dense urban and suburban living, the 1900s were characterized by strategies to exclude Latino/as from residing near Anglo homeowners. In the 2000s, undocumented immigrants have become the prime target of exclusionary tactics that encompass housing, both owned and rented.

The various tools used to exclude Latino/as from housing encompass private as well as government strategies. Private tools range from efforts by ranchers and vigilante groups along the U.S./Mexico border to exclude immigrants from transitory entry onto private lands, to discriminatory agreements among neighboring homeowners to exclude Latino/as from residential subdivisions. Public tools to exclude Latino/as include ordinances directed at preventing undocumented immigrants from renting housing, as well as ordinances that are seemingly neutral but aim to discourage racial minorities and more generally the impoverished from residing in the community by denying affordable housing or regulating the density of residential units.

The discussion of these public and private tools of exclusion is enlivened by the tension posed by legal constraints on these strategies. Almost all exclusionary practices operate outside or barely within the law, and the history of exclusion is marked by ongoing legal battles. Much of the ammunition for challenging exclusionary practices comes from state and federal constitutional provisions, ranging from equal protection challenges against private restrictive covenants to attacks on zoning ordinances relying on the liberty interest of the due process clause and rights to privacy. Legal limits against policies targeting housing or free movement of undocumented immigrants may be rooted in federal preemption of local ordinances, or even in constitutional guarantees of free speech.

Although petitioning courts for injunctive relief is sometimes the first line of defense against exclusionary practices, the historical record demonstrates that litigation-based remedies are no panacea for Latino/a housing.

(The shortcomings of attacking exclusionary tactics through litigation are addressed by the reforms proposed in Part IV.) Some once-effective legal protections against housing inequities have been watered down by conservative courts. Previously invoked to combat the unequal provision of such government services as water, sewer, paved streets, and sidewalks to Black neighborhoods,[1] the constitutional standard of equal protection might have helped ease deprivation among Latino/a residents in today's colonia housing. Such judicial application, however, is now impeded by the need to establish that government intended to discriminate on grounds of race against the neglected neighborhood.[2]

Judicial relief tends to be reactive and rarely sets the tone for meaningful change in the Latino/a community. Legal victories in the housing arena frequently are short-lived, as strategies often emerge in their wake that survive legal challenge and accomplish similar ends of exclusion. For example, in the first half of the twentieth century, Anglos aiming to live in neighborhoods free of Latino/a neighbors might have opted to restrict entry by means of openly discriminatory private restrictive covenants barring sale or rental to Latino/as. Although the Supreme Court denied enforcement of such covenants in 1948, communities might now surreptitiously exclude most Latino/as using local zoning ordinances, or even private covenants among neighbors, that protect against entry by the lower economic class. Requirements intended to raise the cost of entry, such as those mandating large lots and homes, fall disproportionately on minority groups such as Latino/as. However, they often withstand legal challenge given their facial neutrality and the willingness of courts to allow the creation of ostensibly idyllic neighborhoods. Density restrictions enacted by local governments in the form of minimum square footage per resident similarly might survive judicial scrutiny, suggesting the need for more comprehensive reform toward equal housing opportunity.

6

Exclusion of Undocumented Immigrants

[T]he individuals . . . deprived of housing by [municipal ordinances targeting undocumented immigrants] are not asking any unit of government to provide them with housing. Nor are they asking private individuals to supply them with housing free of charge. They are simply attempting to procure housing for themselves, at their own expense, on the private market. An analogy between food and housing, both basic necessities, might be instructive here: Even though many people in America may believe that unauthorized immigrants should not be eligible for food stamps, how many would argue that they should be prohibited from buying food? There is something particularly inhumane about a legal regime that prevents people from obtaining shelter, even those who are illegally present in the country.
—Rigel C. Oliveri, "Between a Rock and a Hard Place: Landlords, Latinos, Anti-Illegal Immigrant Ordinances, and Housing Discrimination," *Vanderbilt Law Review* 62 (2009): 55, 108

Latino day laborers in suburban New Jersey caught in the collapse of the national economy in 2009 resorted to crowding under the front porch of an abandoned house. Accessed by removing a wooden grate, the eight-by-twelve-foot cubbyhole that shelters them is the size of a small bedroom, but with a four-foot ceiling.[1] Hunched and huddling in mismatched blankets, as many as ten men at a time shared what they called "Devil's Cave" as work dwindled below the amount needed to sustain their equally crowded occupancy of squalid rental units that at least allowed them to stand rather than crawl and offered the prospect of a hot shower.

Undocumented immigrants, primarily those from Mexico, are the new targets of exclusionary tactics that stretch north from desolate borderlands to cities across the United States. Most of these tactics aim broadly beyond housing to discourage undocumented immigrants from entering the United States or, once here, to hasten their departure from the territory of the American dream.

Courts have long protected the possessory rights of landowners against unauthorized entry onto their property under the English doctrine known as trespass. Not limited to enclosed structures such as houses, trespass protects barren Southwest ranchland just as it does lush gated subdivisions. As one influential English source put it, "every man's land is, in the eye of the law, inclosed and set apart from his neighbors."[2] Nor does trespass require entry by force or injury to the land unlawfully entered. Rather, "[a]ny unauthorized entry on land in the actual or constructive possession of another constitutes a trespass, irrespective of [the] degree of force used or whether actual damage is done."[3] Yet trespass law does not encircle private property with an impenetrable fortress of protection, as the doctrine occasionally gives way to imperatives of entry by the uninvited. In England, for example, exceptions to the trespass prohibition under the common law allow the poor to enter farmland after the harvest to glean what they can,[4] and by statute allow the public to wander over the "open country" land that comprises about 12 percent of England and Wales.[5]

The Southwest has a rich history of Anglo squatting. As detailed in chapter 2, owners of Spanish and Mexican land grants, particularly during northern California's gold rush frenzy of settler migration, faced threats from squatters who occupied their lands, stole their cattle, built improvements, and conducted farming or ranching operations as interlopers. The U.S. government tried to appease land-hungry western settlers by passing the Homestead Act of 1862, providing 160 acres of federal land to each settler who agreed to cultivate the land for five years. Anglo immigrants and migrants were its primary beneficiaries. Still, although the U.S. population increased by 32 million between 1862 and 1890 and some 98 million acres were available under the program for settlement, during that time settlers claimed only about 372,000 homesteads under the act.[6] Because of the arid climate and sparse vegetation of some parts of the Southwest, ranchers needed several thousand acres rather than just 160, and the custom emerged among Anglo ranchers, as it had among Spanish and Mexican ranchers, to graze livestock on adjoining government-owned lands. Congress encouraged this practice by tolerating trespassory grazing on unclaimed ranchlands, but through laws such as the Taylor Grazing Act of 1934 Congress ultimately shifted to a policy of allocating and charging for grazing privileges on federal lands.[7]

In recent years, America's broken and misguided immigration policy and the common law of trespass have collided in the unforgiving southwestern desert. Replacing once extensive Latino/a rancho landholdings, Anglo-owned ranches and farms dominate the rural Southwest. The roles have reversed since the 1800s, as Anglo landowners now face Latino/a trespassers. But the dynamics of trespass have changed, with Latino/a undocumented immigrants merely crossing the terrain rather than staying to contest and oust the Anglo owners from title, and with some Anglo owners and vigilante groups taking up arms to resist Latino/a entry.

The Immigration and Nationality Act of 1965 halted unlimited immigration to the United States from other Western Hemisphere nations by placing numerical restrictions on citizenship. About the same time, Congress terminated the Bracero guest-worker program. U.S. employers kept beckoning workers, and millions of undocumented immigrants crossed the southern border, seeking a chance at the American dream. Until the 1990s, these immigrant crossings took place near urban entry points on the U.S./Mexico border such as San Diego. In 1994, the United States launched the border-arming strategy known primarily as Operation Gatekeeper, beefing up urban entry points such as San Diego and El Paso with fencing, walls, technology, and manpower under the assumption that immigrants would not undertake crossings in more remote, treacherous areas. But policymakers tragically underestimated the resolve of immigrants seeking economic opportunity, and the death toll mounted as border crossings shifted to desolate, dangerous terrain in the deserts of California, Arizona, New Mexico, and Texas.

In the wide open spaces of the Southwest,[8] ranchers and vigilante groups embrace the legal doctrine of trespass to oust these desert crossers, who out of desperation will traverse private lands in this cruel, mostly roadless terrain. Armed with tracking dogs and rifles, some of these vigilantes exceed the boundaries of trespass law. A landowner's ability to defend her land and eject trespassers has common-sense limits. Deadly force ordinarily cannot be employed. Rather, the landowner may use only the force reasonably necessary to remove a trespasser, and exceeding the bounds of the privilege by using excessive force can result in criminal prosecution. For example, teenagers protecting a California grapefruit orchard in the 1940s were prosecuted after they shot and killed a Mexican national while trying to scatter a group of trespassers taking fruit.[9]

The shift in border crossings to rural areas in the 1990s was accompanied by an increase in demand by U.S. employers for cheap, immigrant labor, luring huge numbers of undocumented workers. Vigilante groups such as the Minutemen and Ranch Rescue began patrolling the border passages. The Ranch Rescue group solicited volunteers to interdict undocumented immigrants on private ranchland (at the invitation of the landowner), either by evicting them or by purporting to make a citizen's arrest for criminal trespass.[10] Despite claiming the privilege of protecting against unlawful trespassers, some of these border vigilantes have faced lawsuits for using excessive force. The most prominent vigilante rancher, Roger Barnett, conducts his own patrols with an M-16 automatic rifle on 22,000 acres (thirty-five square miles) of Arizona cattle ranchland a few miles from the border, which he owns or leases from the state. Immigrant rights groups sued Barnett, among other vigilantes, accusing him of harassing and unlawfully imprisoning some of the undocumented immigrants he confronts. One suit contended that he kicked a woman and threatened a group of captured undocumented immigrants with his dogs, allegedly yelling at them in Spanish, "My dog is hungry . . . for buttocks." The jury awarded the immigrants $73,352 in damages in early 2009.[11] In 2006, another jury found Barnett liable to a family of U.S.-born Mexican Americans for nearly $100,000 stemming from a confrontation when Barnett caught them hunting on his property and allegedly threatened to shoot them with his assault rifle while hurling racial slurs.[12] Following a lawsuit against the former leader of the Ranch Rescue group, Casey Nethercott, two undocumented immigrants from El Salvador gained title to the leader's seventy-acre ranch in Arizona, located two miles from the Mexican border. The immigrants' lawsuit accused Nethercott and others of threatening them and hitting one with a pistol in an encounter on a Texas ranch in 2003.[13]

Opponents of undocumented immigration often cast these immigrants as dangerous outlaws, justifying the threat or use of deadly force to repel them. For example, in the 2006 trial Barnett's lawyer unsuccessfully portrayed him as a rancher justifiably protecting his property rights. Local sentiment seemed to agree—among the many pro-Barnett comments in the local newspaper following the verdict against him was one opining, "I think most of the people of Cochise County support Roger Barnett in principle, as far as rightfully protecting his family and property from the invasion of illegal immigrants."[14] While running a single-issue anti-immigrant campaign for the presidency in 2008, Tom Tancredo painted a menacing portrait of border-crossers, justifying self-defense:

Because many of the people coming across the border are carrying large quantities of illegal drugs for resale, guards with automatic weapons accompany them. These are not people who simply drop everything and run when they are confronted by a rancher or a Border Patrol official. They opt to open fire, and many times have done just that.

Some of the illegals who are not directly connected to drug trafficking have been very indifferent, very aggressive, and very antagonistic to the ranchers in the area. Ranchers have been threatened physically, assaulted, family members threatened, had their wells vandalized, or endured break-ins at their homes, barns, or outbuildings. And so almost everyone on this [border] area is armed. Children go to school armed because their parents are afraid to send them alone.

Ranchers are forced to keep shotguns or other firearms by their doors. And they do this out of necessity, not because they're gun freaks.[15]

The boundary separating permissible and unlawful force to exclude trespassers is not a clear one. Further clouding the issue of undocumented border crossings over private ranchland is the trespass privilege of private necessity. As described by the Restatement (Second) of Torts, this privilege enables entry onto private property in emergency circumstances, allowing one to enter private land "if it is or reasonably appears necessary to prevent serious harm" to the entering party or his property.[16] The most common example of the privilege is docking one's boat at a private dock when a sudden storm arises, perhaps spawning the expression "any port in a storm." But the privilege of necessity is problematic when applied to border crossers who presumably have already broken the law by entering the country. Although once in the United States, the absence of borderland roads and the urgency of reaching food and water make trespass inevitable, perhaps the privilege will be denied because, arguably, the immigrant created the life-threatening emergency. But in some cases culpability is less clear. For example, a family breadwinner may be crossing to secure a job and finances needed for the survival and medical expenses of his family in Mexico. Or the misrepresentation of a coyote (smuggler) as to the distance or route to be traveled might prompt an immigrant to enter a U.S. ranch in search of water. Moreover, like the typical exercise of private necessity, the border crossing is transitory. The landowner ordinarily need not worry about sustained possession that might, over time, ripen to adverse possession and loss of title.[17] The closest legal precedent supporting the necessity of passage of border crossers comes from decisions recognizing a privilege sourced in public policy or free speech rights for legal aid lawyers, health services workers, union organizers, and the like to enter an employer's property to aid and communicate with migrant farm workers who reside there.[18] Although there is no similar communicative purpose surrounding the borderland crossing, or any expectation of visitors providing social services, the health and safety of the future U.S. worker is at risk in this perilous passage.

These are some of the questions sparked by America's broken immigration system, which lures immigrants to risk their lives by crossing the border for a chance at the American dream in cities, towns, and fields throughout the United States.

As of March 2008, an estimated 11.9 million undocumented immigrants resided in the United States, about four out of five of them Latino/a, and most of them from Mexico. Once these immigrants reached the relative sanctuary of the public streets and sidewalks of Anytown, U.S.A., the intersection of undocumented immigration and trespass law resurfaced. Criminal trespass laws enable police to enforce private property rights that do not involve other crimes such as vandalism or burglary. These laws may encompass public spaces too, such as entering a public park after hours. Ordinarily these laws contemplate a relatively neutral application—they apply evenly to the public regardless of citizenship or ethnicity. In 2005, however, police chiefs in two New Hampshire towns attempted to stretch criminal trespass laws to prosecute undocumented immigrants for their mere presence in the town without lawful immigration documents. As one of the chiefs put it, if someone was in the country illegally, then he was in their town illegally.[19] The other agreed that "from now on, anybody who . . . is an illegal alien . . . will be cited [for trespassing]."[20] New Hampshire's criminal trespass statute encompasses any person who "enters or remains in any place" while "knowing that he is not licensed or privileged to do so."[21] Under this broad legislative language the chiefs' interpretation was not too far-fetched, yet it raised troubling policy and constitutional concerns. As the director of the American Civil Liberties Union's New Hampshire office pointed out, the state's criminal trespass law was "clearly directed toward private property" rather than mere presence in a public place.[22] Moreover, as with any local efforts to penalize the undocumented, wielding criminal trespass law against them would require establishing their undocumented status, probably in part by racial profiling. Mexicans would come under special scrutiny in the search of public spaces for "trespassers" on American turf. The immigrants cited for trespass in New Hampshire included an undocumented immigrant from Mexico, living and working locally in construction, who had pulled off the road to make a cell phone call. After he acknowledged that he was undocumented, the man was charged with criminal trespassing and held in jail overnight. Although law professor Kris Kobach opined that the charge was appropriate because the federal government "has always been careful to invite and encourage local assistance with immigration arrests,"[23] a New Hampshire judge found otherwise and dismissed the charges as an unconstitutional local attempt to augment federal enforcement of immigration crimes.[24]

Although the New Hampshire judge's ruling derailed momentum in other towns to use state or local trespass laws against undocumented immigrants, an Ohio legislator subsequently introduced legislation aiming to create a trespass offense for undocumented immigrants entering the state.[25] Arizona's legislature enacted such a "state trespass" crime in 2006, but then-Governor Janet Napolitano vetoed the bill. Republican Governor Jan Brewer, in contrast, signed a 2010 law that criminalized the status of being an undocumented immigrant in Arizona.

Apart from trespass, efforts at the local level to exclude undocumented immigrants from public and private spaces have creatively invoked other legal frameworks, such as loitering (which usually encompasses occupancy of public places) and criminal nuisance laws (discussed in chapter 8), as well as local ordinances targeting the renting of property to undocumented immigrants.

Day laborers who gather in urban spaces seeking temporary employment are primarily male, undocumented, and Latino. Employers hire them as unskilled labor for jobs such as construction and landscaping. These laborers congregate on sidewalks and in parking lots, especially those near convenience and hardware stores, to await prospective employers. Backlash against day laborers comes from the businesses at which they gather, as well as from local residents and law enforcement. For example, a 7-Eleven store in Southampton, New York, posted signs reading "No Formar Grupos" [Don't Form Groups] and "No Loitering" to dissuade the day laborers who gathered there by the hundreds each morning.[26] Residents of the Long Island town of Farmingville harassed day laborers as they solicited work on streetcorners.[27] In Virginia, police arrested twenty-two day laborers outside a 7-Eleven and charged them with loitering.[28] The application of loitering laws to day laborers, however, stands on shaky constitutional ground. The Supreme Court has struck down loitering laws under the due process clause of the Fourteenth Amendment when they are too vague and supply police with open-ended discretion. Loitering laws contemplate authorities making judgment calls on

Exclusion of Undocumented Immigrants | 65

the bona fides of presence in a public place, providing a gateway to racial profiling. In a leading case, the Supreme Court struck down as unconstitutionally vague a Chicago ordinance used by police against suspected Latino/a and African American gang members who loitered in any public place "with no apparent purpose."[29] The First Amendment's constitutional protection of free speech also comes into play, and prompted a preliminary injunction obtained by the Mexican American Legal Defense and Educational Fund against enforcement of a Baldwin Park, California, ordinance that required day laborers to leave a three-foot space for pedestrian traffic when seeking work on public sidewalks. A federal judge in California also invoked the First Amendment to permanently enjoin enforcement of a Redondo Beach ordinance making it "unlawful for any person to stand on a street or highway and solicit, or attempt to solicit, employment, business, or contributions from an occupant of any motor vehicle."[30] In 2004, the city had wielded that ordinance against day laborers by using undercover police officers recruiting workers from their cars. Another federal judge issued a preliminary injunction in 2008 against a similarly worded day laborer ordinance in the Arizona town of Cave Creek.[31]

While day laborers often pursue work in urban public spaces, by night they retreat to the shadows and margins of the American dream. Housing costs in some urban areas are so expensive that many day laborers and their migrant farm worker brethren must resort to makeshift housing. Latino/a laborers near San Diego, for example, "drag tarps, crates, and spare wood into the hills and canyons," where they "can see the glitter of million-dollar homes that brush against tomato fields and hills and ravines less than a mile away, at a closeness that has made some residents of these homes uncomfortable."[32]

Those fortunate enough to have decent shelter may be targeted by local ordinances designed to discourage undocumented immigrants from living in rental houses and apartments. Although several cities have assumed the role of local immigration enforcers, most national attention has been focused on Hazelton, Pennsylvania. An influx of Latino/a immigrants, many coming from New York and New Jersey, and many of them undocumented, sparked a backlash in this community. Although the 1990 Census counted only 249 Hispanic residents, by 2005 Latino/as amounted to nearly one-third of Hazelton's 30,000 residents, reversing steady population declines in the latter half of the twentieth century that accompanied industry's exodus from the area. Reflecting the diversity of the national Latino/a demographic, these residents hailed from the Dominican Republic, Mexico, Guatemala, Honduras, and Puerto Rico, among other places. In 2006, Hazelton enacted ordinances that embraced English as its official language, prohibited employing or harboring undocumented immigrants, and required occupants of rental units to provide proof of legal citizenship or residency. Hazelton's harboring ordinance punishes any landlord or other person who harbors an "illegal alien" in a dwelling unit. Under this ordinance an official or resident—presumably someone who overhears Spanish or sees a Mexican-appearing person living next door—can lodge a complaint, upon receipt of which Hazelton officials will investigate. If the tenant is found to be an undocumented immigrant, the landlord must correct the violation (evict the tenant) or face fines. Occupants of rental units must also obtain an occupancy permit from the city's Code Enforcement Office, which requires showing "proper identification" of "legal citizenship and/or residency." Landlords must ensure their tenants have occupancy permits or face fines.

Hazelton's mindset was to attack undocumented immigrants where they work and live, using housing laws to displace them. Cities such as Escondido, California (near San Diego), and the Dallas suburb of Farmers Branch, Texas, have enacted similar laws. Like Hazelton, these localities experienced substantial jumps in Latino/a population—from 20 to 37 percent in Farmers Branch during the 1990s, from 16 to 42 percent in Escondido since 1990. Their housing ordinances also share a similar purported rationale of protecting public safety. For example, the Escondido ordinance stated that "crime committed by illegal aliens harm [sic] the health, safety, and welfare of legal residents in the city," and the Farmers Branch ordinance sought to "promote the public health, safety, and general welfare of [its] citizens."[33] Sometimes such ordinances are grounded in the stereotypes identified in chapter 4, as with a Farmers Branch councilman who justified the law because "I saw our property values declining . . . [due to] what I would call less desirable people mov[ing] into our neighborhoods, people who don't value education, people who don't value taking care of their properties."[34]

Despite municipal claims of police power, local housing laws targeting immigrants collide with several constitutional and statutory protections that have thus far derailed these local efforts. For example, a federal judge in 2006 temporarily halted enforcement of an Escondido ordinance that called for suspending the business license of any landlord who rented to a person knowing or in reckless disregard of the tenant's undocumented status.[35] Escondido's city council responded by permanently halting enforcement of the controversial ordinance. A judge blocked a similar law in Farmers Branch that required landlords to verify the immigration status of their tenants.[36] A judge in Valley Park, Missouri, enjoined a local ordinance that fined landlords who rented to undocumented immigrants.[37] And a federal judge in Pennsylvania permanently enjoined enforcement of the Hazelton employment and housing ordinances. Among other things, the Hazelton housing ordinances conflicted with federal immigration law and violated the constitutional guarantee of procedural due process—for example, they could result in eviction without notice to the tenant and failed to sufficiently describe the "identity data" required for landlords to verify their tenant's immigration status. Not all of the constitutional challenges to these laws were successful, however. Significantly, the challenge to the Hazelton housing ordinances under the Equal Protection Clause failed because the legislation was found to be rationally related to the aim of preventing public safety problems allegedly triggered by undocumented immigrants.[38] The Hazelton case appears destined for the U.S. Supreme Court on these constitutional questions. Regardless of the resolution there, federal preemption is a constitutional hurdle that Congress can surmount by legislation authorizing local governments to join immigration enforcement through housing ordinances. Alternatively, the local measure might pass constitutional muster if it uses federal standards to determine undocumented status. After a judge enjoined the Farmers Branch ordinance for usurping a federal function, the city council aimed to overcome the constitutional hurdle by reenacting the measure in early 2008 to require the city to verify each renter's immigration status with the federal government rather than rely on the city's own determination. Still, the federal government does not maintain a comprehensive database for these purposes, and the revised ordinance has been embroiled in costly litigation.[39] Alternatively, targeting the housing consequences of impoverished undocumented immigrants might avoid immigration preemption, as by ordinances discussed in chapter 7 specifying maximum occupancy levels and banning street parking. And procedural due process defects similarly might be remedied by carefully drafting the ordinances to provide more definite standards for determining undocumented status and to ensure procedural protections of notice and a right to contest an adverse determination. So the tactic of using local housing ordinances to attack undocumented immigration, while at least temporarily immobilized, still has a pulse. Lawmakers in California did manage to slay this dragon by passing legislation in late 2007 that prohibits a city or county from compelling landlords to obtain information on the citizenship or immigration status of their tenants, and also prevents landlords from seeking such information on their own initiative from tenants or occupants.[40]

Apart from the constitutional infirmities, the Hazelton housing ordinances raise serious policy concerns. Latino/a immigrants often are accused of refusing or being unable to assimilate into the mainstream of American life. The Hazelton English-language ordinance reflects the view of many that Latino/as are unwilling to learn English because they are here temporarily with no plans to put down community roots. Some of these xenophobes believe that Latino/a immigrants are threats to the community who bring crime and violence to neighborhoods. Latino/a immigrants are attacked for taking jobs from Americans, yet sending the fruits of their labor back to Mexico and beyond. Whether these concerns are false, wildly exaggerated, or legitimate, housing can serve as a gateway to the assimilation and community engagement that many claim are lacking in today's immigrants. Homeownership earned through hard work—the quintessential American dream—can be the anchor that injects Latino/a immigrants into community affairs and offers them a stake in the future prosperity of the United States. But many of the voices criticizing Latino/as for their supposed failure to assimilate also rail at the idea of encouraging Latino/as to attain the American dream of homeownership. They bristle at delivering mortgage information in Spanish, and denounce lenders and brokers who service Latino/a immigrant customers.

While former CNN host Lou Dobbs, former Congressman Tom Tancredo, Hazelton's mayor, and others decry the presence of undocumented immigrants in our landscape, quietly and in the shadows many of these immigrants have begun to realize the dream of owning homes in the United States rather than just laboring to construct them for others. Although a potential roadblock to homeownership might be the absence of a Social Security number (SSN) or the nonpayment of federal taxes, undocumented immigrants can obtain an Individual Tax Identification number (ITIN) from the Internal Revenue Service that enables them to pay taxes and thus verify the income needed to qualify for a home mortgage.

Lenders with publicized loan programs for noncitizen Latino/as, however, have drawn harsh criticism and threats that stymied these offerings. For example, Bank of America faced calls for a boycott in 2007 when it marketed a credit card to customers without an SSN so long as they had maintained a checking account in good standing for three months.[41] A Birmingham, Alabama, federal savings bank canceled its "Casa Mia" program of fixed-rate mortgage loans designed to help newly arrived Latino/a residents in the South with an ITIN and a steady job when it received menacing emails and calls threatening legal action and contending it was aiding undocumented immigration. Although federal law does not require banks to verify the immigration status of mortgage borrowers, anti-immrant groups argue that such loan programs violate federal law prohibiting aiding and abetting the undocumented for commercial gain, as well as laws requiring financial institutions to report illegal activity. In 2007, John Doolittle, Republican Congressman from California, sponsored an amendment to the Federal Housing Finance Reform Act seeking to prohibit federally sponsored mortgage loan enterprises such as Fannie Mae and Freddie Mac from acquiring home loans made to borrowers without an SSN. The amendment was directed at undocumented immigrants using their ITIN for borrower identification purposes. In order to facilitate the purchase of second homes in the United States by wealthy foreigners, however, the prohibition would have applied only to those purchasing a primary residence. Although the House adopted the amendment, the legislation floundered as the failing economy and outside pressures undercut the impetus for ITIN loans. By 2008, most lenders voluntarily abandoned ITIN loans despite the irony that home loans previously made to undocumented immigrants were holding up well in the mortgage meltdown, with delinquency rates significantly below the national average for all U.S. borrowers. According to one report, the ITIN loan default rate was less than 1 percent at a time when 6.4 percent of U.S. mortgages were in default,[42] and almost one in ten (9.3 percent) subprime mortgages were delinquent.[43]

Ironically, the outcry over immigration and the resultant tightening of border security have provided incentives for undocumented immigrants to purchase homes in the United States. Prior to Operation Gatekeeper and similar enforcement efforts, Mexican immigrants could travel more freely across the border to their primary residence in Mexico. Their employment in seasonal jobs such as field labor facilitated this ebb and flow without the incentive for placing permanent roots in the United States. But enhanced border security prompted many undocumented Mexican immigrants to forgo the treacherous and expensive passage back and forth across the border for more permanency in the United States. Once here, these immigrants might travel deeper into the U.S. heartland and work in more steady occupations to sustain their living expenses. Further from Mexico and employed year round, these immigrants are now more motivated to deepen their roots and aspire to own homes in the United States. Increasingly, undocumented immigrants might be dreaming in Spanish, but they are dreaming the American dream of homeownership, a job, and a future for themselves and their children, all in the United States.

Constraints on foreign ownership or rental of land in the United States have deep roots that predate the rash of local restrictions in Hazelton and elsewhere. Dating to the 1880s, when Congress restricted foreign ownership of land in U.S. territories by nonresident aliens under the Territorial Land Act of 1887, several states have restricted alien land ownership.[44] Anti-Japanese sentiment prompted another round of these laws in the early 1900s, this time focused on the West Coast and on agricultural holdings. Known as Alien Land Laws, these statutes and initiatives generally restricted ownership by those ineligible for citizenship. Because immigration laws at the time barred naturalization for Chinese, Japanese, and other Asian immigrants, the Alien Land Laws were, in essence, anti-Asian laws. California's Alien Land Law, enacted in 1913, was shored up by a citizen initiative in 1920. The voter's pamphlet from that year failed to disguise the prevailing discriminatory intent, arguing that the law's "primary purpose is to prohibit Orientals who cannot become American citizens from controlling our rich agricultural lands." It further warned that "Orientals, largely Japanese, are fast securing control of the richest irrigated lands in the state," and that "control of these rich lands means in time control of the products and control of the markets."[45] These Alien Land Laws initially survived court challenges. For example, the U.S. Supreme Court upheld the state of Washington's statute against constitutional challenges of due process and equal protection, reasoning that the restriction of ownership to all aliens was neither capricious nor arbitrary, and that states could properly ensure the allegiance of those who own land.[46] But the judicial tide eventually turned against the Alien Land Laws, with the Supreme Courts of Oregon and California striking down laws in 1949 and 1952, respectively.[47] California's decision acknowledged the racist intent of its law:

> The California alien land law is obviously designed and administered as an instrument for effectuating racial discrimination. . . . There is nothing to indicate that those alien residents who are racially ineligible for citizenship possess characteristics which are dangerous to the legitimate interests of the state, or that they, as a class, might use the land for purposes injurious to public morals, safety or welfare. Accordingly, we hold that the alien land law is invalid as in violation of the Fourteenth Amendment.[48]

Despite such judicial backlash, new laws restricting foreign ownership were enacted, particularly during the Cold War and into the 1970s, sparked by concerns of increased foreign investment.[49] Such laws remain in effect in several states and tend to target nonresident aliens, particularly owners of agricultural property.[50] Like recent municipal laws aimed at undocumented immigrants, these state laws are facially neutral and avoid singling out a particular immigrant group on grounds of race or ethnicity.

Just as Alien Land Laws historically tended to target Asian immigrants, it is evident from the timing of their adoption and the discourse surrounding them that recent municipal laws regulating the undocumented aim to exclude Latino/a immigrants from the local townscape. Recognizing the scarce financial resources of most of these immigrants, ordinances targeting the undocumented, such as those adopted in Hazelton, tend to outlaw immigrant rentals rather than ownership. But outcry over loan programs that enable the undocumented to purchase U.S. homes suggests that some local sentiment opposes both rentals and purchases by the undocumented. As people of good conscience regret laws to exclude Asians from property ownership in the twentieth century, we may someday regret as a nation these efforts directed at the housing of undocumented immigrants who come to the United States at great expense and risk, motivated to better their lives and those of their families through hard work in jobs most Americans won't undertake. Those attempting to undercut their housing fail to recognize that these immigrants represent our best hope for continuing the vitality of the American ideal that hard work is the gateway to comfortable housing.

In locations experimenting with restrictive housing laws, local economies have suffered—in Hazelton "there are 'for rent' signs . . . everywhere both for stores and apartments because people have moved out, they've left, both legal and those presumably illegal as well."[51] By chasing away these newcomers from housing markets, communities are choosing to gray and wither rather than embrace the vitality and opportunity of potential new homebuyers to replace their aging Anglo homeowners. Already hemorrhaging its native residents, Hazelton has scant prospects for a vibrant future if it drives away immigrants and their ideals of homeownership.

7

Exclusion by Public Law

Zoning Laws

On Long Island, New York, some local residents organized in the 2000s against overcrowded immigrant housing. Protesters in the Farmingville-based group Sachem Quality of Life carried signs with slogans such as "Let's address overcrowded housing." The group's website maintains that local government allows disintegration of quality of life through "overcrowded slum housing."[1] The Elmont Quality of Life Committee, formed in 2001, collects and forwards complaints of suspected unlawful dwellings to city officials. A 2005 investigative report described one of those crowded Elmont homes, which a Honduran immigrant shared with sixteen others, filling the basement, the two main floors, and the attic. Renovating basements for a living, the twenty-eight-year-old Honduran immigrant shared a bedroom with two men, together paying $550 a month. Six residents used the same bathroom. Back home in Honduras, his wife and two children occupied a house they own.[2]

As examined in chapter 6, cities such as Hazelton, Pennsylvania, have attacked undocumented immigrants explicitly by outlawing their rental of living space. The Hazelton ordinance denies housing to undocumented immigrants by demanding that renters present proof of legal citizenship or residency in order to obtain occupancy permits. Zoning and building codes are another weapon local governments have turned against Latino/a immigrants and Latino/as generally. Though they appear neutral on the surface, such laws can reach beyond undocumented immigrants to target the living arrangements of impoverished Latino/as regardless of their immigrant or citizenship status. Historically, zoning laws have played a role in excluding nearly every minority group from Anglo neighborhoods. The recent imperative of excluding undocumented Latino/as is just the latest application of laws meant to ensure the prevailing perceptions of property value, even at the cost of equality.

Well-entrenched zoning techniques to exclude the impoverished (and, not by coincidence, minority groups) include prohibiting or restricting manufactured housing and multifamily dwellings, particularly public housing projects, as well as restrictions whose effect is to increase the cost of single-family residences. For example, zoning might require large lot sizes (as does the suburban Phoenix enclave Town of Paradise Valley, which requires at least one acre per dwelling unit) and substantial setbacks and dictate the minimum square footage of homes.³ Even a seemingly benign ordinance requiring new homes to include a certain percentage of brick or stone masonry façade instead of cheaper vinyl or wood siding might price many minority buyers out of the neighborhood, as home builders and the National Association for the Advancement of Colored People (NAACP) contended in an unsuccessful 2008 lawsuit brought under the Fair Housing Act against a suburb of Austin, Texas.⁴

These types of exclusionary zoning are often seen in suburbs, which may have sufficient land to support large-lot ordinances, as well as the discriminatory motivation to exclude certain "undesirables." As one set of commentators observed, "[T]here is strong support from case law, popular accounts, and the academic literature that local governments adopt large-lot zoning, minimum house size requirements, and bans on secondary units [such as converted garages or mother-in-law apartments] precisely to make their housing more expensive and thereby exclude lower-income racial and ethnic minorities."⁵

Exclusionary zoning tools include low-density requirements that hamper multifamily housing, which research has found thereby "limits the number of Black and Hispanic residents."⁶ Suburban communities have been notoriously hostile to public housing projects, leading to their concentration in crumbling inner-city landscapes.⁷ After Hurricane Katrina's devastation, the New Orleans parish of St. Bernard employed the novel discriminatory tool of restricting home rentals to blood relatives of the owners absent parish consent. Because 93 percent of those owners were Anglos, a fair housing suit was brought that prompted repeal of the ordinance. The parish later prohibited multifamily housing construction, until a federal court ruled that the moratorium had an unlawful disparate impact on African Americans.⁸

Latino/as might overcome a shortage of multifamily housing by crowding into residences. Municipalities, however, readily resort to zoning laws to defeat these arrangements. Local zoning and housing codes employ occupancy restrictions to exclude group-living arrangements deemed undesirable, such as group homes for the developmentally disabled, communes, student housing, and even Latino/a residences where several low-wage workers pool their funds toward rent. Several density techniques can effectively exclude or restrict group housing. Most straightforward is an occupancy ceiling per residential unit—for example, barring more than eight residents from occupying a single-family home or apartment. However, such a standard might exclude families with many children, as well as fail to take account of the size of the home and its number of bedrooms and bathrooms. Thus, some local governments have pinpointed dwelling size by ordinances requiring a minimum dwelling footprint for each occupant. One such law, enacted in Cobb County, Georgia, in 2005, requires fifty square feet of sleeping space per occupant, excluding bathrooms, hallways, and closets.[9] Other localities, such as Santa Ana, California, abandon the measuring tape and more simply limit occupancy to no more than two people per bedroom.[10] In addition to restricting the number of occupants in a dwelling, many localities also wield setback, minimum lot size, and other requirements to constrain homeowners from making additions such as mother-in-law apartments, converted garages, and even additional bedrooms that could accommodate extended family or renters.[11]

Some local governments protect family occupancy while targeting non-family group-living arrangements, most often by prohibiting occupancy of more than a specified number of unrelated occupants, while ensuring that a small housekeeping staff can reside on the family premises. In the feverish anti-immigrant climate of late, some jurisdictions have gone further by narrowing their definitions of family occupancy to exclude extended family members. For example, before repealing the ordinance in early 2006 (one month after its adoption) under threat of legal action, the city council of Manassas, Virginia, restricted occupancy (apart from one unrelated person) to those persons related "to the second degree of collateral consanguinity by blood, marriage, adoption, or guardianship," thus excluding aunts, uncles, cousins, nieces, and nephews.[12] State law already restricted overcrowding by prescribing minimum living-space requirements per occupant, moving the city council to further regulate Latino/a undocumented immigrant households by barring extended-family living arrangements. The vice-mayor of Manassas explicitly attributed the local law in part to addressing undocumented immigration and the problems thought to flow from it—parking, garbage, school budgets, and the like.[13] But the enforcement experience under the short-lived ordinance ran counter to prejudiced expectations of

Latino/as living in squalor.[14] Rather, as reported in the *Washington Post*, "most of the time inspections turned up neat and orderly houses of perhaps eight extended [Latino/a] relatives living together to help with the high cost of housing."[15]

Zoning restrictions have an inglorious legacy of enforcement against racial and immigrant groups, though the groups most hurt by them have changed over the years. Enforcement efforts targeted Chinese immigrants in San Francisco in the 1880s and Eastern European immigrants in New York in the 1920s,[16] while Blacks moving into White neighborhoods prompted many U.S. cities to adopt explicitly segregationist zoning ordinances in the early 1900s.[17] Today, however, restrictive zoning disproportionately impacts Latino/as. Latino/as are disproportionately poor (the Latino/a poverty rate is 22 percent, compared to 9 percent for Anglos), and modern zoning restrictions are weighted against the poor. Moreover, some of the Latino/a population, particularly undocumented immigrants, is transitory and moves with work opportunities. By necessity, these groups often need temporary living arrangements that are best served by dormitory-style housing. Further, many undocumented immigrants either left property behind in their country of origin or intend to return there to purchase property, so their mindset while in the United States is to save as much money as possible to expedite that return. This expectation lends itself to economy in living arrangements, as does the reality that the undocumented worker, rather than having leisure time around the house, works or seeks work outside the home almost around the clock. Moreover, many undocumented immigrants left families behind and thus as single men or women have trouble justifying the extravagance of their U.S. dwellings.

For many immigrants, the only option for affordable housing is through the economy of numbers. Entry-level, service-oriented jobs such as landscaping and domestic service are often found in wealthy communities with few or no convenient options for affordable housing other than overcrowding. For example, in Los Angeles, home to a disproportionate number of undocumented immigrants, housing costs are twice those of the average U.S. metropolitan area.[18] Recent immigrants are particularly susceptible to these costs, with a study finding that only 3 percent of native-born Los Angeles residents lived in overcrowded housing, while almost half (47.9 percent) of recent immigrants did so.[19]

The disproportionate impact of residential density restrictions on Latino/as, particularly immigrants, also has a significant cultural dimension—especially with regard to zoning ordinances that regulate the number of occupants per bedroom. Several writers have identified a "robust esteem" among Latino/as for their extended family.[20] Anthropological research suggests that countries such as Mexico emphasize interdependency rather than individualism, so that their citizens are more comfortable with crowded sleeping arrangements as opposed to bedrooms as places of isolation.[21]

Given these economic and cultural circumstances, Latino/a households tend to be much larger than Anglo households. Almost one-quarter (23 percent) of Latino/a households contain five or more residents, compared to just 8 percent of non-Latino/a households. Almost one-third (32 percent) of Latino/a households include relatives who aren't immediate family members, in contrast to only 19 percent of non-Latino/a households. Thirteen percent of Latino/a households have nonrelative boarders. Thus, overall, almost half (45 percent) of Latino/a households contain residents outside the immediate family. In addition to extended family and boarders, some 50 percent of Latino/a households contain children, compared to just 30 percent of non-Latino/a households.[22] Predictably, about one-quarter of all Latino/a households—and more than one-third of those foreign-born—are overcrowded, compared to only 4 percent of Anglo and 8 percent of Black households.[23]

In early 2007, *USA Today* reported that "overcrowded housing is emerging as a battleground in the national debate over immigration."[24] No doubt recent local efforts to police overcrowded housing are largely directed at and prompted by Latino/a housing arrangements. Seemingly legitimate enforcement aims often mask animus against Latino/as. By contrast to Hazelton-style ordinances explicitly singling out undocumented immigrants, local governments attribute density zoning and related housing codes to health and safety concerns such as overtaxed electrical systems, cluttered home escape routes, sanitation, and the suitability of garages[25] and basements without opening windows as bedrooms. Neighborhood impacts range from increased traffic, trash, and demand for local services such as schools, to the aesthetic issues created by automobiles that exceed garage parking spaces due to overcrowding or conversion of the garage to a residential unit. The latter concern led Virginia's Fairfax County to prohibit paving residential front yards in 2002.[26] As one Virginia official opined on the prohibition of overcrowded housing, "our focus is on health and safety."[27] A Long Island official characterized overcrowded immigrant housing arrangements as "gross firetraps and health hazards," dismissing claims of racism: "The concerns [of local enforcement officials] have nothing to do with race and everything to do with quality of life and zoning patterns."[28]

Given the toxic anti-immigrant climate, however, one must question whether the health-and-safety rationale is a pretext for discrimination. Latino/as often face discrimination delivered in the guise of protection, such as workplace English-Only restrictions sometimes falsely claimed to protect them from injury due to impaired on-the-job communication. U.S. historical experience belies the safety justification in zoning affecting minority communities. For example, San Francisco's late-nineteenth-century zoning law requiring permits for laundromats in wooden structures was ostensibly justified on grounds of public safety because of open fires used in their operation. The Supreme Court struck down the San Francisco ordinance as violating the constitutional guarantee of equal protection, given the discriminatory motivation for its enactment, as well as the discriminatory history of the officials who dispensed operating permits.[29] The permit applications of Chinese residents, who ran the majority of the city's laundry facilities, were all denied under the new zoning procedures, while all applications for Caucasians were granted. San Francisco's 1870 "Lodging House" ordinance, requiring boarding houses to provide at least 500 cubic feet of air space per resident, facially protected against overcrowding but was also a proxy for anti-Chinese sentiment.[30] Municipal zoning ordinances mandating residential segregation in the early 1900s were ostensibly justified on safety grounds. A 1914 ordinance in Louisville, Kentucky, for example, prohibited "colored" persons from moving onto city blocks with a majority of White residents in order "to prevent conflict and ill-feeling between the white and colored races in the city of Louisville, and to preserve the public peace and promote the general welfare."[31] Attempting racial symmetry to uphold the ordinance, its terms equally barred Whites from moving onto a "colored" block.[32] The Supreme Court struck down these facially discriminatory zoning ordinances in 1917, concluding that while preventing racial conflict was "desirable," this end could not be accomplished by unconstitutional means.[33]

The anti-Latino/a animus of modern zoning ordinances is indicated by their selective enforcement. Latino/a organizations and housing rights advocates point out that non-Latino/a group uses are tolerated while raids on Latino/a households are commonplace. For example, the legal director of the Puerto Rican Legal Defense and Education Fund (now known as LatinoJustice PRLDEF) blasted the enforcement practices of the Long Island community of Farmingville, contending that despite the frequency of overcrowding and of houses in poor condition there, "the town wasn't going after any housing except that occupied by Latino day laborers."[34] A local immigrant advocate alleged "ethnic cleansing" and observed that "there are hundreds and hundreds of mother-daughter apartments [illegal apartments within homes] and dozens of group cottages on Fire Island that are just as illegal."[35] The president of the National Fair Housing Alliance echoed this sentiment of selective enforcement: "We . . . view it as an anti-immigrant issue. You can't have a deed restriction saying, 'No Latinos.' But they're trying to have local ordinances that say immediate families [only]. . . . Are they going back to the white families to see if a cousin is living there? The answer is no. It truly is directed at the new Latino immigrant population."[36]

An example of suspicious reliance on health-and-safety and related justifications comes from Escondido, California. In 2006 a federal judge barred enforcement of the city's ordinance prohibiting rentals in knowing or reckless disregard of the renter's undocumented status. After expensive legal challenges prompted the city to agree to abandon enforcing the rental ordinance, it attempted to chase away Latino/a immigrants by enforcing facially neutral quality-of-life laws outlawing junk cars and converting garages into residences, as well as by considering new ordinances such as one restricting overnight street parking, which would have disproportionately affected tenants of overcrowded homes and apartments.[37] Similarly, when a judge in 2007 blocked enforcement of a Farmers Branch, Texas, rental ordinance requiring verification of citizenship, some residents tried to secure an ordinance barring bright house-paint colors that would have disproportionately impacted Latino/a homeowners.[38] As with Escondido, this approach was intended to overcome legal challenges with a novel but seemingly neutral tactic to impede or quash Latino/a residences.

Zoning and housing code enforcement against Latino/as is further complicated by the reality that while their living arrangements are prompted by economic necessity, sometimes landlords take undue financial advantage of immigrants and others unable to provide security deposits or commit to long-term leases. Many Latino/as earn poverty-level wages. Some may have poor credit histories in U.S. markets, and therefore cannot qualify for housing in their own names. Others are undocumented or have language barriers, making them hesitant to deal with landlords. To their supposed rescue come transitory housing arrangements without long-term obligation or credit checks. But sometimes these arrangements exploit the immigrant's desperate circumstances. For example, in 2005 an outcry arose in the Farmingville Latino/a community over displacement from the 2005 raid of a 900-square-foot single-family dwelling housing up to sixty-four male Latino laborers. Tenants there paid $225 to $250 monthly for a bunk space, and authorities estimated the monthly gross rent at $9,000 for this tiny home. Under any reasonable conception of affordable housing, even in New York's expensive Long Island, the tenants were being victimized with exorbitant rent for miserable conditions. In the 1990s, a Champaign, Illinois, plant nursery owner housed Mexican workers in apartments he owned that were described in court proceedings as "virtually unfit for human habitation, with trash strewn about, bugs and insects scurrying everywhere, and a penetrating foul odor." Sixteen Mexican men occupied one squalid apartment with only six beds, paying $1,600 monthly in rent. The nursery manager claimed that "this was the way Mexicans lived and . . . they would not complain because they were illegal."[39]

Given the oft-declared health-and-safety justifications for zoning and building code restrictions, Latino/a housing advocates face a daunting task in challenging enforcement absent vivid indications of anti-Latino/a animus—in other words, a "smoking gun."[40] Specifically, the variety of zoning restrictions that plague Latino/a immigrant communities tend to pass constitutional muster, at least when challenged under federal law. This suggests that housing solutions for embattled Latino/a communities often are found in the political arena and the marketplace, rather than in the courtroom.

Courts generally uphold zoning regulations that dictate a minimum lot size or floor space.[41] Challenges to those ordinances as discriminating against Latino/as or the poor typically have failed on procedural grounds[42] or on the merits. One such lawsuit brought in federal court in the early 1970s by a group of Mexican American organizations illustrates the difficulty of attacking large-lot ordinances. These organizations challenged the constitutionality of the zoning ordinances in Los Altos Hills, California, requiring that each housing lot encompass at least one acre and specifying that no lot contain more than one primary dwelling unit, effectively quashing multifamily housing.[43] The organizations contended that these ordinances discriminated against Mexican Americans and the poor, and thus to survive scrutiny under the constitutional equal protection standard the town would have to demonstrate a compelling governmental interest to justify the discrimination. But the trial court found Mexican Americans were not excluded from Los Altos on the basis of race because wealthy Mexican Americans could live there. The appeals court rejected the contention that given the correlation between Mexican Americans and poverty, discrimination against the poor constituted discrimination against an ethnic minority. The standard of strict scrutiny for a government action might apply in extremely limited circumstances where a law discriminates against the poor by completely denying their ability to pay for some desired benefit and thus depriving them of a meaningful opportunity to enjoy that benefit.[44] Here, the organizations failed to establish that the poor had no meaningful opportunity to obtain low-cost housing in the rest of Santa Clara County proximate to jobs and services in Los Altos. Therefore, the court reviewed the zoning ordinances under the more lax standard requiring only a showing that the ordinances bore some rational relationship to a legitimate government interest. Because the ordinances were "rationally related to preserving the town's rural environment," they survived the equal protection challenge.[45]

More successful was a landmark lawsuit on behalf of poor Blacks and Latino/as against the New Jersey township of Mount Laurel, claiming its zoning scheme unlawfully excluded low- and moderate-income families. Zoning in Mount Laurel specified a minimum lot size in more than half the town of at least one-half acre as well as a minimum dwelling size and lot width. Single-family housing was the norm. For apartment projects, the city restricted both the number of bedrooms and the number of school-age children per bedroom. Relying on the state constitution, the New Jersey Supreme Court held that the municipality must make housing available for all categories of people, including those of low and moderate income. This meant permitting "multifamily housing, without bedroom or similar restrictions, as well as small dwellings on very small lots, low cost housing of other types and, in general, high density zoning, without artificial and unjustifiable minimum requirements as to lot size, building size, and the like, to meet the full panoply of these needs."[46] Prompted by this protracted litigation, New Jersey's Fair Housing Act implemented a system designed to meet the affordable housing needs of each municipality as well as its fair share of the regional need for affordable housing.[47]

Federal antidiscrimination law proved insufficient to protect existing affordable housing against attack from another local strategy to exclude the impoverished and minorities—urban renewal. For example, a federal court in New Jersey ruled in 2009 that redevelopment of low-income, blighted housing does not violate the federal Fair Housing Act, which regulates race rather than income discrimination. Although the plaintiffs contended that the redevelopment project disparately impacted African American and Latino/a residents, the court rejected a claim of race discrimination because the renewal also displaced existing Anglo residents in the same way.[48]

Zoning ordinances regulating the number of unrelated residents appear to be on shakier constitutional ground, but nonetheless have enjoyed considerable latitude in the federal courts. For example, the Supreme Court upheld a Long Island village ordinance restricting occupancy to a single family, thus excluding boarding and fraternity houses. As defined in the ordinance, family meant "one or more persons related by blood, adoption, or marriage, living and cooking together as a single housekeeping unit, exclusive of household servants." Although as many as two unrelated persons were allowed to constitute a family, the litigation involved six unrelated college students living in a single rental house who thus exceeded the legal limit. In upholding the zoning ordinance against the landlord's constitutional challenge, the Court broadly articulated the bounds of the police power justifying exclusionary zoning:

> The regimes of boarding houses, fraternity houses, and the like present urban problems. More people occupy a given space; more cars rather continuously pass by; more cars are parked; noise travels with crowds.
>
> A quiet place where yards are wide, people few, and motor vehicles restricted are legitimate guidelines in a land use project addressed to family needs. This goal is a permissible one. . . . The police power is not confined to elimination of filth, stench, and unhealthy places. It is ample to lay out zones where family values, youth values, and the blessings of quiet seclusion and clean air make the area a sanctuary for people.[49]

Three years later, however, the Supreme Court struck down an Ohio municipal zoning ordinance that defined family narrowly by limiting occupancy of a single dwelling unit to certain specified immediate family members. This complicated ordinance prohibited, for example, the living arrangement of a woman with her son and her two grandsons who were not brothers but cousins. Rejecting the city's contention it was akin to the valid Long Island ordinance, the Court in a plurality opinion distinguished the Long Island ordinance as affecting only unrelated residents, while the Ohio ordinance chose "to regulate the occupancy of its housing by slicing deeply into the family itself," by selecting "certain categories of relatives who may live together and declar[ing] that others may not."[50] This intrusive regulation of the family unit conflicted with the liberty interests protected under the Due Process Clause of the Fourteenth Amendment. Although the city identified "legitimate goals" of preventing overcrowding, minimizing parking and traffic issues, and avoiding an undue financial burden on local schools, the ordinance failed to sufficiently serve these purposes. To illustrate this disconnect, the Court pointed out that "the ordinance permits any family consisting only of [a] husband, wife, and unmarried children to live together, even if the family contains a half dozen licensed drivers, each with his or her own car.

At the same time it forbids an adult brother and sister to share a household, even if both faithfully use public transportation."[51]

Litigation brought by the United States during the Clinton Administration to enforce the Fair Housing Act prompted the Illinois city of Waukegan to agree by settlement in 1997 to stop enforcing a family-composition ordinance and to pay $175,000 to the Latino/a victims of its prior enforcement. That ordinance allowed occupancy by parents, their children, and no more than two additional relatives, regardless of dwelling size. Evidence suggested an anti-Latino/a animus, as city officials declared their intent to prevent Latino/as from "taking over" the city. The 1990 Census revealed that for every one hundred Latino/a households in Waukegan, fifty-seven other relatives, such as grandchildren or siblings of the parents, lived with the nuclear family, compared with only eight other relatives for the same number of Anglo households, suggesting the burden fell more heavily on Latino/a households. Moreover, city records demonstrated that only Latino/a families had been forced to vacate their homes under the ordinance. With this background, the lawsuit alleged that the city in enacting the housing ordinance purposefully sought to curtail its Latino/a residents.

Some state courts take an even tougher stance on these family-oriented zoning limits,[52] recognizing the legitimacy of ensuring a desirable environment for residential living, but questioning whether limiting occupancy to family members accomplishes that goal. For example, a California Supreme Court decision applied the state constitutional right to privacy in striking down a Santa Barbara ordinance that restricted nonfamilial living arrangements to five persons, thus barring a twelve-person commune. Because the ordinance did not limit the number of related residents and their servants, it did not appear designed to prevent overcrowding.[53] Similarly, the New Jersey Supreme Court struck down a local zoning ordinance that prohibited more than four unrelated persons from sharing a single dwelling. Although a municipality is free to "designate certain areas as exclusively residential" in order to "preserve a family style of living" and to "minimize congestion and overcrowding," the ordinance prohibited uses (such as occupancy by five unrelated widows or widowers) that would not further those goals.[54] At the same time, a group of ten distant cousins could occupy a residence without prohibition.[55]

As a generalization, occupancy limits tend to be upheld as an enforceable means of preserving a family-friendly neighborhood, whereas prohibitions of unrelated residency arrangements may be legally vulnerable. Although a showing that local officials targeted a minority group in enacting or selectively enforcing a zoning ordinance would expose the illegitimacy of the ordinance or its enforcement,[56] such smoking guns are rare in practice. As suggested above, strategies to protect Latino/as from discriminatory zoning enforcement are best directed at the marketplace and the political process rather than the courtroom. In addition to rallying against the selective enforcement or enactment of laws that unduly hamper Latino/a living arrangements, activists should focus their efforts on creating affordable housing through marketplace incentives and political maneuvering. In an analogous context, some localities responded to congestion and livability issues raised by day laborers gathering to seek employment by constructing hiring halls for them that were designed to minimize neighborhood impact. A similar approach can help tackle the immigrant housing problem through construction by municipalities or incentivized private developers of dormitory housing arrangements proximate to public transportation. Some of the same objections would no doubt emerge—predominantly whether the construction of such housing, as with hiring halls, will draw additional undocumented newcomers to the city and pose an unreasonable burden on social services.

Other political and marketplace strategies are needed to address the broader issues of affordability that underlie much of the overcrowded or substandard housing faced by Latino/as, whether undocumented day laborers, documented immigrants, or citizens. These strategies are addressed in detail in the final section on reclamation and reform.

8

Exclusion by Private Law

Restrictive Covenants

In the first half of the twentieth century, private landowner covenants played a direct role in ensuring neighborhood segregation between Anglos and "undesirables" such as African Americans and Latino/as. Following the Supreme Court's 1917 invalidation of explicitly racial zoning laws, discussed in chapter 7, property developers and neighbors turned to private landowner covenants presumably immune from the same constitutional attack. When the Supreme Court nonetheless deemed judicial enforcement of the blatant variety of these covenants as unconstitutional in 1948, landowners resorted to other techniques to foster segregation, such as tacit unwritten agreements to discriminate among sellers, lenders, and brokers. Today, as with zoning, although overtly racial covenants are unenforceable, more subtle techniques can help ensure the continued segregation of residential neighborhoods. This history signals the persistence and ingenuity of racist ideals, even within the confines of the American dream.

Although most racial property covenants targeted African Americans, Mexican Americans were not immune from exclusion. Examples of overtly racist covenants from judicial decisions include one enforced by a Texas appeals court in 1925 that specified the property "shall never be sold or in any manner transferred or conveyed to Mexicans or negroes."[1] A covenant burdening property in California's Alameda County in the late 1940s stated: "No person or persons of the Mexican race, or other than the Caucasian race shall use or occupy any buildings or any lot, except that this covenant shall not prevent occupying by domestic servants of a different race domiciled with an owner, tenant, or occupant thereof."[2] Anglo families could retain their Mexican maid, but she could not aspire to a home of her own in a neighborhood burdened by such a covenant. Generally, state courts enforced these overtly racist covenants; after all, a deal was a deal. Although some courts did hold that constraints on sale to specified races were an illegal restraint on alienation, they distinguished and enforced legal restrictions on mere occupancy by certain groups, thus inspiring covenants such as the example above from Alameda County that prohibited Mexicans from occupying or using, but not from owning, the home.[3] In this permissive legal climate, many homes in northern San Antonio fell under covenants preventing sale to or occupancy by those of Latino/a descent, helping to preserve racial segregation there.[4]

As mentioned in chapter 5, the Federal Housing Administration (FHA) furnished governmental support for these covenants, going as far as drafting a model restrictive covenant for homes the agency financed[5] and routinely suggesting to residential developers that they include covenants against non-Whites.[6] Apparently the FHA was convinced of the connection between racial segregation and neighborhood property values. Bolstering this opinion was a 1933 report provided to the FHA by a well-known consultant who concluded that residents of English, German, Scotch, Irish, Scandinavian, and North Italian background had the most favorable impact on property values, while "Negroes" and "Mexicans" exerted the most detrimental influence.[7] Based on such findings, the FHA redlined the heavily Latino/a district of Boyle Heights in Los Angeles in 1939 and refused to issue federally backed loans there and in surrounding areas.[8] The FHA's Underwriting Manual for 1936 and later years incorporated these racist findings by prescribing a formula for property appraisers giving 20 percent weight to the neighborhood's "Protection from Adverse Influences." Principally, this meant the potential for change in the neighborhood's racial occupancy, determined by whether the neighborhood was safeguarded from "infiltration of . . . inharmonious racial groups" by such mechanisms as zoning ordinances and deed restrictions.[9] Under these standards, pigpens and racial minorities were equally objectionable in federally subsidized neighborhoods.[10] Against this historical background of discrimination, reform measures to boost Black and Latino/a housing and housing finance can be seen as reparative, rather than as singling out Latino/as and Blacks for special treatment.

During this time, Anglos were slightly more inclined to tolerate a Mexican American neighbor than a Black one, but the rates of intolerance were still shocking. A 1952 study in one Southern California suburb found that almost half (45 percent) of Anglos would tolerate a Mexican American living next door, but only a quarter (23 percent) felt the same about an African American neighbor.[11]

Countering this history of private and governmental collusion against racial equality in residential neighborhoods, an enlightened Supreme Court in the 1948 decision of *Shelley v. Kraemer* concluded that enforcing a racially restrictive covenant against African Americans in St. Louis was unconstitutional. That covenant was "intended hereby to restrict the use of said property for said period of time [fifty years] against the occupancy as owners or tenants of any portion of said property for resident or other purpose by people of the Negro or Mongolian Race." (At the time, the Latino/a population in St. Louis was small enough to escape mention.) The Court held that state judicial enforcement of the restrictive covenant denied Black property owners equal protection of the laws and therefore the covenant could not be enforced.[12] Although the case involved African Americans, the Court's reasoning in *Shelley* extended more broadly to other racial and ethnic groups such as Mexican Americans, thus ending state enforcement of race-based covenants that were facially discriminatory. The Court took note of the extensive reach of discriminatory property covenants, remarking in its decision that such agreements were directed at "Indians, Jews, Chinese, Japanese, Mexicans, Hawaiians, Puerto Ricans, and Filipinos, among others."[13] Thus, for example, a Texas appellate court applied *Shelley* to protect a U.S. citizen born in Mexico who faced an action to forfeit his property because a restriction in his chain of property title prohibited sale or lease to "persons of Mexican descent."[14] Although after *Shelley* courts no longer enforced racially restrictive covenants, these covenants remain dormant in the land records for many properties. Pending legislation in California, proposed by state assemblyman Hector De la Torre of South Gate, would require such covenants to be stricken from the public record by the title company whenever the property is next sold. The son of Mexican immigrants, De la Torre proposed the procedure after finding a covenant on his own home, built in 1948, that would have barred occupancy by anyone, aside from servants, "whose blood is not entirely that of the Caucasian Race, and for the purpose of this paragraph, no Japanese, Chinese, Mexican, Hindu or any other person of the Ethiopian, Indian or Mongolian Races shall be deemed to be a Caucasian."[15]

In their heyday, racially restrictive covenants were just one facet of the overt segregation gauntlet faced by African Americans, Mexican Americans, and other groups. Private (nongovernmental) segregation was practiced freely against Mexican Americans and others in the United States by service-oriented businesses ranging from funeral homes to restaurants and movie theaters. For example, a Texas funeral home refused to bury a decorated World War II veteran because of his Mexican heritage. Movie theaters and swimming pools throughout the Southwest were segregated—Mexican Americans might be relegated to the theater balcony, with the main floor reserved for Anglos, or might be allowed to swim only on "Mexican Days," usually right before the pool was drained and cleaned.[16] Government discrimination was reflected most noticeably in Latino/a communities by segregated schools under the "separate but equal" doctrine prior to the Supreme Court's 1954 *Brown v. Board of Education* decision. But that decision failed to address discrimination in private settings, save for the Court's refusal to enforce private restrictive covenants in *Shelley v. Kraemer*. Congress finally confronted private discrimination and segregation in 1960s civil rights legislation, including Title II of the Civil Rights Act of 1964, which tackled discrimination in public accommodations such as hotels, restaurants, and theaters, and the Fair Housing Act of 1968, which outlawed discrimination in real estate transactions on the basis of race, color, and other specified grounds.

In a landmark U.S. Supreme Court case from 1954 stemming from a challenge to the exclusion of Mexican American jurors from local jury pools, the Court recognized that Mexican Americans in Texas were a group separate from "Whites" and thus entitled to protection from discrimination under the U.S. Constitution's Equal Protection Clause. In acknowledging the need for protecting Mexicans as a group, the Court relied on prejudicial attitudes in the community—among other things, at the time of the Texas court hearing there were two men's bathrooms on the courthouse grounds, one unmarked and the other with a sign reading "Colored Men" and "Hombres Aqui" (Men Here). Therefore, the Court concluded that it was unlawful group discrimination for local officials to exclude Mexican Americans from the local grand jury and criminal jury pools.[17]

Although the Supreme Court has not wavered from its ruling in *Shelley*, the Los Angeles Realty Board, among others, took the decision poorly and urged a constitutional amendment to restore enforcement of racially restrictive covenants. The board argued that these covenants had "become a traditional element of value in homeownership," and that the resulting loss in value should minorities infringe on traditionally White neighborhoods would "necessarily create racial tensions and antagonisms and do much harm to [the] national social structure."[18] Following the *Shelley* decision, communities such as South Gate in Southern California, as well as developers, realtors, and homeowners, resorted to other tactics to deny entry of Mexican Americans into Anglo neighborhoods. Some were overt—for example, the fines briefly assessed by the South Gate Realty Board against realtors (for both buyer and seller) who arranged any sale to a Mexican American family. The board relied on a purported violation of the National Association of Real Estate Boards requirement at the time that "[a] realtor should not be instrumental in introducing into a neighborhood a character of property or use which will clearly be detrimental to property values in a neighborhood."[19]

Despite an eventual decrease in overt discrimination against Latino/as, chapters 6 and 7 revealed that discrimination against Latino/a housing simply assumed more covert forms, with local governments enacting ordinances targeting rentals by undocumented persons and zoning restrictions on density, parking, and the like to discourage Latino/as from taking up residence in the community. Private restrictive covenants similarly can operate covertly to exclude impoverished and minority residents through requirements that lower density and increase cost. Covenants might preclude construction of apartments, duplexes, triplexes, and the like,[20] or they might regulate the cost of homes through mandates on minimum lot size and permissible building materials. Covenants might limit the number of occupants of homes or condominiums, or exclude nonfamily residents aside from domestic servants.[21] Rentals might be banned, thus limiting occupancy to owners. Covenants might establish an architectural committee to approve or reject any proposed garage conversions, bedroom additions, enclosed porches, and other improvements to increase capacity of the home. Private covenants often regulate or prohibit home gardens, a common feature in older, unrestricted Latino/a neighborhoods such as the Boyle Heights area of Los Angeles, where residents grow and barter corn, citrus, chili peppers, and tropical fruits.[22] Private covenants might even constrain cultural expression through rigid architectural approval requirements that encompass paint color and decorative features. Enforced through homeowner associations, these facially race-neutral covenants can help maintain segregated neighborhoods without the need for unenforceable racially restrictive covenants. Since 1948, then, developers and homeowners merely shifted their means of regulating the racial character of residential neighborhoods from overt to covert approaches, particularly those excluding lower-class residents. As Evan McKenzie argued in his landmark work *Privatopia*:

> In this manner, homeowner associations and restrictive covenants shifted their emphasis to class discrimination, which is legal, from race discrimination, which is not. Less affluent families, who might be able to afford a house only by pooling resources or renting out rooms, would be prohibited from buying. Lifestyle restrictions were justified with such familiar euphemisms as "preserving the character"—or "integrity" or "stability"— of a neighborhood rather than by referring to race or class. Nonetheless, the principle is still the same: certain groups of people are considered a

threat to property values and are excluded. The result is still increased homogeneity, and, given economic disparities between white and non-white Americans, this approach inevitably contributes to continuing racial segregation.[23]

Closely related to exclusion through restrictive covenants is what Professor Lior Jacob Strahilevitz termed "exclusionary amenities"—the potential for developers to repel or lure certain racial groups and better circumvent fair housing laws by offering amenities that signal racial homogeneity—for example, golf courses that residents are required to join.[24] A developer might also channel Anglo and Latino/a buyers into separate but similarly priced developments by such marketing devices as the name of the subdivision, the style of architecture, the number of bedrooms, and the presence or absence of recreational amenities such as soccer fields and playgrounds for children.

The distinction McKenzie draws between permissible class discrimination and illegal racial discrimination is mostly, but not absolutely, true. For example, public policy and even state and federal antidiscrimination law may restrict enforcement of some of the pernicious varieties of restrictive covenants described above, or similar provisions in residential leases, particularly those that discriminate based on family status. Under the Fair Housing Act, federal authorities have pursued landlords who impose unreasonable occupancy restrictions that burden families with children. For these purposes, the U.S. Department of Housing and Urban Development (HUD) follows a guideline that landlords generally may limit occupancy to two persons per bedroom, although special circumstances (e.g., tiny bedrooms or limited capacity of sewer or septic systems) may justify more stringent limits.[25] Even these reasonable and therefore legal restrictions will fall more heavily on Latino/a occupants. Recall the study of farm worker housing mentioned above in which two-thirds of the farm workers in the Salinas and Pajaro valleys in California, nearly all of them Latino/a, lived in residences with more than two people per bedroom.

While courts in the early twentieth century were enforcing restrictive covenants explicitly targeting African Americans, Mexican Americans, and other groups, residents were using the judicial doctrine of nuisance to pursue legal actions against neighbors seen as undesirable.[26] Some of these legal complaints focused directly and primarily on the racial status of the neighbors, while others mentioned racial status as incidental to the claim. Nuisance is a legal doctrine that protects a landowner's quiet enjoyment of property. Courts employ varying tests for declaring noxious activity a nuisance and prohibiting its continuance, with some invoking a balancing test that looks at the degree of harm to the landowner plaintiff, as well as the social value of the defendant's actions.[27] Wielding this amorphous doctrine, litigants once contended that African American or Mexican American households injured surrounding neighbors, and that their presence should be enjoined. If successful, such an abominable claim would have created the equivalent of a neighborhood covenant against the entry of Mexican Americans by judicial action, even in the absence of deed covenants. Fortunately, courts generally declined to apply the nuisance doctrine in overtly discriminatory terms. For example, in the 1920 Texas case of *Worm v. Wood*, neighbors who lived in "nice and comfortable dwelling houses" sued neighbors erecting closely spaced two-room wood "shacks" that were an alleged fire hazard. The plaintiffs contended that the shacks were built for occupation by "negroes and Mexicans and a low class of white people, which will greatly injure and practically destroy the social conditions of said neighborhood" unless enjoined. But the court refused to halt construction, concluding that the houses were not a nuisance per se, despite being out of character with the neighboring residences:

> Houses of the character of those which plaintiffs allege the defendants are threatening to build will not constitute a nuisance per se, even though they may be out of keeping with the kind and quality of plaintiffs' residences, and unsightly in appearance, and even though they may increase the danger of loss of plaintiffs' residences by fire, and also increase the cost of fire insurance thereon.[28]

Still, the court cautioned that if the shacks, once built, were used in a manner that created a nuisance, that use would be prohibited.

A few years later, the potential of nuisance to regulate different cultural and class lifestyles was invoked in a 1925 Texas decision that enjoined a Mexican labor camp as a nuisance. Among the factors mentioned by the court was that forty-five or fifty "Mexicans of the peon type" were living in a house and a stable converted into small rooms, situated in a White residential section of town. The court pointed out the possible hazard of cooking fires, the unsanitary conditions of inadequate sewer facilities, and the infringement of musical instruments, wood chopping, and noisy animals on quiet enjoyment of nighttime.[29] Although the court focused more on the manner of usage than on the race of the tenement dwellers, it nonetheless signaled the relevance of race in noting that the residents were Mexicans in an otherwise White neighborhood.

Private restrictive covenants today might accomplish covertly what most of these courts were unwilling to allow. For example, the owners of the "nice and comfortable dwelling houses" by agreement might permissibly bar construction of any smaller, closely spaced homes by specifying a minimum square footage for each home and building lot while avoiding overtly discriminatory language. Alternatively, they might specify a more expensive building material than wood framing.

In 2007, an Arkansas mayor made headlines for his proposal to use the related doctrine of public nuisance to confront the city's undocumented immigrants. No doubt the proposed nuisance ordinance was a proxy for restricting Latino/a newcomers. Although the proposal was never explained much beyond the superficial appeal to some residents of classifying undocumented immigrants as a nuisance, consider that most cities so classify noxious weeds, dangerous animals, and junk cars and target them for removal and eradication.[30]

While courts today may point to safety hazards and threats to quiet enjoyment in declaring a nuisance, one wouldn't expect them to consider the racial background of the residents relevant, regardless of racial tensions in the neighborhood. But race still plays at least a covert role in property zoning enforcement, and the vestiges of racial segregation from the days of restrictive covenants have been slow to depart. After the Supreme Court's *Shelley* decision in 1948, courts no longer enforced such covenants, but realtors and lenders worked in concert to maintain segregation by refusing to lend or by steering buyers to neighborhoods in character with their racial background, thus impeding upward mobility and integration. As one commentator observed, although the federal government eventually entered the fray in the 1960s and 1970s with civil rights legislation directed at lenders, brokers, landlords, and sellers, "all this legislation came too late, and it did too little to reverse the patterns of racial segregation in urban areas that had been initially sponsored and sanctioned, and later ignored, by federal policies."[31] Indeed, between 1970 and 1990, one study found that segregation between Latino/as and Anglos increased in forty of ninety metropolitan areas studied.[32] Situating Mexican Americans within the sorry legacy of racial segregation and restrictive covenants, a commentator observed that judicial enforcement of racial covenants in the early twentieth century "had a lasting effect on many Mexican-American communities and the effects of these racially restrictive covenants remain visible."[33] Analyzing their impacts in San Antonio, this commentator concluded:

The poverty that many Mexican Americans experience today is partly the result of residential segregation created by racially restrictive covenants. . . . Today, San Antonio is still divided geographically along ethnic lines. This type of residential segregation has helped . . . perpetuate poverty. . . . Traditionally, Mexican Americans living in San Antonio have been less educated, poorer, and have lived in worse housing conditions than their Anglo-American counterparts. In addition, studies conducted in the 1970s showed that Mexican-American neighborhoods received lower levels of municipal services than Anglo-American neighborhoods.[34]

Among the connections between residential segregation and poverty in communities of color are inadequate funding and facilities for education and substandard public transportation, as well as stunted employment opportunities and potential for wealth acquisition through property appreciation. The strategies for reform suggested in Part IV address some of these engrained obstacles to progress for Latino/as and other communities of color. But first we will examine the geographies of the three primary Latino/a groups in the United States—those of Mexican, Cuban, or Puerto Rican descent.

Part III

Geographic Examples of Loss and Exclusion

Latino/as in the United States are a diverse group that encompasses immigrants or native-born residents with roots in many Central or South American countries. The focus below is on the geographies of the three subgroups that have dominated the discourse on Latino/as—residents of Mexican, Cuban, or Puerto Rican background. Fittingly, this section examines the housing landscape in the urban epicenters of these three subgroups—respectively, Los Angeles, Miami, and New York City. With the addition of Chicago, some 28.6 percent of U.S. Latino/as live in these four metropolitan areas. For example, about half of the U.S. Cuban population lives in the Miami area, and the Latino/a population (4.7 million) in Los Angeles County, comprised mostly of residents of Mexican background, is the largest of any U.S. county. Overall, California, Florida, New York, and Texas account for nearly two-thirds of U.S. Latino/a households. At the same time, particularly in the case of Mexican Americans, the Latino/a diaspora extends beyond these cities and states to urban and rural landscapes throughout the United States. Other Latino/a subgroups are also substantially represented in these featured cities. For example, there are as many or more residents of Salvadoran descent in Los Angeles as in San Salvador, the capital and largest city of El Salvador, and New York City has as many Dominicans as Santo Domingo, also the capital and largest city of the Dominican Republic. Miami is a destination for immigrants from Nicaragua, Colombia, Venezuela, and other Latin American countries.

The three urban landscapes examined below share the legacy of segregation that Blacks and Latino/as have long endured. Segregation is particularly evident within Mexican American neighborhoods, with a majority of Latino/as in California and Texas, most of them Mexican Americans, living in neighborhoods that are more than half Latino/a.[1] But the Puerto Rican and Cuban American experiences also exhibit segregation in housing, as detailed below in regard to New York City's Spanish Harlem and Miami's

Little Havana. A 2000 study identified two metropolitan areas in the United States as what it called "hypersegregated" for Latino/a residents—Los Angeles and New York.[2]

Recent Latino/a immigrants have overwhelmingly favored urban destinations. Overall, nine of ten Latino/as live in metropolitan areas, many of them in segregated neighborhoods.[3] Contrary to the popular belief that racial segregation is limited to inner cities, however, significant segregated and distressed suburban neighborhoods exist in many areas of the United States. In fact, there are more minorities, and more impoverished people, living in suburbs than in inner cities.[4] Latino/as are often geographically concentrated, with the 100 U.S. counties with the largest Latino/a populations home to 73 percent of Latino/as. A 2008 study found that Latino/as might be even more concentrated than Blacks in the United States.[5] On the positive side, growth among Latino/a groups in these urban settings is credited with revitalizing U.S. cities that would otherwise be shrinking in population. On the negative side, the urban crush of Latino/as, both native-born and immigrant populations, has stressed housing markets in cities that were not equipped for the increase, driving up prices and contributing to low homeownership rates for Latino/as. Housing quality deteriorated in these strained markets. Reform strategies for Latino/a housing must therefore confront these urban settings and their unique histories of loss and exclusion.

9

Born in East L.A.

The Legacy of Loss and Exclusion in Southern California

My mother's childhood home in East Los Angeles was tiny and humble. Purchased for about $500 in cash in the early 1930s, it was home to my mother and her four siblings for some twenty years. My grandparents, both immigrants from Mexico, shared a small bedroom, and my mother shared the second petite bedroom with her sister. Her two brothers slept on a davenport couch in the living room. A third newborn brother slept in my grandparents' room. When relatives with children came to stay, my mother remembers sleeping sideways on her bed to accommodate more sleepers. Los Angeles winters were colder then, as a small fish pond in the front yard routinely froze. Without any heat source in the house, no one wanted to be the first to use the bathroom in the morning. My grandmother Ramona would heat the only bathroom with an old-fashioned toaster by opening its sides. As my mother reminds me, "We were poor but we didn't know it." My grandmother's brother Silviano and his family fared worse. For a time the four of them lived beneath my grandparents' house in a basement with dirt and cement floors and a wide trap door to the upstairs. My grandparents kept extra mattresses down there, hauling them upstairs to the living room floor for company. Silviano (whose nickname was Chivi) lived a migratory life. In the California border town of San Ysidro, across from Tijuana, he eventually put down roots by converting chicken coops into small apartments, which he rented while living in a small adjacent home. My grandparents lived more comfortably. My grandfather Fernando worked hard and consistently as a musician, jeweler, and auto painter, and, after he completed trade school, as an electrical switchboard mechanic. Eventually, a neighbor built a small addition to the back of their house to provide a third bedroom. The household got smaller as one of my uncles left for the military and other siblings moved out. In

1955, my grandparents moved to a larger, two-bedroom house in East Los Angeles, with a tiny cottage in the backyard, which I describe later in this chapter.

Originally christened Nuestra Señora la Reina de los Ángeles de Porciúncula (Our Lady the Queen of the Angels of Porciúncula [meaning small portion of land]) when founded by Latino/as in 1781, the second-largest city in the United States grew up around a central plaza area with Olvera, named for a mid-1800s Mexican American judge, as its central street. A few miles east of the Plaza lies the unincorporated area of East Los Angeles and surrounding neighborhoods such as Boyle Heights, which today form the core of Los Angeles's vast Mexican American population, second only to that of Mexico City. The Mexican American experience in East Los Angeles and the greater Los Angeles area is a story of diverse sources of displacement that illustrate the historical and current challenges for Latino/as pursuing the American dream.

Before the Mexican-American War of 1846–48, Los Angeles was home to Mexicans who held expansive land grants, but their tenure as landowners was short-lived. As detailed in chapter 2, a mass divestment and shift to Anglo land ownership followed the Treaty of Guadalupe Hidalgo in 1848. In 1850, 61 percent of Mexican heads of families in Los Angeles owned land, but by 1870 only 21 percent did, and the median value of their holdings had dropped from $2,105 to $1,072.[1] Mexican immigrants arriving after 1850 accounted for some of these landholders, helping to soften a remarkable decline in land ownership—of Mexicans who owned property in Los Angeles in 1850, only 10 percent did so in 1860.[2] By 1870, those Mexican property owners remaining, or those newly arriving, tended to own tiny homes in the Plaza area just northeast of present-day downtown Los Angeles. In the early 1900s, however, several factors converged to drive Mexican residents toward the new haven of the adjoining East Los Angeles area. With the upheaval of the Mexican Revolution, Mexican workers came to the United States to fill the labor void during World War I. Between 1910 and 1920, the Mexican population of Los Angeles jumped from 5,611 to 31,172, and in the next decade it tripled to 97,116, with another 70,000 living in Los Angeles County.[3] When the Great Depression struck in the late 1920s, Mexican workers were unwanted and soon became targets of mass repatriations that uprooted Mexican families from their U.S. homes.[4] In the throes of this cycle of invitation of Mexican laborers and their exile to Mexico whenever the U.S. economy deteriorated,[5] the Plaza area emerged as a coveted site for commercial and industrial development such as the Union

Pacific train station. Land prices and rents rose, helping drive out Mexican residents. Mexicans were ripe for displacement, given the poor condition and low value of their tiny homes. Similar to today's colonia housing on the U.S./Mexico border, many of the homes were self-built by Mexican immigrants, sometimes on leased land, using "flattened oil cans, cardboard cartons, lumber discarded in repairing box-cars, or other refuse of American economic life."[6] Often the shacks were built by extended families that lived together, sharing community toilets. A 1919 study found that almost four of five Mexican families in Los Angeles lived in homes without bathrooms.[7] Most of these Mexican American–owned houses in the downtown Plaza area were overcrowded.[8] A historian depicted the squalid conditions:

> A [housing] court there consisted generally of ten to twenty houses, half on each side of the lot, with toilet facilities in the center. Lots were usually 40 by 170 feet and offered only limited space for children to play or for social activities. In 1920 tenants paid six dollars per month for a 300-square-foot two-room house. Residents of a typical court had the use of ten hydrants with sinks and six toilets. Overcrowding was prevalent. . . .
>
> Families of four or more typically lived in these small [two-room] habitations, which often sheltered eight or nine individuals each. City regulations required only that the house courts have at least one men's toilet for every ten men and one women's toilet for every ten women.[9]

Pollution was an everyday problem, as many of these homes abutted train tracks and packinghouses. Eventually, commerce and industry prevailed over residential uses, and Latino/as were pushed out to other Southern California areas by an early form of urban renewal.

Acting in concert with local officials, developers remade the Plaza as a commercial and industrial center and recast its main thoroughfare, Olvera Street, as a tourist area. On its reopening on Easter Sunday 1930, Olvera Street was touted as "A Mexican Street of Yesterday in a City of Today." As one historian put it:

> The lesson was clear: Mexicans were to be assigned a place in the mythic past of Los Angeles—one that could be relegated to a quaint section of a city destined to delight tourists and antiquarians. Real Mexicans were out of sight and increasingly out of mind. Physically farther away from the [downtown] center of power, Mexican immigrants remained close enough to provide the cheap labor essential to industry and agriculture.[10]

Uprooted Mexican residents, as well as guest workers and immigrants who arrived when the economy revived with the onset of World War II, were steered clear of substantial sections of Los Angeles by means of racialized zoning practices and private restrictive covenants. Evidencing the segregationist ideals of these times, promotional responses to an inquiry in 1927 by the Los Angeles Chamber of Commerce included one from coastal El Segundo boasting that it "had no negroes or Mexicans," and another by Lynwood reporting that "Lynwood, being restricted to the white race, can furnish ample labor of the better class."[11] East Los Angeles became a haven for both displaced Latino/as and new arrivals from Mexico, as did neighboring Boyle Heights, another area free of the restrictive covenants that plagued the rest of the basin.[12] Once home to substantial numbers of Anglos and Jewish Americans, East Los Angeles and Boyle Heights browned in the mid-1900s as Mexicans arrived and Anglos and Russian Jews departed to midtown and West Los Angeles.[13]

Another significant episode of displacement occurred in the 1950s, with the removal of Mexican American residents from the Chávez Ravine neighborhood, initially as urban renewal but ultimately for housing America's favorite pastime, professional baseball. The story of Chávez Ravine well encapsulates the Los Angeles housing experience for Latino/as, suggesting that commercial and municipal interests will trump those of Latino/a residents as needed. Chávez Ravine is a hilly area just north of downtown bounded today by the Hollywood, Harbor/Pasadena, Golden State, and Glendale freeways. Its original owner, Julian Chávez, obtained the property around 1840 as a land grant from the Ayuntamiento (city council).[14] By the 1940s, Chávez Ravine was home to three residential neighborhoods—La Loma, Bishop, and Palo Verde—each populated primarily by Mexican Americans, but also home to some Chinese, Blacks, and Anglos. As compared to the rest of downtown Los Angeles, Chávez Ravine was sparsely populated, with only about 40 percent of its hilly terrain occupied. Given their proximity to downtown, the lower neighborhoods were already decimated by freeway construction. But above the fray on Chávez Ravine, Mexican American residents enjoyed a near-rural lifestyle, growing their food and raising pigs and even cattle.[15] Most of their homes were small, wooden structures, many with porches. As with colonia settlements near the U.S./Mexico border, municipal services were absent. Roads were unpaved and the neighborhoods lacked sewer and water facilities. Also like the colonia settlements, homeownership in Chávez Ravine (43.6 percent in 1948) exceeded the city average.[16]

With the passage of the federal Housing Act of 1949 to provide funding, Los Angeles officials planned a series of public housing projects to ease the city's shortage of affordable housing. Chávez Ravine would anchor the flagship project. At the time, Chávez Ravine housed about 3,769 people living in 1,145 mostly single-family dwelling units. The public housing plan for Chávez Ravine (to be known as Elysian Park Heights) anticipated more than 10,000 people living in over 3,300 units, consisting of 24 thirteen-story apartment towers with private balconies and 163 two-story buildings—with a total of 481 one-bedroom, 1,922 two-bedroom, 742 three-bedroom, 202 four-bedroom, and 18 five-bedroom units.[17] Larger families would enjoy private garden areas, and each apartment floor would have a recreation area. In order to accommodate the project, the hillside would be leveled in half and thus its residents needed to vacate. Many left voluntarily, with the guarantee from the Housing Authority that they would receive first priority for the new units, with rent scaled to income, and no racial discrimination.[18] Those refusing the offer faced government condemnation proceedings to pay them the supposed fair market value of their homes. Bulldozers leveled most of the homes after their fixtures of value were auctioned off, but ambitious plans for the Elysian Park Heights housing project fell apart amid accusations of "creeping socialism" and of Communist influence in the Housing Authority during the peak of the Red Scare.

Subsequently, the Chávez Ravine acreage changed hands from the federally funded Housing Authority to the City of Los Angeles, on condition that the land be used for a public purpose. A few years later, the city transferred the land to the owner of the Dodgers professional baseball team to persuade him to move the Brooklyn Dodgers to Los Angeles and build a private stadium. In return for the land and its promise to spend $2 million on street and site improvements, the city received a small, dilapidated minor league baseball stadium, along with the owner's promise—never fulfilled—to build a forty-acre public recreational area.[19] Although outcry ensued over the absence of a discernable public purpose for the transfer, the California Supreme Court eventually upheld this contractual exchange.[20]

Ostensibly awarded fair market value for their land and homes contributed toward the baseball stadium, residents of Chávez Ravine faced hardship in replacing them in the smaller and more expensive lots of surrounding neighborhoods. One Mexican American homeowner in his sixties received $9,600 for his home and thought he was "making a killing," until he bought a replacement home in adjacent Lincoln Heights for $15,000.[21]

When a television special celebrating the thirtieth anniversary of the Dodgers' move to Los Angeles implied that the stadium site formerly was a wasteland, a Mexican American former resident wrote, "Every time anyone talks about Chávez Ravine before the Dodgers came along they seem to forget that many families made their homes there! . . . Alright the people have all moved away and the houses are all gone. But please don't keep referring to it as a dump or wasteland. The people all loved their homes."[22] No doubt, popular conceptions of Latino/as as poor stewards of the land played a role for policymakers and Los Angeles residents in legitimizing these destructive events. Latino/a neighborhoods are consistently slated for renewal, but the results often benefit Anglos. Whether for new homes or industrial or commercial development, displacement demarcates the history of Latino/a housing in the United States.

The most blatant appropriation of Latino/a neighborhoods in the name of progress occurred in East Los Angeles in the 1950s and 1960s, not for any building, but for construction of freeways that severed the barrio. Around the same time as the Chávez Ravine upheaval, Anglo residents fled the downtown area for predominantly White suburbs where the culture of the automobile took hold. Addressing their need to reach jobs and recreational opportunities such as beaches and the new Chávez Ravine baseball stadium, freeways were built throughout downtown, cutting swaths through the soul of the barrio, with brutal effects on its residents:

> In the late 1950s the massive construction of freeways linking the Anglo suburban communities with the central business core began. High overpasses and expansive six-lane freeways crisscrossed the [Los Angeles] east side. Thousands of residents from Boyle Heights, Lincoln Heights, City Terrace, and surrounding neighborhoods were relocated. The freeways divided the neighborhoods without consideration for the residents' loyalties to churches, schools, businesses, or family. Residents, especially the young and the aged, became increasingly isolated from other areas of town as the massive layers of grey concrete and asphalt eliminated the trolley lines and disrupted public transit service. The daily trek of hundreds of thousands of autos left a gloomy grey cloud of smog hanging over the east side.[23]

Another commentator summed up the emasculation of the East Los Angeles area by freeway construction as having "destroyed massive tracts of affordable housing, devastated the local economy, and forced the dislocation of thousands of families," as well as causing "a loss of social cohesion and a severe increase in air pollution."[24] The Golden State/Santa Ana, Pomona, Long Beach, and San Bernardino/Santa Monica freeways each dissected the area, with the East Los Angeles interchange connecting some of these roadways touted as the world's busiest. Periodic freeway widening claimed thousands more homes. Federal policy enabled suburbanization, particularly the Federal-Aid Highway Act of 1956, which funded 41,000 miles of national interstate and spurred a freeway construction boom in the Los Angeles basin. From 1960 to 1970 alone, the East Los Angeles area lost 1,172 housing units to freeway demolition.[25] Freeways displaced more than 10,000 residents of the adjoining neighborhood of Boyle Heights between 1946 and 1965.[26] In contrast to other cities such as New York, Chicago, and San Francisco, Los Angeles grew by design as a single-family dwelling city, connected by automobile rather than by mass transit.[27] The 1941 Master Plan for Los Angeles County, for example, dedicated only 2 percent of the city's land to multiple-family dwellings.[28] This legacy leaves today's immigrants searching for affordable housing in Southern California, while they temporarily crowd into converted garages and basements in East Los Angeles and beyond.

The most recent displacement in Los Angeles is the upheaval of the subprime mortgage meltdown, which is claiming Latino/a-owned homes in the raft of foreclosures. My grandparents' house, where I spent considerable time as a child, was caught in this maelstrom. Although the public perception of the East Los Angeles area may be of multifamily and public housing, the reality is a landscape of single-family neighborhoods with smaller, older homes, of which my grandparents' last home is typical. Built in 1923, the Spanish-style house near the busy corner of Whittier and Atlantic boulevards was home to most of my family's last three generations. It was larger than my grandparents' first tiny home, described in the narrative that opens this chapter. Although the main house of 1,200 square feet has only two small bedrooms, the luxury of a tiny one-bedroom guest cottage with its own bathroom allowed as many as five of my family members to claim their own house at the same time. My mother and her siblings eventually inherited the house and sold it cheaply. A few years later, in mid-2007, they were shocked when my uncle looked up the house on the popular real estate website Zillow.com and discovered that it had sold for $460,000 in late November 2006 and was currently valued at $500,000.[29] By spring 2008, however, the home was listed for sale at $460,000 and advertised as a potential short-sale.[30] Given the sale price and content of the broker listing, it is apparent the home was purchased at the height of the recent subprime mortgage frenzy with financing for all or nearly all of its purchase price—a common attribute of subprime loans. By

August 2008, in the heart of the subprime crisis, Zillow estimated its value at $338,500, an economic freefall. Although the house eventually sold for $390,000 in late October 2008, the Zillow website estimated its value at only $247,000 in April 2010.

Despite Los Angeles's origins as a city of owner-occupied, single-family homes, today only New York City has a higher proportion of renters. Many Southern California renters occupy single-family houses, crowding into bedrooms and ancillary buildings such as garages. More than a quarter of all Los Angeles households are overcrowded, reflecting the economic conditions in which more than 28 percent of working families in Los Angeles devote in excess of half their income to housing.[31] In this climate, at least six of ten Los Angeles residents are renters (61.4 percent), compared with seven out of ten (69.8 percent) in New York City. The rate for Los Angeles County is split between renters and homeowners (49 percent), but still exhibits the lowest homeownership west of the Mississippi River.[32] Los Angeles, then, has become a city of renters, particularly as its Latino/a population has surged. That population surge, consisting of native births, immigrants from Mexico, and immigrants fleeing upheaval in Central America since the 1980s, has created a Latino/a-dominated urban residential sector that now stretches from the San Fernando Valley to the San Gabriel Valley. With their increasing political influence in Los Angeles County and beyond, Latino/as may be poised to pursue some of the reforms discussed in chapters 14 and 15, particularly those that depend on local political power.[33]

Most homes in the East Los Angeles area date to the first half of the 1900s. As can be expected, given crowding and the financial stresses on residents, many of these homes are in disrepair. The decline in housing values and pressures in credit and employment markets associated with the subprime crisis will make home equity improvement loans scarce. The history of Latino/as in the Los Angeles area documented above suggests an unhappy ending for this region. Displacement of Latino/as tends to occur when competing uses with a higher assumed economic value, such as industrial and commercial downtown development, sports stadiums, and freeways,[34] target economically depressed neighborhoods ripe for so-called urban renewal. The homes in Chávez Ravine were mostly run-down, and the landscape was relatively uncrowded. Although the shanties in the early 1900s Plaza area were crowded together, their dilapidated condition was the gateway to renewal. With the subprime housing crisis driving down home values, and with much of its housing stock aging and in poor condition, the East Los Angeles area is primed for a new upheaval, this time from gentrification.

Several factors signal the potential for gentrification of East Los Angeles. Continued delay in enacting comprehensive immigration reform with a pathway to citizenship for undocumented workers will further destabilize Latino/a communities and create opportunities for Anglo buyers. These buyers will be looking to move closer to the downtown area as part of the new green urbanism, which attracts upwardly mobile, younger workers in pursuit of a lifestyle where proximity to jobs and public transportation replace the lengthy automobile commutes of the post–World War II "drivable sub-urbanism" model.[35] Trendy margarita bars and burrito stands will keep a dash of spicy Latino/a influence in the neighborhood. Dilapidated single-family housing in East Los Angeles would give way to Spanish-styled multifamily renewal projects offering condominiums and luxury apartments with on-site recreational facilities and upscale amenities intended for these new city dwellers. Perhaps a greenspace plaque will someday memorialize the occasion of renewal as "A Mexican Park of Yesterday in a Green City of Today." Latino/a workers servicing the needs of this twenty-four-hour neighborhood will commute home on the same freeways that once ripped apart their barrio neighborhoods to their destination in otherwise emptying suburban neighborhoods where the McMansions of recent vintage will house Mexican and Latino/a worker families crowded into their many bedrooms.[36] Spanish-speaking Latino/as may find humor in the trendy names of these subdivisions and their streets, many of which butcher the Spanish language by making up nonsense names with a Spanish feel, by misapplying gender (as with San Maria Drive instead of Santa Maria, the proper form for a female saint), or by leaving out articles used in correct Spanish, such as Calle de Amigos instead of the proper Calle de los Amigos.[37] As Anglo buyers head for the green urban core, the predicted national surplus of twenty-two million large-lot suburban homes may lead to deterioration in these neighborhoods, along with an eroding tax base, that threaten their schools and the delivery of municipal services.[38]

10

Little Havana

As reported by the 2000 Census, Cuban Americans constitute about 4 percent of the U.S. Latino/a population. Prompted by geography and other factors, the Miami metropolitan area is the hub of this population and is known more broadly as the de facto capital of Latin America. The U.S. Census Bureau estimated Miami's population in 2005 as 361,701, with about two-thirds (243,874) of its residents Latino/a. Miami's metropolitan area population is similarly composed—with Latino/as constituting about 1.3 million (57 percent) of the 2.2 million residents. About half of Miami's Latino/a residents are Cuban American. The rest of its Latino/a population includes significant numbers of immigrants from Nicaragua, Colombia, Venezuela, and other Latin American countries. An estimated 72,892 African Americans and only about 39,819 Anglos called Miami home in 2005.[1]

Cubans arrived in Miami primarily as a result of two events—the Cuban Revolution of 1959 and the Mariel boatlift of 1980. About 135,000 Cubans came between January 1959 and April 1961; another 125,000 arrived in 1980 during the boatlift.[2] From December 1965 to April 1973, when Fidel Castro terminated the flights, some 340,000 Cuban refugees from the Revolution arrived in the United States by plane. Initially exiles came from Cuba's elite class, but gradually the emigration became a more representative cross-section of class and race in Cuba.[3]

Particularly in the early stages of the migration to Miami, arriving Cubans found a city with pronounced segregation between Black and Anglo residents. Cubans accentuated this segregation by forming enclaves in the older middle-class residential neighborhoods in Miami as Anglos left for newer neighborhoods.[4] For example, Latino/as comprise more than 90 percent of the residents of Miami's so-called Little Havana neighborhood, with its famous main artery, Calle Ocho (Eighth Street). Cubans settled primarily in modest single-family homes, but the pressures of overcrowding led to conversions or demolition and rebuilding of homes as multifamily units where zoning restrictions would allow.[5] Jewish residents relocating from the northeastern United States during the Depression held a strong presence in this neighborhood until Cubans arrived as the newest group in what is known as a modern-day Ellis Island. Little Havana continues that tradition today, as Cuban residents give way to other Latino/a arrivals, particularly Nicaraguans.[6]

The Cuban American diaspora now extends well beyond Little Havana to cities throughout Florida, as well as to other states, particularly New Jersey, home to the Cuban American U.S. Senator Robert "Bob" Menendez. Florida cities with half or more of their population comprised of Cuban Americans include Hialeah (62.12 percent) and Sweetwater (49.92).[7] Sweetwater is also home to such a significant Nicaraguan population that it is known locally as Little Managua, named for the Nicaraguan capital.

Owing in part to their relatively recent arrival, most of which took place in the era of fair housing protections, Cuban Americans faced neither the severity of loss nor the exclusion that imperiled Mexican Americans in the Southwest. Moreover, prior to the toughening of immigration policies toward Cubans in the mid-1990s that allowed refugee boats to be intercepted on the high seas, Cuban immigrants enjoyed the special status of "political refugees" and thus were shielded from the perils many Mexican immigrants faced. Nevertheless, Cuban Americans confronted some familiar tactics of exclusion in housing markets, as real estate brokers steered them away from select Anglo neighborhoods such as Coral Gables. They also suffered the loss, not of land and homes in the United States, but of their Cuban residences and agricultural land lost through government expropriation.

Fidel Castro's regime stripped Cuban Americans (and others) of their real estate by several means. First, Cuba's Agrarian Reform Law claimed large landholdings, initially those in excess of 400 hectares (one hectare equals approximately two and one-half acres). Subsequently, the government claimed farm acreage in excess of five *caballerias* (one caballeria is about thirty-three acres). Before 1959, fewer than 3,000 individuals and corporations owned almost three-quarters of Cuba's total arable land. At the same time, most of Cuba's farm workers (about 70 percent) were landless renters.[8] A 1951 World Bank report found sharecropping, tenant farming, and squatters commonplace in the rural Cuban landscape.[9] Pursuant to the post-Revolution agrarian reform, the government distributed confiscated lands to those owning farmland of less than two *caballerias*. Ultimately, the government confiscated and redistributed about 63 percent of the arable land in Cuba.[10] Although the Agrarian Reform Law specified a system of compensation using twenty-year bonds, the lands expropriated were undervalued in issuing the bonds, and no compensation was actually paid to the former landowners.[11] Bonds were expected to be paid with U.S. sugar quota purchases, but Congress scuttled the sugar quota and any other benefits to Cuba in the 1961 Foreign Assistance Act. Many U.S. property owners, primarily corporate interests, were stripped of their Cuba holdings in the agricultural upheaval. The U.S. Foreign Claims Settlement Commission eventually adjudicated these claims, certifying in 1972 that $1.8 billion in property, agricultural and otherwise, was expropriated from U.S. owners, constituting the largest certified seizure ever of U.S. property. The lion's share of this loss was corporate, as the top ten U.S. corporate claims of loss alone accounted for half of this $1.8 billion.[12]

Cuban citizens suffered perhaps an even greater financial loss of their own expropriated property, particularly those who left for the United States.[13] Many Cuban exiles lost their homes pursuant to the draconian Confiscation of Abandoned Property Law, which captured without compensation properties owned by counter-revolutionaries or anyone who left Cuba for a specified period of time. Some exiles were able to save their homes from expropriation by placing title in relatives' names. Expropriated homes still raise some cautionary flags for buyers, some of whom are fearful that in a post-Castro Cuba a title battle might ensue.[14]

Through its Urban Reform Law in 1960, the Cuban government expropriated rental dwellings from landlords and offered them for sale to the renters, who could eventually become owners through monthly payments at government-determined prices. This law proscribed all leasing except for hotels, hostels, and the like. Owners of expropriated rental properties were to be compensated in amounts determined by government appraisers.[15]

Despite its Marxist foundations, Cuban law sought to encourage private ownership of homes after the dust of the upheaval of redistribution had settled. Cuba's 1984 Housing Law declared that Cubans have the right to own their residence and one vacation home, and it fostered self-building by individuals and housing cooperatives.[16] Transfers of homes are tightly regulated, with house exchanges rather than outright sale as the method of transfer. An underground economy of transfer has arisen, however, whereby homes of disparate value are illegally traded with compensation to even the deal.[17] Mortgages of homes are impermissible, because loans in Cuba are personal rather than asset-based.[18] As one Cuban resident opined to a U.S. reporter while her son, a Florida transplant, was struggling with house payments: "I prefer our system. We don't have mortgages and so we're not facing foreclosure like so many of you are [during the subprime loan crisis]."[19]

Cuba's 1992 Constitution aspires to ensure that all families have an adequate place to live.[20] Consistent with this ideal, Cuba has the highest rate of homeownership in the Western Hemisphere, jumping from about 50 percent at the time of the 1984 Housing Law to an estimated 90 percent of adults in 2004.[21] However, the underbelly of this impressive statistic is the poor condition of Cuba's housing stock—totaling about 2.2 million urban units and 835,000 rural units in 1999—as well as the severe shortage of housing Cuba faces. Seventeen percent of Cuban housing is officially rated as in bad condition, and one government report in 1999 found nearly half of Havana's units in moderate to bad condition, with some 4,000 in danger of collapse.[22] The occupancy of unsafe structures can be explained by the absence of access to capital, a scarcity of building materials, and other factors, which have combined to create a housing shortage and consequent overcrowding. Thus, despite Cuba's high rate of homeownership, many residents there face housing situations that approximate those of most U.S. Latino/as—living in crowded and dilapidated conditions.

Cuban land reform is headed in the opposite direction from that in Mexico and the United States. As detailed in chapter 2, extensive Latino/a landholdings in the United States gave way in the second half of the nineteenth century to Anglo ownership, mostly in smaller chunks carved up by lawyers, courts, marriages, sales, and squatters. As discussed in chapter 12, the Mexican Revolution similarly launched the breakup of large ranchos in Mexico, though in contrast to the U.S. experience, recipients of these rancho properties were landless Mexicans. Similarly, agricultural land devolved in the Cuban Revolution to landless Cubans. As addressed in chapter 12, land reform in the United States and Mexico, however, has since shifted direction as large agri-business and corporate interests have amassed landholdings. At the same time, Cuban reform has maintained its momentum of breaking land ownership into smaller pieces. Chapters 12 and 14 offer ideas to implement a similar equitable shift in U.S. land ownership, by boosting Latino/a collective ownership of, or income from, agricultural and forest lands.

As with much of the Southwest, Florida was once owned by Spain, which began conferring land grants on settlers there in 1790. Effective in 1821, the Adams-Onis Treaty transferred ownership from Spain to the United States with these land grants intact. As it did for the Southwest, Congress created a land grant commission to resolve the legitimacy of Spanish land grants in Florida.[23] Now, almost two centuries later, Latino/a immigrants arrive in Florida without any prospect of a government land grant. Wealthy international buyers own a considerable stake in the Florida residential real estate market, with about one-third of international buyers of Florida homes hailing from South America, Central America, and the Caribbean.[24] But most immigrants arriving in Florida are cash-poor Latino/as who pursue their dream of homeownership without ready access to capital. These immigrants are the lifeblood of the American dream and ambition—a tradition of hard work in exchange for the reward of comfortable living.

11

Spanish Harlem

> At home we grouped into a tight knot, two adults and seven children inside [an apartment of] two rooms. . . . The front room was just big enough for a table and two chairs, and Héctor and Raymond's fold-out cot. The girls' beds were along the walls of the back room. Mami and Papi's bed was against the paneled wall, a curtain separating it from our side of the room.
> —Esmeralda Santiago, describing one of her childhood residences in San Juan, Puerto Rico, in *When I Was Puerto Rican* (1993), 156

> All those white yuppies want to live in Manhattan, and they think Spanish Harlem is next for the taking. When they start moving in, we won't be able to compete when it comes to rents, and we'll be left out in the cold. But if we build a strong professional class and accumulate property, we can counter that effect.
> —Conversation between Nuyoricans in Ernesto Quiñonez, *Bodega Dreams* (2000), 106–7

Officially a territory of the United States, the Puerto Rican islands are regarded by many scholars as a colony given their lack of legal and political sovereignty.[1] Following the seizure of Puerto Rico by the United States in 1898 during the Spanish-American War, Puerto Ricans became U.S. citizens in 1917 under the Jones Act. As citizens, Puerto Ricans are free to travel and reside anywhere in the United States without regard to immigration procedures and limits. Initially, few Puerto Ricans came to the mainland United States, but with the advent of affordable air travel (with flights in the late 1940s costing Puerto Ricans between thirty and fifty dollars) and the lure of jobs, Puerto Ricans came in substantial numbers following World War II.[2] Most headed to New York City, initially a port for those arriving by sea, but eventually a home for later migrants. New York's popularity as a destination point transformed these mostly rural, farm worker Puerto Rican migrants into urban industrial and service workers. The rise of unskilled or low-skilled jobs in the New York garment and hotel industries, coinciding with declines in the Puerto Rico sugar industry, brought thousands of Puerto Ricans to New York and elsewhere in the mainland United States.[3] In 1945, only about 13,000 Puerto Ricans resided in New York City; by the following year, it was more than 50,000. By 1955, almost 700,000 Puerto Ricans had migrated to the U.S. mainland. In 1953, the peak year for migration, some 69,000 Puerto Ricans arrived.[4] According to the 2000 Census, more than 3.4 million Puerto Ricans resided on the mainland, and nearly 4 million more resided in Puerto Rico. By 2009, there were more Puerto Ricans living on the mainland than in Puerto Rico.[5]

Within New York City, the area known as East Harlem emerged as the epicenter for Puerto Rican migration. East Harlem in the late 1800s and early 1900s was home to German and Irish immigrants, and later to such substantial numbers of Italians that it was known briefly as Little Italy. Jewish immigrants arrived later, as did Puerto Rican migrants who eventually cemented the neighborhood's identity as Spanish Harlem or El Barrio. Running north from 96th to about 129th Street, and situated between Fifth Avenue on the west and the East River, Spanish Harlem at one time constituted an enclave that was nearly 85 percent Puerto Rican.[6]

On the island of Puerto Rico, the impoverished residential area of La Perla, just outside the walls of tourist destination Old San Juan, is reminiscent of U.S./Mexico border colonias with its sometimes self-built housing and an absence of government services. Puerto Rico's homeownership rate of 74.1 percent significantly outpaces the rate for Latino/as in the mainland United States, and even that of all groups in the majority of U.S. states—only Minnesota and Michigan have higher overall ownership rates. But many Puerto Rican residents strain their budgets to achieve homeownership—only California (51.8 percent) has a higher percentage than Puerto Rico (47.2 percent) of homeowners with mortgage loans who spend more than 30 percent of their household income on housing costs. Moreover, Puerto Rican residences are more crowded than those in all U.S. states except Alaska, California, and Hawaii.[7] These statistics reflect dismal education and poverty rates. Puerto Rico's rate of high school completion is lower than that of any U.S. state, and its individual poverty rate is 45.4 percent, more than three times the overall rate in the United States. Puerto Ricans living in Puerto Rico are the poorest group of all U.S. citizens, and the poverty of Puerto Ricans defines their housing options as migrants in Spanish Harlem and elsewhere in the mainland United States. Given their overwhelming poverty, they have few housing choices in one of the world's most expensive cities. Spanish Harlem faced a poverty rate of 36.9 percent in 2000, with a distressing unemployment rate of 17.1 percent. As expected, the neighborhood has an abysmally small percentage of owner-occupants, with renters constituting 93.6 percent of its residents.[8] It is also home to the second-highest concentration of public housing units in New York City, with almost two-thirds of the population dependent on publicly subsidized housing.[9]

Rental units in Spanish Harlem are perennially dilapidated and overcrowded, ushering in urban renewal and gentrification that pose a different threat to the wellbeing of impoverished residents.[10] Foreshadowing the onset of urban renewal efforts, a commentator in 1965 reported that almost half the privately owned dwellings in Spanish Harlem were dilapidated and nearly one-third overcrowded.[11] Another report in the 1950s described decrepit conditions for Puerto Ricans in Spanish Harlem, including eighteen people occupying a three-room unit, thirty people sharing a single broken toilet with no seat in a building laced with rat holes, and twenty-five residents sharing a dark, airless, coal cellar converted into crowded sleeping quarters.[12] Absentee landlords contributed to the decay, as resident tenants had little incentive or ability to undertake repairs of common areas or even within their units.

Urban renewal projects in the form of public housing initially displaced more Puerto Ricans in Spanish Harlem than they housed:

> [T]hey were initially intended for the "submerged middle classes," those "worthy" of help, not the minority, unemployed, or "untraditional" large, extended families. Through this discriminatory admissions policy, Puerto Ricans had to struggle for due and equitable access to public housing, which became a marker for class distinctions among East Harlemites through housing policies that included interviews for tenant suitability, apartment inspections for hygiene, wait lists for apartments, and other forms of tenant surveillance.[13]

Not until the late 1960s and 1970s did Puerto Ricans gain adequate access to public housing projects in Spanish Harlem.[14] As entire city blocks were razed, displaced Puerto Ricans instead found themselves accepted in housing projects outside El Barrio.

The economics of the supercharged housing market in Manhattan eventually reached Spanish Harlem, with working-class Anglos from Manhattan seeking cheaper rentals and even ownership in newly built condominium and cooperative housing. While rising rents drove Puerto Rican residents to more affordable cities in Pennsylvania and Connecticut, or forced them to double or triple up in rental units, new condominium projects displaced tenements by offering affordable housing by New York standards.[15] In 2007, the average price per square foot in the Spanish Harlem area was about $629, affordable compared to downtown Manhattan.[16] These condo projects offer such upscale amenities as concierge service and roof decks. Heralding the new playground for the Anglo bohemian are real estate brokers and developers aiming to de-race the neighborhood by rebranding it with geographical references such as Upper Manhattan, Upper East Side, Upper Carnegie Hall, or Upper Yorkville that eliminate the specter of Puerto Ricans (Spanish) or African Americans (Harlem). From 1990 to 2000, the Spanish Harlem Anglo population jumped 20 percent, and since then the growth rate is likely greater.[17] By 2005, Puerto Ricans, once a significant majority in Spanish Harlem, comprised only 35.3 percent of the neighborhood's population, at 37,878, down from 39.4 percent in 1990, when 40,542 Puerto Ricans resided there.[18] Although New York City remains home to about 800,000 Puerto Rican residents, roughly 20 percent of the mainland population, the fastest-growing Puerto Rican areas on the mainland are in the South, especially the Orlando area, where about 220,000 Puerto Ricans reside.

Gentrification to the detriment of Puerto Rican migrants has not been limited to Spanish Harlem. In Manhattan's Hell's Kitchen neighborhood, for example, tensions between resident Puerto Ricans, Irish, and Italians became the blueprint for the violent Puerto Rican gang members depicted in 1961's *West Side Story*. The movie was filmed in the area that became Lincoln Center—a transition marking the development pressures that ultimately displaced Puerto Ricans and some of the other groups residing in this desirable neighborhood adjacent to midtown Manhattan.[19]

Another factor from the opposite side of the income spectrum worked to decrease the Puerto Rican population in El Barrio in the 2000s—resurgent immigration of poor minority groups, particularly Dominicans in the 1980s and Mexicans since 1990. Dominicans are expected shortly to surpass the Puerto Rican population in New York City. From 1990 to 2000, the number of Mexicans in Spanish Harlem grew from less than 3,000 to more than 10,000, 80 percent of whom were Mexican-born.[20] Many of these Mexican immigrants are undocumented, sharing with Puerto Rican residents a lack of tierra—as renters in an urban landscape—and an absence of libertad, with both groups facing a complex identity of imperiled sovereignty and liberty. Undocumented Mexicans, on the one hand, can return to their home country to escape the shadows of undocumented existence and gain the right to participate fully in their communities. Despite being U.S. citizens, Puerto Ricans pushed out of Spanish Harlem by the real estate market and other pressures, however, would still lack self-determination and U.S. political representation should they migrate to Puerto Rico.

In comparison to owners losing their homes to subprime mortgage lenders, and Mexicans who lost their vast rancho properties in the Southwest, the Puerto Rican experience in Spanish Harlem presents a different degree of loss.[21] As a community of renters, most displaced Puerto Ricans did not lose property as a result of economic pressures, but they did lose membership in the vibrant community of arts, culture, language, merchants, and family that was El Barrio. Moreover, the benefits of the rapid price appreciation in Manhattan in recent decades fell mostly into Anglo hands, and not those of the Puerto Rican tenants who kept the tenements in business for generations until the superheated Manhattan real estate market swept into Spanish Harlem. The Puerto Rican experience in Manhattan suggests that a focus on boosting Latino/a homeownership must not ignore housing imperatives of renters trapped in higher-priced markets while earning substandard wages.

The Puerto Rican legacy of loss in El Barrio also resonates with the gentrification experience of African Americans in neighboring Harlem, in which new condominium developments replaced aging brownstones and retail catering to upscale residents replaced dollar stores. By 2008, the average price for new condominium units in Harlem was $900,000, despite an average household income in the area of less than $25,000.[22] From 2004 to the market's peak in 2007, the median sale price for Harlem area town homes increased about 150 percent, from $554,250 to $1.4 million.[23] As with the experience in El Barrio, gentrification in this African American cultural center led many to lament the loss of community and soul. Their shared experience of upheaval, however, can augment the basis for coalition between Latino/as and African Americans, addressed in chapter 15, to confront and reform the underlying structural causes of inadequate housing, whether owned or rented.

Part IV

Reclamation and Reform

Blending efforts to reclaim or recover compensation for lost land, to ensure adequate and affordable rental housing, and to boost homeownership, the final chapters chart strategies new and old in the pursuit of Tierra y Libertad. These strategies avoid relying on judicial relief and instead point primarily to legislative measures, such as passage of comprehensive immigration reform, as well as laws to create jobs, finance education and affordable housing initiatives, and ensure consumer education. At bottom, most of these measures will hinge on what Latino/as have failed to galvanize over the years—political prowess. Even dramatic expressions of Latino/a political promise—particularly the immigrant rights rallies that brought millions to the streets across the United States in 2006 and subsequent years—belied political roadblocks faced by Latino/as, such as the inability of noncitizens to vote in most jurisdictions and the backlash from hate groups and hate radio prompted by such visible displays of Latino/a political angst and urgency. Reform must also overcome perceptions raised in chapter 4 that Latino/as are improper stewards of land and homes and therefore undeserving of housing opportunities.

Despite a history of muted political influence by Latino/as, there is reason for optimism on progress related to housing policy. First, as discussed in chapter 15, African Americans share much of the same mistreatment in the housing market, and along with it the urgency for reform, particularly structural changes to increase educational and wage equality as the gateway to fair housing. Interracial coalitions between Latino/as and African Americans on these crucial issues can merge two of the fastest-growing voting groups, who with working-class Anglo voters might effectively launch a strategy to attain broadscale economic reform. Further, opportunities exist for interest convergence with middle-class Anglos in encouraging homeownership for Latino/as. Addressed in chapter 13, these include the need for a continuing wave of entry-level homebuyers to propel existing homeowners up the housing ladder. The demographics of America's youth population make it abundantly clear where these homebuyers of tomorrow must emerge from in order to benefit the predominantly Anglo homeowners of today.

Connections among housing, labor, and education offer indirect means for meaningful reform in housing. Enhanced support of public education that fuels wage advances ultimately will lift housing markets. Reform efforts might therefore concentrate on whichever arena—housing, labor, or education—holds the most interest convergence and political traction. Education and wage reform have been sought for decades without success, while schools and wages continue to erode. As chapter 14 details, the housing market has found political favor, at least for purposes of upper-middle-class beneficiaries of tax subsidies such as the mortgage interest and real property tax deductions. Reforms to boost the entry levels of the housing market will be a tougher sell, but are vital to ensure the American dream isn't relegated to history.

12

Tierra y Libertad

Reclaiming Individual and Collective Space

In the less than two hundred years since they owned huge rancho properties in the Southwest, Latino/as find themselves relatively landless. Although the dispossession of Latino/as might be seen as egalitarian because lands were disbursed to smaller landholders, U.S. corporate interests and wealthy Anglos eventually commandeered huge stakes in land, to the exclusion of such groups as Latino/a newcomers and family farmers. The federal government stands out as the nation's largest landowner, controlling nearly one-third of U.S. land.[1] Industries such as oil companies and agri-giants own massive land interests. The paper industry owns a significant chunk of the state of Maine. Led by media king Ted Turner, the ten largest individual landowners possess more than ten million acres, amounting to 1 out of every 217 acres of land in the United States.[2] Latino/as are invisible within this landscape of gigantic landholdings as they struggle for recognition of ongoing land claims that may date back to the nineteenth century.

Protest has been a familiar strategy in land disputes involving Latino/as, just as it has been for the United Farm Workers union in labor disputes and for Latino/a activists seeking comprehensive immigration reform through street rallies. When land is at stake, group occupation is readily employed as a means of protest, particularly when rights to community use are involved.

The most famous land occupation in recent history, the Native American occupation of Alcatraz Island from 1969 to 1971, no doubt inspired some of the Latino/a occupations. Yet the history of Latino/a protest through occupation precedes the Alcatraz takeover. For example, when the Arechiga family was forcibly evicted from their humble residence in Chávez Ravine in the 1950s to clear the way for construction of Dodger Stadium, the family hung on in a makeshift campground. Ten minutes after the last family member was evacuated, a bulldozer crushed the home they owned for thirty-six years, but the family was not easily swayed. Along with some forty friends and family members, they camped across the street. The next day, the family moved their tent to the site of their bulldozed home, declaring that authorities would have to carry them off the land as they were carried from their home.³ With a media spotlight on the encampment and a host of spectators, the family received the gift of a trailer and chemical toilet to help them comply with health department threats to remove their children. After ten days of occupation while fending off government officials, the family broke camp but continued to pursue their legal claims in local courts without success.

Although the Arechigas had an individual stake in the land they occupied, most notable land occupations in Latino/a history are collective, community-based struggles in which the occupied property was chosen strategically to convey broader goals. Given the specter of trespass laws, these occupations eventually prompted local authorities to intervene, and thus tended to be short-lived, albeit dramatic events in the history of Latino/a land struggles that deserve discussion for their potential advantages and shortcomings as strategies in the quest for land and housing reform.

Three examples of occupation in the 1960s and 1970s illustrate this strategy of land occupation toward broader land reform. In 1977, the Puerto Rican activist group and political party the Young Lords seized the Statue of Liberty for a day to protest the occupation of Puerto Rico by the United States and the imprisonment of Puerto Rican nationalists for using violent tactics in their freedom-fighting campaign. In addition to serving as a New York landmark, the Statue of Liberty was emblematic of the self-determination many Puerto Ricans desired for their island territory, as well as for their extensive community in Manhattan. Acting according to a script, twenty-eight Young Lords members evacuated Liberty Island of tourists and federal workers and unfurled a huge Puerto Rican flag on the statue's crown. That same night federal authorities moved in to arrest the protesters, charging them with trespass on a federal facility. Ultimately, each was fined $100.⁴ Still unrealized, the Young Lords' 1969 party platform included broad goals of libertad: "We want self-determination for Puerto Ricans—Liberation of the Island and inside the United States. . . . We want community control of our institutions and land." The latter aspiration was accentuated with the platform's imperative "Land Belongs To All the People!"⁵ Related to the Mexican Revolution imperative of Tierra y Libertad is the logo of the Partido Popular Democrático de Puerto Rico (Puerto Rico's Popular Democratic Party, which supports continuance of its status as a commonwealth), depicting a farm worker silhouette with the slogan "pan [bread], tierra, libertad."

The campaign for redress of the loss of Latino/a farm and ranch land in the wake of the Treaty of Guadalupe Hidalgo led to occupations during the Chicano Movement of the late 1960s and early 1970s—most prominently, of California's Santa Catalina Island and of the Carson National Forest in northern New Mexico. Armed with an awakening historical consciousness from the burgeoning Chicano Studies movement in schools, the Chicano/a youth activist group and community security force known as the Brown Berets embraced land reform in its community agenda. Reading the Treaty of Guadalupe Hidalgo as granting to the United States just that portion of Mexico's territory that extended along the current U.S./Mexico border "to the Pacific Ocean,"[6] the Brown Berets believed that the Channel Islands off the California coast remained Mexican territory excluded from the treaty.[7] Selecting the most populated of the eight Channel Islands, the Brown Berets planned to occupy Santa Catalina Island as a means of "restitution of the land for those who need a place to be free. As of now, we [Chicanos and Mexicans] have nothing. We are poor. But land is like gold. The land can feed the people. There is a great deal of animal game there, and a bountiful supply of fish surround[s] the island. On the land, we can develop an institute of study."[8] In late August 1972, twenty-six Brown Berets established camp on a hillside of the island and hoisted a large Mexican flag, issuing a press release proclaiming the Channel Islands as "Mexican lands."[9] Although their occupation lasted nearly a month, their encampment within the jurisdiction of the Los Angeles County Sheriff's Department ultimately prompted sheriff's deputies to issue the ultimatum that they depart or face arrest for illegal camping. The occupation proved one of the last actions of the Brown Berets, who were escorted off the island by deputies and disbanded shortly thereafter. Subsequent to the occupation, federal courts finally addressed the underlying legal question and concluded that the United States acquired the Channel Islands in the Mexican-American War.[10]

Led by controversial activist Reies Tijerina, the occupation in northern New Mexico stemmed from a slightly different application of the Treaty of Guadalupe Hidalgo. Although the territory in question clearly was within the reach of the treaty and thus within the legal jurisdiction of the United States, much of the area had once been held in communal land grants. As explained in chapter 2, these grants were issued to small groups of settlers, who shared common rights to water, grazing, and timber to supplement small individual plots of land for residences, vegetable gardens, and orchards. Although the Spanish and Mexican land grant systems recognized these communal grants as owned by the community of farmers, the

U.S. Supreme Court decided that the ownership of the communal portion remained with the sovereign, and thus passed to the United States under the Treaty.[11] Tijerina targeted the Carson National Forest, named after pioneer Kit Carson, as communal land of Mexican villagers that still belonged to the community despite this Supreme Court ruling. Forming La Alianza Federal de Mercedes (the Federal Alliance of Land Grants) around 1963, Tijerina gained a considerable following, although some New Mexico Latino/as, including then-Senator Joseph Montoya, viewed him as an outsider and criticized his tactics and aims. The Alianza organization's manifesto on Spanish land grants expressed disdain for the court-controlled property certification procedures of the 1800s and advocated the right to defend the community land: "The true owners of these lands have the legal right to use all the force necessary to oust these trespassers [on the Spanish grant lands], without running into an Anglo controlled and orientated court for a 'Qui[e]t Title Action' wherein title to the property is up for grabs."[12] Adhering to these principles, in October 1966, Tijerina and 350 Alianza members occupied the Echo Amphitheater public campground area of the Carson National Forest in the name of a sovereign Mexican American nation they called Republica de San Joaquín del Río de Chama. They elected as mayor a direct descendant of the communal land grant of San Joaquín, and claimed all rights conferred in 1808 by the King of Spain in the original grant.[13] To evidence their sovereignty, Alianza members replaced national forest signs with placards proclaiming the name of the old land grant. A week into their symbolic camp-in, the group seized two park rangers and tried them for "trespassing and being a public nuisance" in impromptu court proceedings on a park picnic table.[14] The de facto judge levied a fine of $500 along with suspended jail sentences. As the Alianza occupiers dwindled a few days later, federal and state officials cleared them out and charged Tijerina and some Alianza members with assaulting federal officials, conversion of government trucks, and conspiracy.[15]

The backdrop of these occupations was similar—in New York City, Southern California, and northern New Mexico, the local Latino/a communities were impoverished and poorly served by local, state, and federal governments. Prompted by these circumstances, community activists looked to land as a potential solution to the needs of the impoverished, under-served community. But meaningful transfers of land were not forthcoming. Somewhat more successful have been struggles targeting smaller, better-defined tracts of land for specific community aims, such as a school or parkland. An example is the occupation in 1970 of what became Chicano Park in a predominantly Mexican American area of San Diego known as Barrio Logan (or as Logan Heights). Having ignored for decades community requests for dedication of parkland, San Diego rezoned the neighborhood after World War II as mixed residential and industrial, allowing an influx of uses incompatible with a residential neighborhood. The eight-lane Interstate 5 sliced through Barrio Logan in 1963, displacing some 5,000 barrio families,[16] and the Coronado Bridge connected affluent Coronado Island[17] with Interstate 5 in 1969, leaving dozens of unsightly concrete support pillars to the roadway overhead defacing the heart of Barrio Logan. When construction began in 1970 for a Highway Patrol parking lot under this jungle of freeways, a few hundred community members gathered to evict the construction crew and occupy the site. Planting cacti, vegetation, and trees, the neighbors remained on the construction site for twelve days while negotiating for creation of a park. Evidencing that few advances in Latino/a neighborhoods come without struggle, the occupation succeeded in relocating the Highway Patrol facilities and gaining approval for what is now Chicano Park, resplendent with vibrant Chicano artist murals on the many freeway pillars.[18] Chicano Park stands in contrast, however, to Belvedere Park in East Los Angeles, which was decimated and stripped of more than half its acreage by construction projects, including localized services such as an elementary school and a sheriff's office as well as by the Pomona Freeway that tore through the park's core in the 1960s.[19]

Less successful was the occupation in South Los Angeles of a fourteen-acre parcel known as South Central Farm, which was used by predominantly Latino/a families as a cooperative urban farm. Reminiscent of the saga of Chávez Ravine but with a twist, the city acquired the parcel in 1986 for $4,786,372 through condemnation, intending to build a trash incinerator that community opposition soon scuttled. Following the 1992 riots, spurred by the acquittal of the police officers who beat African American motorist Rodney King, a nonprofit food bank gained permission to use the vacant site as a community garden. For years, Latino/a families farmed the land through a communal structure whereby they shared costs and decision-making. Typically these families were poor laborers who worked the land evenings and weekends to grow vegetables and herbs for their food and medicine. Whereas the Arechiga family[20] of Chávez Ravine was unable to reclaim their condemned property when the city abandoned plans to build a public housing project, the former owner of the South Central Farm property reacquired his condemned acreage. Paying a below-market price of $5,050,000,[21] the owner settled his court action against the city that invoked a clause of the original condemnation allowing repurchase should the city sell the land for nonpublic purposes. Fighting their subsequent eviction in court, the community farmers lost their lawsuit and resorted to occupying the property. Attracting celebrities to their cause, the Latino/a farmers gained national attention during their few weeks of occupation, defying the judge's order to vacate. They built an encampment on the farm, with a kitchen and medic station, but ultimately their efforts to persuade the developer to sell the parcel to the cooperative at a huge profit failed. On June 13, 2006, county sheriffs in riot gear forcibly arrested and removed the protesters—among them actress Daryl Hannah, who had chained herself to a walnut tree. Once the property was stripped of protesters, the developer hired a private security force to keep out trespassers while workers bulldozed the farm and its improvements. The arrival of bulldozers often marks the end of Latino/a ownership or occupation of disputed land, as evidenced by the Chávez family homestead lost during the Depression, Latino/a homes in the path of Southern California freeways, homes perched on Chávez Ravine, and old downtown multifamily buildings in many cities demolished in the name of urban renewal.

Two years after the developer's bulldozers leveled the farm, the property captured headlines again as plans emerged to erect a warehouse distribution center on the site for a women's apparel company, Forever 21, which had earlier been the target of a three-year boycott by Latino/a garment workers, who contended that the retailer was responsible for the unfair labor conditions of its subcontractors.[22] Community advocates urged the city to require an environmental impact study before allowing a warehouse that would draw 2,400 trucks daily to the neighborhood. In rejoinder, the company threatened to leave the Los Angeles area if a suitable location was not found, taking manufacturing jobs with it. An entry on a blog site maintained by the *Los Angeles Times* reflected the sentiment of Angelinos who sided with the developer and regard Mexican Americans as interlopers:

> The property owner has every right to do what he wants to do with his property as long as it comply [sic] with the zoning code. If I recall the protesters are 3rd world Mexicans. If they want to farm, [then] move back to Mexico and live like pigs. Horowitz [the developer] has the right to do with his property what he wants to do.[23]

Here again is the conception of the dirty Mexican undeserving of land or housing reform, an image that has long constrained policymaking and trumped protest and other efforts toward equality.

As a strategy for redress of housing and land grievances, the tactic of protest by occupation has merit, but ultimately falls short of a panacea for Latino/a land woes. On the plus side, some past occupations have drawn considerable publicity, particularly the Young Lords' brief takeover of the Statue of Liberty, as have those infused with celebrity participation, such as the South Central Farm occupation and the protests of U.S. military operations in Vieques, Puerto Rico, which drew celebrities such as Edward James Olmos to the civilian encampments on Navy turf and helped end military exercises there.[24] In the case of South Central Farm, widespread publicity secured funds sufficient to purchase the property at its fair market value, but the developer rebuffed the purchase offer.[25] Moreover, occupations are connected to a rich history of protest and supply a vehicle for the involvement of the Latino/a community in disputes.

The inadequacy of the strategy is evidenced by the fact that most occupations, however well publicized, and however much they galvanized a movement, ultimately failed to secure their immediate goal. The Carson National Forest is no less federal property today; Santa Catalina Island remains a playground for the wealthy, and is no refuge for Mexicans and Mexican Americans; and Puerto Rico remains under U.S. control. The rule of law tends to intervene swiftly in these property disputes, particularly when government land is at stake. This is especially true in the wake of the September 11th attacks, as threats to government property generally are perceived as terrorist in orientation. Even the occupation of private property in the case of the South Central Farm drew police in riot gear to arrest the trespassers. Interlopers had far more success in the 1800s, when Anglo squatters occupied Spanish and Mexican land grant acreage and the government looked the other way. Particularly in the current climate, with hate radio warning of a de facto or even de jure takeover of the Southwest—the territory of Aztlán— by means of a *reconquista* that returns the Southwest to Mexican control, Latino/as do not have the political winds of change or even tolerance at their backs for widespread land acquisition.

Most land disputes of community consequence are decided by power, demanding political, legal, and financial clout. For example, the Cuban American population has helped influence U.S. policy toward Cuba through its economic clout. In contrast, the Puerto Rican population on the U.S. mainland, despite its ostensible ability to participate politically, has not had as much success dictating U.S. policy over Puerto Rico.[26] Federal and state lands in the Southwest, many of which stem from Spanish and Mexican land grants to Latino/as, are susceptible to control by powerful private interests that desire such uses as grazing, serving tourist populations, mineral exploration, or energy generation. But uses on behalf of the poor, such as collective farming plots, have little political traction. The opportunity for any fundamental change in the land and housing fortunes of Latino/as probably lies in the strategies for comprehensive gains in political and economic clout outlined in chapter 15. In the interim, tactics of protest and occupation may serve as stopgap measures to draw attention to the worst abuses, and perhaps when the stars align to bring some gains to a landscape littered with loss and exclusion.

The history of occupation and protest in Latino/a communities signals the importance of two crucial urban land uses—open space and urban farming plots. Both share the element of collective use that resonates with the history of the community-centered ejido in the Southwest. City planners wondering how shifts in demographics prompted by Latino/a growth will affect urban landscapes would do well to recognize this community theme in Latino/a history and struggles. There is much to be done. In the Los Angeles area, for example, while inner-city barrios have lost their scant open space to freeway construction and government buildings, hundreds of millions of dollars were spent to acquire open space in wealthy Malibu for the enjoyment of the nearby elite.[27] The South Central Farm struggle symbolized the need for allocating urban farming land for neighboring Latino/a families in the same way that the government supplies parkland for recreational use. These plots could be rented out for nominal fees, just as the government licenses public land for other private uses such as grazing, campsites, hunting, and the like. Equally important community spaces in Latino/a landscapes are schools and community centers. As chapter 15 explains, schools should be the centerpiece of a housing strategy for Latino/as that aims to increase homeownership and dignity.

Disputes over some Spanish and Mexican land grants remain active into the twenty-first century. As detailed in chapter 2, most of these extensive landholdings in the Southwest were lost in the late nineteenth century through burdensome certification procedures, greedy lawyers, tax auction sales, intimidation and fraud, and other tactics. Some heirs of the original owners continue to pursue restoration of their property rights, particularly in areas where the land remains relatively undeveloped and still close to its original uses as ranchland or farmland. Therefore, although the subject of land grants rarely is raised in the crowded urban geography of San Francisco and Los Angeles, or in California generally, their restoration is a passion for many in northern New Mexico. New Mexico is home to five national forests, each of which exceeds one million acres, with the Carson National Forest consisting of 1,507,000 acres. Land grant disputes also thrive today in the open ranchlands of Colorado and Texas.

These disputes proceed on two fronts, depending on whether the land is in government or private hands. For land in Colorado and Texas now mostly in private hands, courts are the primary battleground for restoration of rights. In contrast, for land in New Mexico once subject to community land grants but now controlled by the U.S. government and its agencies such as the Forest Service, Congress will likely be the arbiter of claims in the form of restorative legislation.

Recent litigation over private lands has yielded mixed results. Muted success came in a court battle over community rights to a mountainous tract in southern Colorado known as the Taylor Ranch, located in a county that calls itself "Where Colorado Began" and dates its colonization to 1540 when the Spanish explorer Francisco Vásquez de Coronado (1510–1554) traversed the Southwest.[28] Litigation spanning some forty years in federal and state court finally succeeded in the early 2000s in restoring some rights for residents able to establish themselves as descendants of the settlers who were induced in the early 1850s by the ranch owner to inhabit the area in exchange for grazing rights. The land that comprises the Taylor Ranch was originally granted to two Mexican nationals in 1844 as part of a million-acre land grant known as Sangre de Cristo (the Blood of Christ). After these land barons died in the Mexican-American War, their successor, Carlos Beaubien, was one of the few owners able to confirm his title through the Surveyor General and obtain a congressional act of confirmation. The decades-long modern litigation was sparked in 1960 when a North Carolina lumberman purchased 77,000 acres of the grant and began fencing the land to exclude local residents from using the mountainous terrain for grazing and recreation. Applying theories of prescriptive easement, easement by estoppel, and easement from prior use, the Colorado Supreme Court established the right of successors to the early Mexican settlers to graze and gather firewood and timber on the mountain.[29] Still, the epic court battle was a mixed victory, as the court rejected the descendants' claims to use the land for hunting, fishing, and recreation, and also limited common access rights for grazing and timber to just those descendants able to trace their claims to the original settlers, rather than all the landowners in Costilla County. Moreover, even though a federal appeals court had wrongly interpreted Colorado state law in the 1960s to deny all claims of the settler descendants to Taylor Ranch, that court ruling was binding, under formalistic rules of res judicata, on the many landowners personally served and made part of that earlier federal court action, leaving only those descendants served in the prior lawsuit through newspaper notification able to pursue their grazing and timber rights.[30]

Another ongoing land grant battle in the courts has yielded even less success for the claimants and signals the difficulty and expense of pursuing justice in the court system for these old wounds. More than eight hundred court-certified descendants of Jose Manuel Ballí Villarreal are using the judicial system and organized protest in an attempt to restore their claimed ownership of South Texas lands once subject to a two-million-acre land grant from Spain in 1804. The John G. and Marie Stella Kenedy Memorial Foundation, which currently occupies some of the property, took the preemptive step in the 1990s of filing a court action to establish its ownership of a 370,000-acre parcel.[31] The Ballí family contends that title remains in their name and that the Foundation held possession pursuant to a series of long-term land leases, now expired. In 2005, the Texas Court of Appeals sounded the last salvo in the decade-long court battle by affirming the trial court's ruling that the Foundation established superior title to the disputed property. Alternatively, the court ruled that the Foundation had adversely possessed that property for the requisite time period, a doctrine the *New York Times* characterized correctly as "a rough equivalent of squatter's rights."[32] The Ballí family narrowly escaped having to pay the Foundation's significant legal fees.[33] After the court losses, the family was left with the strategy of protesting wind-farming operations on the Foundation-occupied land. At one such protest, in July 2008, family members displayed signs reading, "Your leases have expired; stop renting our land to others!"[34] They presented law enforcement officers at the scene with a "Notice to Vacate" directed at the Foundation, claiming the authority of "applicable law under the lease agreement and Spanish Land Grant authority."[35] As the Ballí family website proclaims: "Today the Ballí Family and the Kenedy Foundation are currently engaged in a dispute as to ownership of La Barreta. We are the heirs of Jose Manuel Ballí Villarreal and we are saying the land belongs to us. . . . What we want is the truth in history."[36] The Ballí family separately pursued land-grant litigation to reclaim rights in Padre Island off the Texas coast. That effort to claim oil and gas royalties on Padre Island failed in 2008, however, as the Texas Supreme Court invoked doctrines of legal formalism such as the statute of limitations to deny the claim.[37]

Disdaining the court system in its battle to reclaim public lands, Reies Tijerina's Alianza Federal de Mercedes organization in New Mexico acted in the 1960s through occupation and protest. The group's manifesto explained its rejection of justice through courts:

> The reason why the Alianza is not seeking at this time, court decisions relative to this Spanish Land Grant question, is due to the fact that the Supreme Council [of the Alianza] . . . has passed a resolution of non-confidence in the Courts of the State of New Mexico and of the United States of America. The reason behind this resolution is the history of these courts, a history of a century of gross denials of justice and of arbitrarily misconstruing of the law, and the inability of these courts to overcome their own corruption, by always invoking their "stare decisis" doctrine as a defense to their frauds and as a denial to give just compensation for their arbitrary confiscation of property.[38]

The 1897 ruling of the U.S. Supreme Court in *United States v. Sandoval* still haunts many descendants of the New Mexico community land grantees for its conclusion that the sovereign rather than the collective owns the shared (community) portion of those lands. As the president of one of the community grants explained in 2004, the U.S. government, through the *Sandoval* decision, "has held the thumb of poverty over us."[39] Because there is little chance the Supreme Court will revisit its 1897 ruling, the community land grant descendants affected by that decision formed the Sandoval Coalition and today are pursuing legislative reform rather than litigation to restore their community rights in public lands. Combined, the seven grants represented in the Sandoval Coalition lost 1.1 million acres of community land to the U.S. government, with only 16,485 acres confirmed following the Mexican-American War. Efforts at reinstatement or restitution were buoyed in June 2004 when the U.S. General Accounting Office, at the request of several members of New Mexico's congressional delegation, issued a report titled *Treaty of Guadalupe Hidalgo: Findings and Possible Options Regarding Longstanding Community Land Grant Claims in New Mexico*. Although the report concluded that the process of confirming land titles in New Mexico complied with U.S. statutory and constitutional requirements, it did opine that "the confirmation processes were inefficient and created hardships for many grantees."[40] Therefore, the report suggested that Congress may wish to consider further action in response, and offered five potential options for federal legislation:

Option 1: Consider taking no additional action at this time because the majority of community land grants were confirmed, the majority of acreage claimed was awarded, and the confirmation processes were conducted in accordance with U.S. law.

Option 2: Consider acknowledging that the land grant confirmation process could have been more efficient and less burdensome and imposed fewer hardships on claimants.

Option 3: Consider establishing a commission or other body to reexamine specific community land grant claims that were rejected or not confirmed for the full acreage claimed.

Option 4: Consider transferring federal land to communities that did not receive all of the acreage originally claimed for their community land grants.

Option 5: Consider making financial payments to claimants' heirs or other entities for the nonuse of land originally claimed but not awarded.[41]

Land grant descendants polled for the report preferred a combination of the last options—transfer of land and restitution. From 1997 to 2001, Congress had flirted with adopting the Guadalupe-Hidalgo Treaty Land Claims Act, which would have established a commission, in the mode of Option 3 above, to determine the validity of community land grant claims and recommend that Congress restore valid claims to grant descendants through subsequent legislation. The Clinton Administration opposed the bill, contending among other things that reopening these claims would create expectations of similar treatment in other regions of the Southwest, as well as disrupt federal land management activities and displace public recreational activities on federal lands.[42] In contrast, then-Speaker of the House, Republican Newt Gingrich, championed the legislation. Chicano historian Rodolfo Acuña was suspicious, however, of support from national Republican leadership:

> [W]e must be reminded that Gingrich and company are the apostles of privatization; the counterparts of Mexican neo-liberals such as Carlos Salinas de Gortari. The history of privatization must be analyzed in the context of both United States and Mexican history. The light of history is the best method to interpret motives. Republicans recognize that the best way to achieve their own goals of privatizing land without seeming to give it to the rich is to give it to the poor and let the market do their bidding.[43]

Similarly, some of Tijerina's critics were afraid that acquiring private control of otherwise protected and beloved forestland might lead to unwelcome private development. Presumably, grant descendants who acquire title to their community land could suffer the same fate as the nineteenth-century grant holders who lost their land to a gauntlet of illegitimate pressures. Ostensibly public lands, then, which the Forest Service regulates, demanding fees for such activities as hunting and fishing, might end up privatized in wealthy hands should the community out of financial necessity sell the right to mineral reserves or other uses of the land. Despite the appeal among some Latino/as of shifting control over lands from a government that they historically mistrust, any legislative proposals to restore the community property should be looked at suspiciously. More sustained and meaningful solutions to the land grant problem may be those that aim to curb rural (and urban) poverty among local Latino/as and other groups. For example, the inequality of obtaining hunting and fishing permits on federal land that are not scaled to income can be as readily tackled by economic reforms as by restorative remedies. Fostering educational and employment opportunities for these impoverished communities can empower them to purchase a family home or homestead. The proposals in chapter 15 toward economic equality, then, hold value for resolving the 150-year-old land title disputes in the Southwest, as well as the dilemma of creating affordable housing for farm workers and others striving for the American dream of homeownership and decent housing.

Mexico's history of compelling and unrequited struggles over land offers insights for Latino/as seeking to reclaim lands in the United States and the challenges they face. Before the Mexican-American War, thousands of Mexicans resided on individual and collective land grant ranchos in the Southwest. Not all these residents were landholders, as a peon class developed of lower-class workers who labored on the expansive lands owned by the upper-class Mexicans. After the Mexican-American War, this separation of rich Mexican landholders and impoverished, often indigenous peasant workers, ignited in the remaining Mexican territory to write Mexico's own story of dispossession and loss. In contrast to the United States, where the wealthy class of Mexican landowners suffered dispossession during the nineteenth century, in Mexico the upper class, with the backing of government, preyed on the poor, and particularly on indigenous occupants.

Dispossession of the indigenous and mestizo populations in Mexico dates back to Spanish control, during which the government would claim indigenous land deemed abandoned or unworked. By 1810, approximately 52 percent of Mexican land was considered abandoned and in government control. Spaniards, many of them residing in *haciendas* and controlling vast ranchos, owned 39 percent of the land, compared to only 9 percent for indigenous communities.[44] Many indigenous residents remained on the "vacant" national land without title. The disparity of ownership widened following the 1862–67 war against French invaders, when the Mexican government sold these lands to raise cash. Beginning in 1883, the Mexican government surveyed vacant government lands, offering one-third of the bounty to the surveyors and selling the remaining two-thirds to "wealthy landowners, foreign investors, and anyone who had money to pay for them."[45] In Mexico, it was the surveyors, rather than the lawyers, who took their one-third fee in the process of dispossession.

Mexican land laws of 1883 and 1894 authorized foreign ownership by U.S. elites, allowing wealthy Anglos to join Mexican land barons in controlling Mexican territory during the railroad boom of the 1880s:

> In [the states of] Sonora and Coahuila sales of vacant lands directly corresponded to the progress made by concessionaires in building the Sonora and Mexican Central Railways, respectively. Sales of vacant lands peaked in Chihuahua as the Mexican Central was completed in 1884–85. Mexican and foreign companies pieced together enormous holdings of 100,000 acres or more. Some, like the Hearst interests and the Palomas Land and Cattle Company, built ranches of a million acres.[46]

Ownership by U.S. residents and other foreigners in some northern Mexican states such as Chihuahua soon exceeded 40 percent of the total territory.[47] By 1911, large hacienda estates of just a couple thousand families owned 57 percent of Mexican territory. In contrast, 95 percent of Mexican rural families, some fifteen million people, were landless.[48]

These conditions set the scene for the Mexican Revolution that began in 1910, in which land and agrarian reform were at the fore of the struggle.[49] Revolutionary leaders emerged such as Pancho Villa (1878–1923) and Emiliano Zapata (1879–1919). Zapata's famous rallying cry, "Tierra y Libertad," heralded communal (*ejido*) land rights for Mexico's rural indigenous population, many of whom had lost their land to sugar plantations.[50] During the Revolution, Villa managed to incite U.S. publishing magnate William Randolph Hearst by looting his huge Mexican cattle ranch, prompting Hearst to editorialize in favor of a Mexican invasion to protect foreign ownership.[51] But the dream of land reform prevailed in Mexico, as memorialized in its 1917 Constitution.

Article 27 of that Constitution embodied land and agrarian reform by providing a system of land redistribution. It imposed constraints on foreign ownership of land and included bold provisions for return of certain indigenous lands:

Article 27 declared all land, water, and mineral rights to be the property of the people of Mexico. It also gave the government a mandate and the requisite authority to expropriate land from large landholders and to give it to eligible agrarian communities. Over the next sixty years, administrators sporadically redistributed lands of varying quality. By 1988, more than three million households lived in over 28,000 rural communes called ejidos.[52]

The Mexican agrarian economy and its landholding culture were thus transformed from massive agricultural estates to community-based ejido farms and small individual landholdings. Experiencing expropriation similar to that of Cubans (see chapter 10), U.S. property owners, including Hearst, lost about 6.2 million acres in Mexico to redistribution between 1927 and 1940.[53] Helping to protect the collective ownership fostered by the 1917 Constitution's program of land redistribution, federal agrarian laws prohibited the rental or sale of ejido lands, thereby effectively prohibiting their use as collateral for mortgages.[54] When reform arrived, Mexico's landless peasants typically lived in one-room thatch huts or cardboard shacks, without utilities or even doors and windows. Their aspiration for property ownership stemmed from their belief that ejido ownership would stabilize their migratory life and enable them to transfer land to their children.[55]

By the 1970s, however, Mexico was importing a significant amount of its food, and critics blamed agricultural production problems on lack of access to credit markets and the inefficiencies of the ejido system. Ushering in the North American Free Trade Agreement (NAFTA), in the early 1990s Mexico's Constitution underwent "modernization" reform. Article 27 was overhauled to remove the power to expropriate and redistribute additional land to ejido peasants, and to liberalize the ownership rights of existing ejidos by authorizing voluntary privatization. Lifting some of the restrictions on transfer and foreign ownership, the constitutional amendments authorized the potential certification and transfer of individual title to other members of the ejido or to outsiders, entering into joint ownership ventures with multinational agriculture corporations, and offering collateral for agricultural loans.[56] The expectation is that smaller-scale community-based holdings will be replaced by multinational efforts with ready access to capital and familiarity with the rigors of the capital markets.

The fruits of the reform thus far have been sour for the *ejidatarios* (ejido owners). Land restored to workers following the Mexican Revolution is being lost in the new agricultural industrialization revolution. Much like those who lost rancho lands in the U.S. Southwest after the Mexican-American War, many ejidatarios have been forced to sell their land at bargain prices, not with the aim of maximizing productivity, but because of financial emergency.[57] The post-NAFTA upheaval of Mexico's rural economy has launched millions of rural Mexicans across the border, leaving behind lands they own or used to own. As one writer described the modern transformation from land owner to migrant:

> [C]ampesinos [farm workers] are becoming minimum wage workers on what were once their own lands. . . . Campesinos are now free to move north to the burgeoning industrial farms of Baja and Sonora, the bustling, if wholly degrading, Maquila districts, and of course [media] have no trouble turning up indentured Zapotec peasants living in converted chicken sheds on flower farms in San Diego and Riverside, and their even less fortunate compatriots living without shelter in the ravines below Southern California's sprawling, faux-Spanish suburbs.[58]

The Mexican government's repeal of land reform in the early 1990s prompted a new revolution by so-called Zapatistas in the Mexican state of Chiapas, led by the elusive Subcomandante Marcos. One percent of the Chiapas population owns approximately 45 percent of the land, as land reform under Article 27 was behind the pace of the rest of Mexico and thus incomplete when that program ended abruptly.[59] At the core of the Zapatistas' thirty-four-point negotiation agenda articulated in 1994 are claims for a return to land reform ideals:

> Land is for the Indians and peasants who work it, not for the large landlords. We demand that the copious lands in the hands of ranchers, foreign and national landlords, and other non-peasants be turned over to our communities, which totally lack land. . . .
> We demand the construction of housing . . . with basic services such as electricity, water, plumbing, telephones . . . and such advantages as televisions, stoves, refrigerators, washing machines, etc.[60]

The Zapatistas recognize that land and housing are connected to structural inequities that must also be reformed for meaningful change, and their struggle has also emphasized labor, health, education, freedom, democracy, and justice among its broad goals for reform.[61] In similar fashion, the strategies in the final chapters of this book construct an agenda for housing reform that goes beyond bricks, mortar, and dirt to address deep structural inequities in the United States.

Mexico's current housing statistics reveal some of the same obstacles faced by Latino/as in the United States, as well as some stark contrasts. Among the contrasts is Mexico's high percentage of homeownership, with a 2004 national survey revealing that only 3.4 million of Mexico's 25.8 million households live in rental units, mostly in large cities.[62] Thus, Mexico's homeownership rate exceeds 80 percent, a vast improvement over the U.S. Latino/a rate of less than 50 percent. Another contrast is the relative absence of mortgage financing in Mexico, with only about 12.6 percent of its housing stock subject to mortgage loans.[63] Thus, on the surface at least, Mexican homeowners are less at risk to lose their homes to foreclosure than U.S. borrowers caught in the clutches of the subprime loan crisis. It would appear, then, that many Mexicans are on much firmer housing ground, having both ownership and equity. But a look behind these numbers reveals a housing market with many of the same (and perhaps worse) stresses as the U.S. market.

Mexico's low rate of mortgage financing is driven by factors that include the low and often unstable incomes of its residents, the indeterminacy of legal title of many homeowners, and the deteriorating condition of much of its housing stock. About half of new homes and nearly two-thirds of existing housing stock are self-built.[64] Like dwellings in the U.S. border-area colonias, these homes are sometimes built with construction scraps. They often rest on land owned by others, for which establishing the firmness of title demanded by mortgage lenders may be impossible. These Mexican colonias have been propelled in part by the country's rapid urbanization, which saw the percentage of city-dwellers swell from 35 percent to 73 percent between 1940 and 1990.[65] Given these circumstances, there may be scant true equity in many of these homes. The high rate of homeownership in Mexico also belies the crowded condition of most of its homes, at least when compared to homes in the United States. As determined by the United Nations, most Mexican homes are overcrowded by U.S. standards, with an average 1.4 persons per room.[66] Thus, Mexico's homeownership rate would plunge if it were adjusted to comport with the average density in the United States. A 2004 housing study found that single-room homes in Mexico were on the rise, accounting for 23.1 percent of the housing stock, while large homes (defined as six rooms or more) had declined to only 6.4 percent.[67] Most Mexicans thus live in overcrowded housing, much of it in deteriorated or deteriorating condition, mirroring the situation faced by many if not most Mexican Americans and other Latino/as in the United States.

As many U.S. residents have decried the entry of considerable numbers of Mexican immigrants, both documented and undocumented, a reverse migration has taken place whereby significant numbers of U.S. retirees and prosperous vacationers have purchased homes in Mexico. Although Mexico's 1917 Constitution prohibited foreign ownership, subsequent laws relaxed the rules. Prompted by the history of loss and conflict caused by foreign settlements, particularly in Texas, the 1917 Constitution established a restricted zone disallowing foreign ownership within a hundred kilometers of the border and fifty kilometers of the Mexican coastline. Outside that restricted zone, foreign purchases were permissible if the purchasers agreed not to invoke the protection of their foreign government in any disputes over the property. The restricted zone is substantial in size, encompassing some 40 percent of Mexico and all of its famous coastal resort towns. To encourage investment in the restricted zone, Mexico enacted legislation in 1971 authorizing foreigners to own property in the restricted coastal and border zones through a trust (known as a *fideicomiso*) created by Mexican banks, which hold legal title to the property. At the expiration of the thirty-year trust, presumably the property would be sold to a Mexican national. Eventually, Mexico further liberalized restricted-zone ownership by permitting a fifty-year trust automatically renewable for another fifty years. Moreover, the NAFTA treaty helped ease concerns of expropriation of foreign-owned property for land reform or other purposes, by providing that no party may "nationalize or expropriate an investment of an investor of another Party in its territory . . . except (a) for a public purpose . . . (c) in accordance with due process of the law . . . [and on payment of fair market value]."[68]

In what came to be known as the Baja Boom, large numbers of U.S. residents purchased homes and condos along the northwest Baja coast, from Tijuana to Ensenada, and the south Baja coast between Cabo San Lucas and San Jose de Cabo. Just before the U.S. and international real estate crisis arrived around 2007, developers planned to construct three twenty-six story oceanfront condominium/hotel towers in Baja, thirty minutes by freeway from San Diego, to be named the Trump Ocean Resort. Another massive residential development under construction in coastal La Paz on 1,700 acres "was designed to emulate the small towns of America while reflecting the spirit and history of Mexico."[69] The largest development was planned seven miles south of the picaresque Baja coastal village of Loreto, on 8,000 acres, with 6,000 homes to be built by 2020. Offering prices for these homes in 2008 were extravagant even by U.S. standards—with two-bedroom, two-bath homes of 1,090 square feet at $375,000, and four-bedroom, four-bath homes of 3,109 square feet available from the mid-$900s.[70] Falling victim to the real estate crisis that stripped potential buyers and developers of financing, the Trump project was canceled in early 2009,[71] followed a few months later by suspension of the Loreto project.

From the mid-1990s to the mid-2000s, the U.S. State Department estimated that the number of Americans residing in Mexico jumped from 200,000 to one million.[72] Some experts look to the more than seventy million U.S. baby boomers expected to retire in the next two decades and predict a vast migration to the warmer and cheaper Mexican coast.[73] Although the market for vacation homes has frozen in the mortgage upheaval, it is too early to speculate whether the current crisis will curtail or even boost these projected numbers. If the projected migration arrives, it would bolster the Mexican economy through local construction and service industries, but at the same time drive out local Mexican residents as land and housing prices rise with demand and the greater buying power of U.S. residents.

In California, meanwhile, oceanfront communities that once were Mexican territory and the home of great ranchos are already too expensive for all but the wealthiest Latino/as. Communities bearing Spanish names (and street names), such as Palos Verdes (Spanish for green sticks or trees) Estates (with an average Zillow home value in May 2009 of $1,417,100), Redondo (round, or perfect) Beach ($618,500), Hermosa (lovely) Beach ($973,300), Laguna (lake or pool of water) Beach ($1,440,400), and Santa Barbara ($816,200), are among the priciest real estate in the world. In contrast, the average value of homes in East Los Angeles in May 2009 was only $248,700. Although the United States has no federal restricted zone for foreign investment akin to the Mexican coastal and border zones, the costliness of these neighborhoods and their gated communities has turned much of the California coastline into a de facto restricted zone for U.S. Latino/a residents. Perhaps the Mexican coastline will soon follow this model, pushing Mexicans inland in both countries except when they commute to their work shifts serving affluent coastal enclaves.

These coastal displacements and exclusions, as well as the exclusions and loss detailed elsewhere in this book, implicate mostly poor Mexicans and Mexican Americans. Ironically, the Cuban and Mexican revolutions expropriated significant holdings of U.S.-owned property, in many cases with little or no compensation, in the broader interest of restoring Cuban and Mexican lands to otherwise landless citizenry. The upheaval following the Treaty of Guadalupe Hidalgo in the United States arguably could be characterized in general terms as consistent with this trend of busting up large landholdings and distributing them more equitably, in this case to the immigrant group of Anglo settlers. With the entrenchment in the United States of a property rights ethos and a flaring anti-immigrant, and particularly anti-Latino/a immigrant, sentiment, combined with the constitutional imperative of paying just compensation for property takings, the likelihood of a similar property redistribution to modern-day U.S. immigrants is scant. Moreover, as noted at the outset of this chapter, large and powerful corporate and individual interests have amassed huge landholdings that realistically will not be wrested from them. Reform, then, must contemplate evolutionary rather than revolutionary ideas. The remaining chapters reflect this political landscape in suggesting more nuanced changes in the housing arena using tax incentives and other pragmatic strategies, while urging more strident changes in arenas, particularly education and labor, where ideals of equality have eroded over time.

13

Policy Considerations in Formulating Housing Reform

Before articulating strategies for housing and land reform, we must confront several policy questions that may temper or shape reform. Foremost is the question some critics may pose of whether Latino/as are deserving of special attention in the housing markets. Raising this concern, one set of commentators otherwise urging expanded housing opportunities for new Californians argued against "special programs just for Latinos," characterizing any such efforts as "divisive and discriminatory."[1] The answer to this initial policy question resonates with history, human rights, and interest convergence.

As detailed above, Latino/as have a far lower rate of homeownership than Anglos. Moreover, whether rented or owner-occupied, their housing is disproportionately overcrowded and deteriorating. Because income and wealth are the primary constraints on Latino/as in the housing market, many of the proposals below seek to foster growth in income potential and actual income. Although a few of the suggested reforms have particular resonance for Latino/as, most of these proposals reach beyond to the impoverished generally, trying to lift all boats. Few can argue with efforts to aid the poor in their pursuit of the American dream of homeownership as a reward for hard work. Although some might criticize the proposals below as redistributionist, a characterization that dominated debate over economic policies in the 2008 presidential election, most government policies in some manner reshape and redistribute scarce resources. My aim here is to ensure and preserve the essence of an American ideal shared by most Latino/as that comfortable homeownership is a natural consequence of hard work, no matter the race or ethnicity of the worker. In an increasingly diverse America, this overarching aspiration can still help define our common identity and goals.

To the extent that the reform proposals that follow are tailored to the special needs of Latino/as, often steeped in language, immigration status, or culture, strong interest convergence justifies this focus. As the fastest-growing minority group in the United States, and as a decidedly young population, Latino/as are poised to serve as the largest source of first-time homebuyers, an important demographic for the housing industry. Demand at the entry stages of the housing market helps propel existing homeowners up the ladder into nicer homes. As the baby boom generation of Anglo homeowners ages, unless Latino/as are positioned to purchase their homes at the prices those senior sellers desire, the housing market will compress and collapse. In the short term, even using a model assuming low immigration rates, minorities are expected to constitute 73 percent of household growth from 2010 to 2020, with Latino/as alone comprising 36 percent of that growth.[2] As one writer suggested:

> The housing market is surely going to transition to a more Latino-dominated mix. That group may be numerous enough to replace the white seniors. The only question is whether enough young households will have the wherewithal to pay seniors the prices they are asking for their homes. A shortfall of buyers in the upper price ranges will compress the entire price structure downward, creating a buyers' market that has not been seen for a very long time.[3]

Other researchers warning of the generational housing bubble on the horizon suggest that "[w]hereas the major housing problem was once affordability, it could now be homeowners' dashed expectations after lifelong investment in home equity."[4]

An additional convergence of interest between Anglo homeowners and Latino/as is grounded in the Social Security system, where advances in education—and thus in income and buying power—among Latino/as will help sustain the top-heavy Social Security structure for retiring boomers.[5] In short, it is in the best interest of all Americans to enhance opportunities for Latino/as to share in the American dream.

Arguments for repairing the broken housing dream faced by many Latino/as are also sourced in human rights. In 2008, the United Nations Committee on the Elimination of Racial Discrimination labeled racial disparities in U.S. housing as violations of international norms of human rights to which the United States is bound by treaty.[6] The pursuit of decent housing for all U.S. residents is viewed properly as a civil rights and a human rights issue. How can the American dream remain vital if structural and other impediments keep it from reach of America's most populous minority group?

Arguments steeped in history support attention to the discouraging state of Latino/a housing. Among other examples, chapter 2 exposed a sorry legacy of redistribution of land in the Southwest from Mexican to Anglo hands in the second half of the nineteenth century through courts, lawyers, squatters, predatory lenders, and even violence, that ought to compel redress. This and other historic examples of discrimination against Latino/as in the housing market, encompassing private efforts such as racial restrictive covenants (see chapter 8) and state action such as discriminatory zoning ordinances and enforcement (see chapter 7), construct a strong argument for reparative relief earmarked for Latino/a communities.[7] Deprived of generational wealth from substantial housing appreciation in the second half of the twentieth century, which was enjoyed almost exclusively by Anglo homeowners, and buffeted by discrimination from an array of public and private actors, Latino/as today stand on unequal ground in their ability to pursue adequate housing.

Still, the role that history should play in justifying or formulating housing and land reform is its own complex policy issue. For example, a relatively small percentage of today's U.S. Latino/a population traces its roots to those holders of Spanish and Mexican land grants in the mid-1800s who lost much of their land unfairly. Rather, today's Latino/a population claims roots in several countries other than Mexico, and even the Mexican-origin population largely began its immigration in the 1910s, when World War I labor demands and the upheaval of the Mexican Revolution combined to pull Mexicans north. Millions of immigrants, documented or not, comprise the current Latino/a population. Should newcomers who cannot trace their roots to land loss or episodes of exclusion such as restrictive covenants benefit from reform prompted at least in part by abuses of the past? The argument might be made that because these newcomers understood the economics of U.S. housing when they chose to immigrate, they are undeserving of reform. Similar arguments have been raised in the arena of affirmative action, which was intended in part as redress for past wrongs against African Americans and other groups, but whose benefits in the workplace and schools also extend to newcomers.[8]

In the case of land and housing, at least, history is relevant in vital ways that demand and shape reform. Primarily, the legacy of loss by and exclusion of the Latino/a community still controls their housing today. For example, the use of restrictive covenants excluding Mexican Americans from occupying certain neighborhoods in San Antonio, among other cities, consigned Latino/as en masse to sectors of the city with less overt prejudice. With the advent of funding schools through local property taxes, the sins of the past still plague Latino/as whose neighborhoods remain largely determined by these old segregationist patterns, to the detriment of their children's future earning potential.[9] History also offers valuable insights for reform efforts. The legacy of land loss in the Southwest in the nineteenth century includes the lesson that expensive credit extended to land owners hastened that loss through foreclosure, a preview of the outcome in the modern subprime mortgage crisis. The blame placed by some historians on Latino/as for improvident borrowing as the trigger for the 1800s land grant loss mirrors that leveled by some on Latino/as for fueling the subprime crisis by their undeserved participation in housing markets. Real property taxation also played a role in that nineteenth-century shift of land from Mexican to Anglo hands. Today, the real property taxation structure poses a different threat to the Latino/a community, with schools in neighborhoods marked by lower home values and overcrowded homes unable to keep pace with funding in the suburbs. As chapter 15 explains, reform of school finance to tap sources other than property taxes is a necessary component of revitalizing Latino/a neighborhoods. Finally, another history lesson relevant to Latino/a immigrants is that of past homestead giveaways to settlers willing to commit to work the land for a specified number of years. As chapter 14 details, today's immigrants deserve a similar boost in housing, although accomplished by tax credits and other incentives, given shortages of buildable land, prerogatives to ensure open space, and the shift away from a ranching and farming economy to an imperative of proximity to other arenas of employment.

A related policy argument that flares in the affirmative action debate is whether reform should be class-based rather than single out Latino/as and other historically oppressed minority groups. As noted above, most of the reforms proposed below extend beyond Latino/as to the impoverished generally, but some do address the unique language, demographics, and cultural needs of the Latino/a community. A narrower focus on equality for Latino/as may be justified not only in terms of remediation of historical wrongs, but also under the so-called diversity justification. As the Supreme Court recognized in the University of Michigan affirmative action cases, student body diversity is a compelling state interest that can support the use of race in university admissions without offending the constitutional imperative of equal protection.[10] In so holding, the Supreme Court extolled the value of diversity in the workforce and the global marketplace, as well as in positions of leadership. The Court recognized the role of higher education as a gateway to these positions of influence and economic power. Equally, initiatives that boost Latino/a housing can help ensure diversity in these crucial venues. As discussed in the Introduction and in chapter 15, stable housing, particularly homeownership, can help ensure educational success. Educational stability during a child's formative years can create a foundation for opportunities in higher education and ultimately in the global marketplace and workforce that will supply the diversity desired by society and recognized by the Court as a compelling state interest. In the most optimistic of visions, affirmative action–like programs in housing markets may foster gains in education and employment that would alleviate the need for such programs in those areas, and which in turn through economic gains would eventually obviate the need for housing stimulus, except for recent immigrants. Still, class-based reforms are touted in the affirmative action arena as having better political potential than race-based measures.[11] Most of the reforms proposed below apply across lines of race and ethnicity to all impoverished groups, and thus might find an easier path to adoption and implementation if these attitudes prevail.

As discussed in the Introduction, homeownership rates and housing conditions are particularly troubling for Latino/a immigrants, many of them undocumented. Among the vexing policy issues in any reform proposal for improving Latino/a housing is this specter of undocumented immigration. As the argument goes, aiding the undocumented to obtain better housing will encourage continued undocumented immigration. Expectedly, there was outcry when some banks in the early 2000s introduced credit and savings programs aimed at the undocumented. Chapter 15 argues that instead of concentrating our efforts on excluding undocumented immigrants from the American dream, as Hazelton, Pennsylvania, has tried to do, we should reform our federal immigration laws to give those who want to contribute and pursue their dream in the United States the opportunity to do so. Comprehensive immigration reform with a pathway toward regularizing status and acquiring citizenship if desired will eliminate the most shrill narrative of many xenophobes against Latino/a housing reforms.

Another contention leveled against Latino/a immigrants, however, would survive comprehensive immigration reform. Some critics of immigration have argued that living conditions of Latino/a immigrants in the United States, however deplorable they are, nonetheless are superior to the conditions they left behind. As the argument goes, these immigrants should be grateful for their enhanced fortunes in the United States, and special programs should not be implemented for their advancement. Classicist and farm owner Victor Davis Hanson suggested in his bestseller *Mexifornia* that "illegal aliens in California are not materially poor"; rather, their rental apartments contain "carpeting, air conditioners, heaters and appliances."[12] He compares the material wealth of a Latino farm worker neighbor to his own, explaining that Humberto's television is nicer, and that Humberto lives in a small wooden ranch home provided by his employer. Hanson decries the ungratefulness of Mexican immigrants, explaining that they might be ten times better off than they were in Mexico, yet be churlish because their residence lacks central air conditioning.[13]

The reform program offered below refuses to accept that miserable housing conditions are justifiable if they are less abysmal than what the immigrants may have left behind. The United States upholds a tradition of its own ideals, values, and promise as a nation. The standard of aspiration for housing and other norms of American life simply shouldn't be lowered for different groups, particularly for immigrants who represent the lifeblood of our national identity and our future in a competitive global economy.[14] The United States undervalues the labor contribution of Latino/a immigrants, as reflected by the race to the bottom of wages in immigrant-intensive industries, and the disdain in local communities for resident immigrants. In this climate it is easy for many to view substandard housing as appropriate for the station of Latino/a immigrants in our national hierarchy of status and entitlement. Chapter 15 confronts these underlying economics with the assumption that Latino/as deserve equal treatment in labor markets regardless of immigration status, as well as the prospect of citizenship to reward them for their labor.

At bottom, most of the housing problems Latino/as face stem from poverty and inadequate earnings, savings, and wealth. Might comprehensive immigration reform legalizing millions of undocumented workers increase competitive pressures in the workplace and send wages further spiraling downward to the detriment of all workers? As part of the structural reforms suggested in chapter 15, wage reform is urged as crucial not only to raise the ability of Latino/as to afford adequate housing, but also to ensure that employers are constrained from unfairly exploiting any short-term surpluses in the labor pool that might follow a legalization program.

As pointed out earlier, one of the challenging questions for housing reform is the diversity of the Latino/a population. No doubt the needs of rural Mexican farm workers in California may differ from those of Puerto Ricans and Dominicans in New York City. Regardless of their background, however, most Latino/as aspire to homeownership, and at minimum to decent housing, whether rented or owned. What matters more are factors such as immigrant status, age, education, class, and geography. As detailed in the Introduction, homeownership is positively correlated with a wide range of benefits to the owners and society, but these benefits may vary depending on the home's location. More likely to own lower-value homes in segregated areas of concentrated poverty,[15] Latino/as may not reap the same benefits as Anglos from ownership. The importance of location suggests that reform should look beyond housing to encompass workplace and education. As articulated in chapter 15, these reforms must better equalize educational and labor opportunities in neighborhoods that still suffer the effects of segregated housing, schools, and the workplaces. Geography plays an important role, as many Latino/as historically have chosen to live in high-cost areas, such as Puerto Ricans migrating to New York City and Mexicans to Los Angeles. As discussed later, rental housing is part of any national housing reform, mindful that some of the structural measures proposed may take generations to implement, and that new arrivals in expensive urban areas and transient workers in rural landscapes will continue to seek affordable rental housing as a gateway to homeownership.

Other policy issues encompass Latino/as, whether immigrants or native born. A defining challenge—raised in chapter 3 with regard to colonia housing—is whether enhanced regulation to ensure safety and minimum standards in housing will price some Latino/as and other disadvantaged residents out of the market. Presumably, these residents would either sacrifice other essential human needs to afford housing, or would elect homelessness, greater overcrowding (unless density is regulated), or illegal housing arrangements that flout stringent local standards. Arguments here are complex, and even reformers with the interests of the Latino/a community at heart might nonetheless differ in their approach. For example, an argument in favor of government-enforced minimum standards for housing quality is that allowing a deregulated race to the housing bottom will backfire by normalizing the status of impoverished housing conditions. In other words, the larger culture may come to view those who live in these shanty communities as deserving of their fate:

> Because of norm theory, we will come to tolerate more and more shanty conditions for those we see as different from ourselves, and these conditions in turn will simply confirm to us that the residents are indeed a different order of humanity, in a self-reinforcing spiral. Eventually, ghetto, barrio, or colonia conditions will seem natural and just—"the way things are."[16]

Policymakers might consider a modified approach by regulating quality of construction and requiring essential infrastructure such as sewers and clean water, but allowing self-help in construction or renovation of homes as well as in affordable housing projects as a credit toward future rent or down payments.[17] The federal government's Self-Help Ownership Opportunity Program embodies this approach in its grants, which fund nonprofits to assist low-income families in purchasing homes at below market rates in exchange for their self-help labor of at least one hundred hours.[18] Others may prefer the policies of the Mexican government in tolerating but incentivizing the improvement of its shantytowns. Rather than outlawing self-built shanty housing and evicting its residents for trespass, the Mexican government introduced measures to purchase and resell the underlying land to the squatters, and to regularize their settlements by providing utility and other government services.[19] In return, residents paid for this public infrastructure through tax and fee assessments, and provided labor to help install the services.

While this incentive-based approach finds favor among free-market advocates, it fails to protect against rampant abuses in the marketplace. For example, in the case of colonia housing along the Texas border with Mexico, almost a quarter of colonia households surveyed reported some deception in their purchase of the land, such as unfulfilled promises about services the developer would install.[20] In the related context of overcrowded housing, discussed in chapter 7, landlords of boarding houses might take advantage of the lack of housing alternatives to overcharge undocumented workers who live in unsafe and overcrowded conditions. At the same time, in the absence of safe, affordable alternatives, cracking down on overcrowded housing might drive tenants onto the streets (or to campsites in nearby hills and ravines).

The choice between increased regulation and free-market approaches arises in settings from substandard colonia housing to overcrowded conventional housing. To resolve this policy conflict, I favor a modified free-market approach that tolerates unconventional housing, from colonias to campgrounds to converted garages, yet employs regulation to combat the worst abuses and to correct imperfections in the marketplace. Today, government regulation of these alternative living arrangements is often a proxy for local regulation of undocumented immigration, with the aim of ridding the municipality of Latino/a day laborers and impoverished immigrant workers. Rather than targeting Latino/a residents living in undesirable or potentially unsafe conditions for ouster, government would aspire foremost to protect these residents from abuses. Revised government policies would follow naturally from this fresh perspective. Instead of relying on safety justifications as a proxy for immigration regulation, local government would concentrate on eliminating the worst abuses of resident Latino/as and other impoverished groups. For example, instead of enforcing density regulations to raid and evict residents from overcrowded dwellings in markets with shortages of affordable housing, government might allow boarding houses to exceed density limits on the condition that they obtain a permit to lease or sublease the space, while implementing rent controls to prevent exploitation and safety inspections to flag and educate about perilous conditions such as overburdened electrical outlets. Regulation would further aim to remedy imperfections in the marketplace. The vulnerability of many Latino/as, particularly undocumented immigrants, in the housing market is sourced in their miserable financial state and immigration status. Undocumented workers remain in the shadows and are hesitant to complain about housing abuses. Poor workers face fewer choices in housing markets, as their inability to afford initial housing deposits may consign them to an overpriced room in an overcrowded house or couch space instead of their own apartment. Following comprehensive immigration and wage reform, Latino/as will be better equipped to navigate the housing marketplace. In this environment, those Latino/a immigrants who willingly choose to minimize their expenses while in the United States and thereby return with extra capital to their families in their country of origin, should within reason be permitted to do so. Given the experience of the last few centuries, however, many of these Latino/as will choose to stay and forge an American dream toward more comfortable living.

Related to the policy debate over whether government regulation or free-market approaches offer the best model for housing reform is the raging subprime mortgage controversy confronted in chapter 5. Pundits disagree on the cause of the crisis, with some free-market proponents blaming government for pressuring banks through regulatory means such as the Community Reinvestment Act to fund risky loans in poor neighborhoods to Latino/as and others. Some even blame undocumented immigrants for fueling the crisis by improperly speculating for profit in U.S. housing markets. In contrast, others place responsibility on unscrupulous mortgage lenders and brokers, spurred by frenzied demand in Wall Street securitization markets for resale of loans to remote investors, who preyed on vulnerable Latino/a borrowers—some of them immigrants, and some with language barriers—to profit from housing loans with unfair and deceptive terms. Accordingly, lack of regulation and enforcement action against unfair trade practices in the mortgage industry is blamed for the foreclosure crisis.

From any of these camps we can expect proposals to rein in loans to Latino/a borrowers with requirements such as ascertaining and ensuring the financial ability of the borrower to repay the loan before it can be consummated, ramping up down payments and debt ratio requirements, and eliminating adjustable interest rate loans. Those blaming immigrants and the undocumented for the subprime crisis may go further and propose restraints on lending to noncitizens, many of them Latino/a. Financial constraints on loans to the impoverished will disproportionately impact Latino/a borrowers. More rigorous and conservative determinations of income history as a condition to making loans will impede Latino/as who might otherwise decide to obtain their steep monthly mortgage payment by renting rooms to others, pooling household income, or taking on additional employment or hours. Similar to the policy choice faced in regulation of overcrowding or dilapidated housing conditions, the tension here is whether it hurts or helps the Latino/a community, and the greater real estate community, to prohibit willing parties from engaging in a risky transaction. Despite their sometimes limited financial resources, Latino/as are strongly motivated to become homeowners. Often they strain their budgets by devoting too large a percentage of their monthly income to mortgage and housing costs. The argument for paternalism could thus be made to constrain their housing choices. Here again, however, I favor a modified free-market approach that aims to cure defects in the marketplace while mostly leaving the parties to their own choices. Later I discuss the need for consumer education in Latino/a markets, particularly in light of research findings that a substantial number of Latino/as who received expensive subprime loans could have qualified as prime borrowers. Critics charge that consumer financial education models are ineffective because they cannot keep pace with rapid-fire developments in financial markets and the bombardment of advertising and marketing ploys consumers face.[21] But the trade-off is worse, as substantive regulatory constraints on loan products would ensure that home ownership and the libertad that accompanies it would remain out of reach for many Latino/a households. The playing field for mortgage borrowers also needs to be leveled by wage reforms to increase the income potential of borrowers. Armed with insight into the mortgage lending process and the ability to save for a traditional down payment, Latino/a borrowers who opt for familiar subprime terms such as no income verification and low or no down payment loans, or loans with elevated ratios of debt to income, should be free to do so if they find any lenders still willing to lend on such terms.

Seemingly contradictory U.S. housing policies endeavor to provide affordable housing for entry-level buyers yet enable homeowners to acquire long-term wealth through appreciation in home values. A silver lining of the subprime crisis is that the national slide in housing prices will present opportunities for new Latino/a homebuyers to enter the market should the credit crunch subside. Looking more broadly at these competing housing policies, there is no reason why housing appreciation models must erode from their past performance. As new immigrant groups have arrived to tap entry-level markets, sellers of those homes have been able to climb the housing ladder. So long as immigration laws are reformed to permit entry consistent with the demands of U.S. labor markets, instead of being allowed to succumb to anti-immigrant sentiment, long-term appreciation should be ensured. Because all boats tend to rise through housing appreciation, including entry-level homes, special attention must be directed at entry-level prices if a disconnect exists between wages in labor markets and entry prices, as it does today in many cities. In such circumstances, government must consider tackling entry-level affordability from both ends, as addressed in chapters 14 and 15. This means that while government works to incentivize construction of affordable housing, it must inject corrections into the labor markets to ensure wages sufficient to meet ordinary household needs, including decent, uncrowded, entry-level housing, whether owned or rented.

Roadblocks to Latino/a housing reform in the political arena pose challenges to reformers in developing feasible proposals. Concurrent with the 2008 Wall Street bailout of $700 billion, the 2009 $787 billion stimulus package, and runaway spending on foreign war, political support for a housing reform agenda that demands additional government spending is unlikely, particularly if it appears to benefit Latino/as, whom some pundits unfairly blame for the subprime crisis. Admittedly, many of the reform proposals articulated below require government spending, such as those urging additional support for public education and affordable housing. On the negative side, many government spending proposals shackle future generations with deficits. But housing and educational opportunities break the mold. Given that 21 percent of the U.S. population under age five is Latino/a,[22] strengthened public education and an uncrowded, safe living environment to enable youth to prosper will deliver economic returns that help them shoulder the load of these fiscal burdens later. The stimulus package approved by Congress in 2009 funded infrastructure reform in critical areas such as transportation and public buildings as essential to our continued economic and social prosperity. Equally, educating our Latino/a youth is an infrastructure issue that will ensure prosperity ahead.

Any reform proposals that emphasize expanding opportunities for homeownership and stabilizing immigrant populations to better situate them for home purchases raise the specter of concern over unsustainable life-styles and conspicuous consumption. As the argument goes, population growth through Latino/a immigration triggers home construction, which imperils natural resources and strains local infrastructure.[23] Wage reforms might further increase opportunities for consumerism, and easing the overcrowding among millions of Latino/a renters might require construction of millions of new residences, gashing urban and rural terrain. With the advent of outcry over global warming and calls for reduction of carbon footprints, a campaign encouraging homeownership for underprivileged groups may face political opposition, some of which may mask ill will toward Latino/as. As I have noted elsewhere, however, it is wrong to implement environmental strategies that hamper or unduly burden Latino/as, who already bear the brunt of human-caused environmental degradation through the discriminatory siting of waste-production and -disposal facilities, and as farm workers through pesticides in the fields.[24] To draw a line in the dirt against decent housing and homeownership for Latino/as now would be unfair given our history of generosity toward past immigrant groups in the form of land giveaways and government-subsidized mortgage loans. Until these national voices of sustainability give up their own comfortable homes en masse for smaller and more crowded dwellings, they have no standing to speak against sharing the American dream with Latino/as, many of whom built or maintain those comfortable homes for scant wages. Government can contribute here, among other ways, by ensuring tax and other incentives for more energy-efficient and less resource-intensive home construction to meet entry-level needs. Venture capitalists in the marketplace can assist by funding green technology initiatives to develop these new construction methods and materials. Moreover, the current housing crisis has left millions of homes vacant, many owned by real estate speculators or their financiers. Rather than relegating partially completed subdivisions to landfills, as some developers have done, Latino/a immigrants can fill these vacant units if government programs better aid entry-level purchasing.

Cities must confront the issue of when and how Latino/a communities fit within modern urban redistribution policies. Today, cities subsidize sports stadiums, conference centers with marquee hotels, housing for urban professionals, shopping centers that generate tax revenues, and other commercial projects. Most of these efforts aim to attract either well-to-do visitors or highly educated permanent residents. As one scholar of urban planning observed, because these subsidies "rarely materialize in barrios . . . [d]ecades of favoritism and elite alliances at the local level have produced a basic redistribution policy where resources are not allocated according to social need."[25] When cities do subsidize barrio construction, it tends to be gentrified projects such as Dodger Stadium. Latino/as must confront decisionmakers and seek their fair share of the urban dollar, which is often thrown at other constituencies while barrio needs are ignored. Affordable housing initiatives for Latino/as are not affirmative action programs. Rather, they are gateways to housing and resource equity in geographies that have long favored other groups.

Finally, in articulating a housing reform agenda, the question of its focus is relevant. Should the core of reform efforts address homeownership ideals, abuses and shortages in transient rental property, or restoration of lost community farm and ranchland? At bottom, homeownership and rentals may be more alike than distinct, given the pervasiveness of mortgage financing. As with late rent payments, missing a loan payment may oust the homeowner from her residence.[26] Moreover, the introduction of forty-year and even longer repayment periods for housing loans, together with the now commonplace home equity loan, the custom of upward housing mobility throughout one's lifetime, and the reverse mortgage designed to fund retirement, ensure that this risk of upheaval may exist throughout the homeowner's adult lifetime. Clashes in policy might nonetheless occur in certain settings—for example, if tax laws further incentivize home purchases over rental housing. Conversely, some government policies, such as rental assistance programs, overlook homeowners. But these conflicts are the exception rather than the rule. Pursuit of all these goals of land acquisition and comfortable homes may therefore be possible without undue conflict. The recurring historic need for transitory migrant labor, for which Latino/as have answered the bell for at least the last hundred years, demands consideration of reform in rental markets to address the reality of shortages and lack of affordability, as well as ongoing discrimination.

At the same time, making the American dream of homeownership more accessible for workers who aspire to it is a laudable goal. I reject the notion that the subprime crisis signals the inherent incompatibility of Latino/as as homeowners, and the reform agenda below thus encourages homeownership as a natural and reasonable expectation of the American working class. I also reject paternalistic arguments that homeownership is more hurtful than helpful to Latino/as and other minority groups. These critics cite widespread foreclosure and loss of value, impediments to job mobility posed by ownership, and the ruptures to overextended families straining to afford a home with inadequate income to address other pressing needs. They assume that Latino/as would be served better as transient renters, with any equity accruing to Anglo landlords. This model of Anglo ownership of infrastructure, with tenants beholden to the landlord's prerogatives concerning tenure of occupancy, family size, rent, improvements, and even pets, is a power dynamic with historically grave consequences for Latino/as. Although the Latino/a community could profit from greater information about the risks and rewards of homeownership, ultimately the choice of subservience to a landlord or of libertad should be left to them, with discriminatory roadblocks and inequities removed.

The reform proposals that follow are divided into two sections. Chapter 14 suggests proposals to drive down the cost of homes and rentals and of credit for home purchases. Many of these proposals are stop-gap, short-term fixes. Chapter 15 builds on those strategies by proposing longer-term, more systemic changes to raise incomes for Latino/as that translate to greater purchasing and rental power. Politically, many of the stop-gap suggestions stand the best chance for adoption, particularly with the urgency of the subprime crisis. In contrast, many of the structural changes proposed in areas such as education and labor have been articulated and urged for decades as anti-poverty measures. Without these major structural reforms, however, Latino/a housing will continue to fall short of the American dream. The subprime crisis exposed the difficulty of sustaining long-term growth of Latino/a homeownership, and many regulatory reform proposals emerging from that crisis, while ostensibly for their protection, may hinder Latino/as from reaching the dream of homeownership. Growth, then, will need to come from advances in income and education as part of a wider anti-poverty campaign.

Most of the reform proposals below emphasize political rather than judicial agendas. Courts have sometimes played a role in advancing the housing agenda of Latino/as, notably in invalidating racial restrictive covenants and overtly racialized zoning laws. However, with isolated exceptions such as the New Jersey *Mount Laurel* litigation,[27] courts rarely take a lead role as agents for progressive social change. Rather, they tend either to defer to the legislature for creation of positive rights,[28] or to deal setbacks to the core of Latino/a housing models.[29]

14

Lowering the Cost of Housing and Credit

Reducing the cost of housing is a delicate balancing act. Because existing homeowners depend on appreciation for wealth creation, reform initiatives to reduce cost might harm that expectation. The suggestions in this chapter generally concentrate on reducing the cost of financing in purchase transactions, as well as protecting Latino/a renters and purchasers from discrimination and misinformation that might cause them to overpay for housing in the marketplace. Rather than marketplace price controls, most involve government-sponsored or -goaded programs to increase the stock of affordable housing and to augment tax incentives for first-time homebuyers.

Whether as homeowners or as renters, Latino/as tend to pay too high a percentage of their income toward their monthly mortgage payment or rent. One study found that despite the recommended ceiling of 30 percent, Latino/a homeowners on average spent 38 percent of their income on a mortgage payment, and more than one-third spent above 40 percent.[1] Among Latino/a renters, about one-third spent more than 40 percent of their monthly household income on rent, while on average foreign-born Latino/a renters paid a distressing 45 percent.[2] Overall, a 2003 study determined that 20 percent of Latino/a households were severely cost burdened, spending more than 50 percent of their income on housing costs.[3]

Contributing to the problem of overspending on housing is the shrinking stock of affordable housing in the United States, particularly in urban areas with significant Latino/a populations, such as in New York City and the Los Angeles metro area. In Los Angeles, the home construction boom in the early 2000s exposed a gap between the intended market for homes being built and the needs of low-income residents. For example, in 2007, most units constructed in Los Angeles chased buyers with above-average incomes, while demand went unmet in the moderate, low, and very low income categories of housing.[4] In Florida, during the early 2000s developers favored upscale units with luxury features, prompting one commentator to remark: "[A]ffordable home construction became passé. What developer wanted to build humdrum houses for teachers and police officers when he could make a killing with waterfront condominiums that promised the glamorous lifestyle of murder suspects on CSI: Miami?"[5] At the same time, subprime lenders schemed to qualify occupants of otherwise affordable housing to purchase these extravagant units.

Ironically, the emphasis on upscale urban homeownership depleted affordable rental housing. In the early 2000s developers were busily tearing down older rental units for new condominium projects, or rehabbing older units into high-end condos destined for Anglo buyers in convenient urban locations. Tending to be smaller, cheaper, and located in the inner cities, these older units are the lifeblood of affordable rental stock: in 2005, one-third of the units in the United States renting for less than $400 a month were built before 1940, and another one-third between 1940 and 1970.[6] But between 1995 and 2005, 9 percent of the pre-1940 constructed units were removed from the rental market, with losses even greater (about 14 percent) among those pre-1940 rental units categorized as affordable. Between 1993 and 2003, the national affordable rental supply shrunk by two million units.[7] The National Low Income Housing Coalition estimated in 2005 that only 6.2 million affordable rentals were available to serve the nine million renter households classified as extremely low income.[8] In this competitive environment, that Coalition was unable to find a single U.S. county where a worker earning minimum wage could afford a two-bedroom apartment while spending only the recommended 30 percent of the worker's income toward housing.[9] In areas of the least affordability, such as San Francisco, the worker would need an income five times the minimum wage to meet this standard.

Developers chasing high-end buyers are not the sole cause of the shortage. Although some xenophobes blame shortages of affordable housing and increases in rental prices on surging immigration, the root causes are more complex. Blameworthy factors include local zoning practices outlined in chapter 7 designed to exclude lower-class renters and homeowners. Cities attempted to avoid creating infrastructure of public schools and parks needed by low-income residents, preferring more expensive homes on larger lots to multiple homes on smaller footprints. In areas of adjoining, competing suburbs such as Southern California, local governments favored big box retail outlets and other generators of tax revenue over homes and apartments for families needing localized services. Demanding significant exactions in the form of infrastructure contributions from developers as a condition to approving their new residential projects, local government thereby encouraged construction targeting more affluent buyers. Low-income workers increasingly could afford homes only on the remote fringes of their employment sources, requiring lengthy commutes or crowding into units closer to the workplace. Aging low-income housing fell short as new construction failed to keep pace with demand, and as renter and buyer incomes sagged due to labor pressures in the globalized economy. With this background, I outline below some of the steps federal, state, and local governments can take toward increasing the stock of affordable housing for purchase and rental.

Federal housing assistance programs have shrunk in the face of other budget prerogatives, falling from 10 to 8 percent of domestic discretionary outlays between 1997 and 2007, despite large increases in those households needing assistance.[10] Affordable housing units in the United States suitable for the nine million households earning between $11,000 and $18,000 annually fall millions short of the number needed to house these struggling families.[11] Federal housing reform strategies, then, should center on increasing funding for affordable housing construction, as well as programs benefiting distressed renters and homeowners. Congress took a positive step toward boosting affordable housing in the Housing and Economic Recovery Act of 2008, creating an affordable housing trust fund and also temporarily raising state limits on federal low-income housing tax credit allocations.

At the state level, more sustainable funding sources for schools, roads, public safety, parks, and other infrastructure must be created to relieve pressure on the zoning policies of local government. Identifying new or enhanced revenue sources is challenging. California, for example, already imposes sales, income, and property taxes, with constitutionally mandated restrictions on property tax increases that are likely politically invulnerable despite their unfairness to newcomers and others buying property after 1978.[12] At the state or local level, affordable housing needs a permanent funding source, such as a real estate transfer tax based on property value or recording fees for property transfers, dedicated to affordable housing initiatives.[13] The City of Los Angeles unveiled an innovative affordable-housing plan in 2008 that relies on public/private partnerships with employers, developers, and others, as well as grants, loans, philanthropy, and other creative sources to fund its proposed $5 billion cost.[14] Private vision and philanthropy also drive the community land trust model active in most states. Related to but distinct from the community ownership model of the ejido, community land trusts acquire real estate and typically sever the land from the homes to ease affordability for home purchasers, who purchase their house but lease the underlying land.[15] Affordability for future buyers is ensured by agreements with the land trust that restrict profit on resale to a specified formula of fair return.[16] The upshot is that the initial and subsequent buyers are able to purchase the home at below-market prices and still retain hope for modest appreciation.

At the local level, relaxed density requirements in regions lacking affordable housing, especially in neighborhoods proximate to public transportation, can help encourage infill development.[17] Environmentalist resistance to affordable housing based on open-space ideals, like those in Monterey County discussed in chapter 4, must be reconsidered in light of the human suffering associated with overcrowded and overpriced housing. Environmental aims can be achieved by means less detrimental to affordable housing—for example, by the wealthy in the community purchasing conservation easements that generate development credits to partially subsidize their cost. In turn, developers with land in designated zones conducive to affordable housing would purchase these credits to avoid otherwise applicable zoning laws that govern setback, height, density, and the like.[18]

Regulatory approvals clog urban development, as in Los Angeles, where twelve departments, bureaus, or agencies must approve each housing development. Local government must streamline the process for building affordable housing, as the 2008 housing plan for Los Angeles proposed to do.[19] Among the more controversial components of that plan is its proposed mixed-income housing ordinance, which requires residential developments above a specified size to include affordably priced units. New Jersey has employed this so-called inclusionary zoning model since the 1983 decision of its state Supreme Court in *Mount Laurel* discussed in chapter 7, as have more than a hundred cities and counties in California, although not without ongoing legal battles over the constitutionality of such zoning.[20]

Affordable workplace housing is important for urban districts, as reflected in the 2008 Los Angeles housing plan, which contemplates collaboration with employers to create nearby housing. In the present climate of global mobility of capital and jobs, most localities are too giddy in their competition for large employers to require construction of affordable housing as a condition to incentive packages offered these new or expanding employers paying wages insufficient for decent housing. But some employers have less leverage of situating their operations elsewhere. For example, Wal-Mart or another retailer aiming to open a new location might be subjected to such requirements, unless a race to the bottom for the site occurs among adjoining municipalities.

Favoring affordable rentals close to public transportation, the 2008 Los Angeles housing plan requires that rent control housing near transit stops be replaced upon demolition. At the federal level, some commentators have proposed a green housing tax credit that would encourage home purchases proximate to public transportation.[21] Prioritizing the funding of public transportation at federal, state, and local levels will in turn boost nearby housing markets.

In addition to creating and sustaining affordable housing in urban environments, rural and farm worker housing must overcome the conditions of despair detailed in chapter 3. Consistent with the green building initiatives of many jurisdictions, workplace housing should situate the rural workforce closer to their jobs. As discussed previously, housing quality enforcement created disincentives for farmers to supply worker housing, given the seasonal nature of the work and the increased cost of maintaining suitable housing in an enforcement environment. Overcoming this hurdle will require federal intervention in at least two venues. In the arena of comprehensive immigration reform discussed in chapter 15, opportunities will exist for requiring large employers who hire noncitizen workers to ensure adequate and affordable housing nearby.[22] Further, the federal government regulates crop production through federal subsidies to farmers that among other incentives may ensure a guaranteed crop price. Decent wages and living conditions for the farm labor force are no less crucial a component of a national food policy than steady income for farmers. Affordable worker housing initiatives might similarly be made the subject of federal farm subsidies, as well as beneficiaries of state income and property tax policies. For example, states could exempt farm worker housing from real estate taxation, thus lowering housing costs to workers who must otherwise bear the carrying cost of the property. Group housing projects for migrant farm workers have faced NIMBY-ism but stand the best chance for approval in rural areas where agricultural employers are sympathetic to needs of their workforce, rather than in nearby cities.[23] Still, siting issues are complex, as rural locations may pose transportation issues for workers' school-age children.[24]

In the modern landscape of agri-business, family-owned farms distributing their products locally have emerged as a more sustainable alternative. With their knowledge of agricultural practices and willingness to undertake the grueling labor of farming, Latino/a immigrants are the gateway to a renaissance in farming that connects the past agrarian culture of the United States to sustainable practices for future generations. As the cowboys and ranchers of Western lore, Latino/as are poised to write a new history in rural landscapes. Strategies to promote acquisition of farmland by first-time buyers are akin to those promoting first-time homeownership. Indeed, oftentimes the family farm includes a comfortable residence in rural terrain. Honoring the rich history and culture of collective (ejido) ownership of agricultural property by Latino/as and the U.S. history of immigrant homestead programs, agricultural subsidies and other legal norms need retooling from those currently in place, which promote and sustain corporate agribusiness,[25] to those that nurture collective agricultural ventures among local families. Programs are needed that offer initial land as well as credit for agricultural improvements in exchange for supplying food at price-controlled levels to government programs that in turn feed the local hungry, rather than the government buying food from agri-business at market prices. In urban areas, municipalities can accomplish similar ends by dedicating open space to collective urban agriculture, allowing the hungry to help feed themselves and their families. Vacant land in private hands might garner real estate tax breaks in exchange for its temporary dedication to community farming use.

Incentives toward desired results in public policy can come from a variety of sources, and through both carrots and sticks. Government catalysts to improve Latino/a housing have included sanctions such as the federal Community Reinvestment Act, which holds banks responsible for their lending record in the communities in which they draw their deposits. Government also doles out incentives toward housing, particularly through the tax code. Some tax incentives, such as the low-income housing tax credit, favor developers but inure to the benefit of lower-income residents. But most existing tax incentives favor higher-income taxpayers, such as mortgage interest and real property tax deductions for those homeowners who itemize their deductions.[26] Combined, these two deductions alone deliver more than $80 billion annually in tax benefits to middle- and upper-income homeowners in higher tax brackets, amounting to almost three times the money spent on all housing programs for low- and moderate-income residents.[27] Adding in the deferral of capital gains on home sales, in 2000, the 2.2 percent of taxpayers who earned more than $200,000 received 22.4 percent of the benefit from these three tax incentives.[28] Critics of these home tax breaks contend they artificially inflate home prices and encourage purchasing of larger homes in outlying areas with larger lots, thus contributing to sprawl.[29] Moreover, the reach of the mortgage interest deduction to seasonal vacation homes offers billions in annual subsidies to affluent families with second homes while millions of families live in overcrowded apartments or are homeless.[30]

Because Latino/as often are situated in the bottom reaches of the housing market, the battle over equality in tax policy holds a particular stake for them. Tax policies ought to favor first-time homebuyers and lower-income earners. To counteract declining federal funding of low-income housing programs, some commentators urge a broader redistribution of housing welfare from the mansion subsidies embedded in current policies to those providing more support for impoverished renters and first-time homebuyers.[31] Government incentives are particularly needed to promote first-time homeownership among underrepresented groups, particularly Latino/as and African Americans. Such affirmative action in the housing market would address the remedial and diversity justifications identified in chapter 13, while providing a market for resale and construction of entry-level homes. Alternatively, shifting from interest and property tax deductions toward tax incentives for purchase of entry-level homes might be structured in a race-neutral manner that aids all lower-income purchasers. Another possibility for facially race-neutral reform would be to direct homeownership deductions or credits toward immigrant homebuyers. Although the federal government boosted previous immigrant groups with homestead property giveaways, current anti-immigrant sentiment (directed especially at Latino/as) makes any tax relief favoring immigrants unlikely. Moreover, reallocating what is by far the most substantial of the tax subsidies, the mortgage interest deduction, will be politically unpopular during the present housing crisis, given the potential for home prices to collapse even more upon repeal of the deduction.[32]

The most politically viable reform may be to shift incentives toward all first-time homebuyers regardless of their class, race, or immigrant status. Because current homeownership dramatically increases as income rises (for example, 92 percent of U.S. households earning more than $119,999 in 2003 owned homes),[33] assisting first-time homebuyers disproportionately favors lower- and middle- income households as well as many Latino/as and immigrant buyers. Demand created among entry-level buyers may also help sustain home prices as the existing mortgage interest deduction is gradually phased out. Because few low-income taxpayers benefit from the itemized mortgage interest deduction, that deduction might be restructured as a tax credit for entry buyers, available primarily in early years following the purchase and then phased out over the life of the entry loan.[34] Revenues gained by repealing the existing deduction and limiting the mortgage interest credit to new homebuyers would fund a substantial credit, particularly as new homebuyers tend to purchase modest homes with smallish mortgages. In defining first-time homebuyers eligible for such tax incentives, government should include foreclosure or short-sale victims of subprime lending who lost their homes within whatever eligibility period is specified to define first-time buyers.

Lowering the Cost of Housing and Credit

Recognizing that neighborhoods where more than 10 percent of the residents are Black start to lose property value, one innovative commentator suggests a tax credit for mortgage interest and property taxes to those purchasing in these neighborhoods.[35] Rewarding those purchasing in a racially diverse or even segregated minority neighborhood, however, raises practical problems of application (for example, how to define a neighborhood's boundaries) as well as policy issues (for example, might a flood of Anglo buyers seeking the credit gentrify a formerly Black neighborhood).[36]

Apart from tax incentives to first-time homebuyers, tax credits directed at mortgage lenders can encourage desirable market behavior to fund new entrants into the housing market. As discussed in chapter 5, subprime loans with excessive closing costs and high interest rates flourished in an environment in which prime lenders had long ignored Latino/a and Black communities and borrowers. Tax incentives might encourage prime lending to minority borrowers otherwise susceptible to subprime terms. For example, tax credits might be awarded to lenders for each loan made to first-time homebuyers, so long as the lender forgoes prepayment charges and excessive closing costs and offers a prime, fixed interest rate.

Several strategies might help with purchaser down payments. For example, federal or state governments might partner with first-time homebuyers in shared appreciation arrangements that offer tax credits upon purchase in exchange for enhanced taxation of any resale profits. Still, the complexity of this tradeoff is a drawback, since few first-time buyers of color have the luxury of professional tax advice at closing.

Congress hoped to jumpstart the housing market with the more straightforward first-time homebuyer tax credit of $7,500 in the Housing and Economic Recovery Act of 2008. Unlike an earlier credit in 1975 legislation, however, the 2008 credit must be repaid to the federal government over time and expired on July 1, 2009. A more effective tax credit would carry no repayment obligation and would target underrepresented groups such as Latino/as and African Americans, or any future groups whose homeownership rates fall below the national average by double digits.[37] This program would operate, in essence, as affirmative action on the housing front to remedy inequities. By addressing only first-time homebuyers and placing a dollar limit on homes eligible for the credit, or an income cap, any such program would avoid much of the critique in educational affirmative action programs that decries potential benefits accruing to children of wealthy parents based on their racial or ethnic background. Enacted in 2009, the American Recovery and Reinvestment Act fulfilled part of these aims by conferring an $8,000 tax credit on first-time homebuyers (defined as a non-homeowner for the past three years) who purchase in 2009 (extended later to April, 30, 2010) that, unlike the 2008 Act, need not be repaid and phases out for larger incomes.[38] Because many Latino/a first-time homebuyers may not have down payment assistance from their families, similar tax credit programs in future years should include a more immediate receipt of the credit on the purchase date.[39] Alternatively, federal law might allow payment directly to lenders for loans resold on federal secondary markets, thus subtracting the amount of the credit from any required down payment standards for federal purchase.[40] The tax credit also needs to be larger to serve as an effective stimulus, as $8,000 is well below a 10 percent down payment on starter homes in almost any jurisdiction.[41] As an example, the dollar value and incentive offered to new car purchasers under the popular federal "cash for clunkers" program were far higher than the first-time homebuyer credit ever was.

Current federal tax law allows withdrawal of monies toward a down payment from a tax-free individual retirement account. A similar program to stimulate home purchasing through tax laws would exempt interest income earned on certain home savings accounts from state and federal taxation, akin to treatment of educational accounts in some states, as long as the principal is used toward a down payment on a first-home purchase below a specified dollar amount. Such laws fostering home purchases have some chance for political traction during the current housing slump. Existing programs employing this approach tend to stimulate homeownership for those with lower incomes, rather than on grounds of race or ethnicity. A federal program administered through the Department of Health and Human Services supplies matching funds through Individual Development Accounts to low-income households saving to purchase a first home, but the program must be reauthorized and supplied with more funds.[42] A similar program fostering first-time affordable home purchases is the federal American Dream Downpayment Initiative, which allocates money to state and local governments to assist first-time homebuyers with incomes not exceeding 80 percent of the area median income. No Latino/a renter should be left behind, as the federal government could complement homeownership aspirations with programs to assist low-income earners with the rental security deposits required to obtain safe, affordable housing as the gateway to eventual homeownership.

Environmental imperatives can help shape tax policies benefiting Latino/a residents. New U.S. homes are steadily increasing in size, from an average of 1,100 square feet in the 1940s and 1950s, to 1,750 in 1978, to 2,479 in 2007.[43] With the decline in average family size during that time factored in, a 1950 home offered 290 square feet per family resident; today's new home provides 893 square feet.[44] In contrast, new homes in countries such as Sweden, Ireland, Italy, Portugal, and the United Kingdom average less than 1,000 square feet, and new Japanese homes average 1,033 square feet.[45] Government gives tax incentives for energy consumption savings, such as for purchases of hybrid cars and installation of energy-saving appliances. Because Latino/as tend to live in overcrowded housing, our tax laws might similarly reward the lesser environmental footprint left by these living arrangements. In essence, the tax code could award incentives for smaller living spaces and greater densities in housing, whether owned or rented. Although overcrowded conditions are detrimental to Latino/a families, and the goal should be moving them to more comfortable housing, nevertheless the tax incentive would address the short-term certainty that overcrowded conditions will demarcate the Latino/a housing experience.[46]

Despite the cultural preference of many Latino/as to forgo incurring debt, ready access to mortgage financing is crucial to most home purchases. As stated above, almost three-quarters of Latino/a homeowners obtain mortgage financing. The current subprime mortgage crisis, however, threatens the growth of Latino/a homeownership. Unsubstantiated contentions that risky undocumented immigrant borrowers brought down the housing market will further squelch the development of mortgage loan products for immigrants. Subprime loan programs that dispensed with income documentation were the catalyst for predatory loans shepherded by mortgage brokers or lender agents that misstated borrower income in order to qualify unsuspecting borrowers for supersized loans for their limited budgets. But some Latino/a borrowers benefited from the no-documentation programs when their income came from nonverifiable sources such as day labor jobs, self-employment, relatives contributing to the household, future overtime or earnings on second jobs, or from expected future rentals of rooms or space in the home being financed. The upshot of the subprime crisis is that most mortgage lenders have discontinued loan programs that relaxed or dispensed with income verification. Moreover, asset-based loans—those relying on the value of the home rather than on the borrower's ongoing income and other assets as the source of repayment—are in legal jeopardy in several states, which now require the lender to determine the borrower's ability to repay the loan.[47] At the federal level, Congress is debating the Mortgage Reform and Anti-Predatory Lending Act (H.R. 1728), passed by the House in May 2009, which requires lenders to ensure that their borrowers have a "reasonable ability to repay." Without asset-based financing, income-constrained homeowners desiring funds for unexpected necessities such as medical expenses or extraordinary home repair will be deflected to potentially more expensive, and less regulated, sources of unsecured money, such as payday loans and credit card cash advances.

In many ways, the dilemma for policymakers here is similar to the enduring question of caps on interest rates for risky borrowers: To what extent should the law intervene to protect borrowers from themselves? The subprime experience suggests that some paternalism is needed because in the absence of regulation, abusive mortgage brokers and lenders will exploit vulnerable borrowers, who in the subprime market tended to be African American and Latino/a homeowners and homebuyers. Too much regulation, however, in practice marks a return to the days of mortgage redlining that excluded large numbers of Latino/a and African American borrowers and neighborhoods from obtaining conventional mortgage loans. The challenge, then, is to ensure the availability of credit at a reasonable cost to income- or credit-challenged borrowers, while weeding out the predatory players in the marketplace.[48]

The reforms and enforcement strategies outlined below try to strike this delicate balance of fostering growth of financing for Latino/a home purchases and home improvement while protecting Latino/as and financial markets from imprudent deals. The political climate for such reforms is treacherous, as some call for abandonment of subprime lending programs and even a halt of lending to minority borrowers by using the proxy of avoiding "risky" borrowers. During the 2008 presidential campaign, federal programs acting as catalysts for home loans to minorities, as well as the groups that support these programs, came under attack. A *Wall Street Journal* editorial blamed ACORN (Association of Community Organizations for Reform Now) for promoting the federal Community Reinvestment Act (CRA), a law it alleged "laid the foundation for the house of cards built out of subprime loans."[49] Fox News anchor Neil Cavuto offered his condescending assessment of the subprime crisis in concluding that "[l]oaning to minorities and risky folks is a disaster."[50] Conservative commentator Laura Ingraham singled out Bill Clinton as blameworthy for pushing loans to minorities. These views are misleading. Motivating banks to meet local credit needs of underserved low- and moderate-income neighborhoods, the CRA did successfully prompt covered lenders to increase their home loans for these often minority borrowers by 39 percent from 1993 to 1998.[51] But blaming the CRA and its advocates for the subprime crisis is misplaced, as the CRA did not compel overpriced or teaser-rate loans. Moreover, 80 percent of the subprime loans were made by lenders not even covered by the CRA. Rather, as one professor testified to Congress, "the worst and most widespread abuses occurred in the [lending] institutions with the least federal oversight."[52] Many subprime loans were unsustainable, and their terms misrepresented, such as those with dramatic jumps in interest rates or with payments that failed to include taxes and insurance, as some borrowers were promised.[53] I refrain, therefore, from leveling blame on programs that encourage loans to minority borrowers. Instead I urge expansion of opportunities for Latino/as in housing markets, while weeding out the bad actors and abusive underwriting practices in lending markets.

Credit scoring systems that underlie the choices between prime and subprime lenders and among loan programs are constructed to the detriment of Latino/a borrowers, particularly immigrants. Many Latino/a immigrants come from countries where banking services are unavailable to low-income residents, and once in the United States they deal in a cash-based economy that utilizes check-cashing stores, cash payments from employers and to creditors, and wire transfer services.[54] The Federal Deposit Insurance Corporation (FDIC) estimates that some twelve million Latino/as in the United States deal almost exclusively in cash.[55] Culturally, many Latino/as disdain using credit cards or incurring debt in the normal course of living. Existing automated credit scoring techniques fail to account for timely rent, utility, and cell phone payments, and thus steer many Latino/a borrowers toward the more expensive subprime market. Alternative underwriting standards should be developed to account for these deficiencies in traditional credit history systems.[56] Toward this end, the federal Housing and Economic Recovery Act of 2008 amended the National Housing Act to authorize a pilot program of automating an alternative credit rating to include rent, utilities, and other nontraditional information, but limited the new system to a five-year test-run and annually to no more than 5 percent of federally insured home mortgages.[57]

For immigrants without Social Security numbers, ITIN loans offer an alternate financing path. Traditional lenders, however, were spooked by an anti-immigrant backlash attacking these loan programs as unlawfully aiding undocumented immigrants. The absence of a secondary market for ITIN loans also hampers their development,[58] and the likelihood of creating a market of buyers of ITIN loans is slight given the blame pointed at secondary markets for fueling the subprime mortgage crisis and the flight of investors from nontraditional real estate–backed securities. Ratings companies assessing the investment risks in ITIN loans would no doubt factor in the risk of payment disruption should immigration enforcement intervene. Under these circumstances, Latino/a immigrants should hope for development of an ITIN loan market as a stop-gap measure, but concentrate efforts toward comprehensive immigration reform to regularize their immigration status. Chapter 15 offers additional housing-based arguments supporting immigration reform.

As contended in chapter 5, many subprime mortgage borrowers, including Latino/as, would have qualified for cheaper prime loans. Among the reasons for this market failure is that many prime lenders do not compete in lower-income and minority communities, essentially ceding that segregated territory to unregulated subprime lenders. Latino/as have called for increased accountability of banks for their localized lending obligations under the federal CRA.[59] Education programs discussed below in connection with anti-discrimination strategies will also serve a role in channeling borrowers to the lenders and loan programs they deserve. But the climate caused by the current mortgage crisis presents challenges for overcoming the lack of lender competition. Blame properly leveled at mortgage brokers and subprime lenders for pushing predatory loans on minority borrowers might cause prime lenders to hesitate to avidly pursue Latino/a customers. Higher default rates among Latino/a borrowers caught in the net of abusive subprime lenders might further discourage such initiative by prime lenders. Yet, the road to Latino/a housing reform requires prime lending institutions setting up shop in Latino/a neighborhoods with bilingual personnel to service local needs.

Discrimination historically has contributed to the dismal state of Latino/a housing. As discussed in chapter 8, restrictive covenants once guarded neighborhoods against entry of African Americans, Latino/as, and other unwelcome neighbors. Chapter 5 discussed how the federal government helped to establish discriminatory mortgage lending practices. Decades later, the federal government reversed course by enacting anti-discrimination laws governing housing and housing finance. As suggested below, further reform is needed to better implement and modernize these laws.

Discrimination in housing has multiple origins, including attitudinal and economic motivations. As examined in chapter 4, derogatory stereotypes depict Latino/as as the "dirty Mexican," as unwilling to undertake or incapable of property upkeep, and overall as undesirable neighbors. Restrictive covenants in the twentieth century channeled these fears that Latino/a residents would lower surrounding property values. Racial restrictive covenants, therefore, were grounded in both attitudes and economics. Predatory mortgage loans singling out Latino/as, particularly Spanish-speakers, are more deeply grounded in economic motivation. As explained in chapter 5, some abusive lenders and mortgage brokers, abandoning the history of refusing to deal with Latino/a borrowers, instead sought them out in order to strike deals that were either unfairly profitable or doomed to fail after generating lucrative origination fees to the broker or initial lender. Fueled by these motivations, discriminatory practices in housing have deleterious economic consequences for Latino/as already handicapped in the housing market. In theory, discrimination in markets reduces choice, and thus increases the ultimate cost for consumers, whether renting or purchasing. Eliminating discrimination in housing markets, then, should lower housing and financing costs for Latino/as, and thus deserves discussion alongside the other means addressed in this chapter.

Discrimination in housing takes many forms, some of which linger today. In the case of home purchases, racial restrictive covenants are no longer enforceable. Moreover, the current housing crisis makes it unlikely that sellers or brokers will refuse to deal with viable buyers of any background. Nevertheless, discrimination lurks in home sales. A study by the federal Department of Housing and Urban Development (HUD) in 2000 revealed that sales agents still tend to steer prospective Latino/a and African American homebuyers toward neighborhoods of their own racial composition.[60] Discrimination also exists in rental markets. The same study found that Latino/a renters were even more likely to encounter discrimination than African Americans. Latino/as received different information than Anglo renters on the availability of the target dwelling, and property managers tended to quote higher rents to Latino/as. Similarly, a 1995 study in Fresno County, California, found 77 percent of Latino/as seeking rental units in predominantly Anglo neighborhoods faced discrimination; a 1997 San Antonio study made similar findings, with 51 percent of Latino/a renters receiving differential treatment in lease terms and conditions, and 21 percent given different information on rental availability.[61] Discrimination is rampant too in mortgage lending markets, despite the abolition of overt forms of discrimination. Using testers, the HUD study found that real estate agents gave Latino/a buyers little or no help in finding mortgage financing. In contrast, agents more often favored Anglo homebuyers with such advice as lender recommendations and discussion of down payment requirements.[62] Lenders also often favor Anglo over Latino/a borrowers. HUD testing, for example, revealed a loan officer who prequalified an Anglo borrower for a loan without a credit check, but then told a Latino/a tester he couldn't give any information before doing so, explaining, "We usually don't meet with anyone without doing the credit check, it would be a waste of time for you and for me."[63] Although federal Home Mortgage Disclosure Act data consistently reveal higher denial rates for Latino/a applicants than for Anglos, even for applicants of equal income, mortgage lenders contend that differences in credit history justify the discrepancy. But studies have found otherwise. For example, a 1992 study by the Federal Reserve Bank of Boston concluded that Latino/as and African Americans were 60 percent more likely to be denied a mortgage loan than Anglo counterparts with equal credit histories.[64]

Discrimination in housing can also be government-initiated. Wielding zoning laws that target or are selectively enforced against Latino/as, as detailed in chapter 7, many municipalities are engaging in government-sponsored discrimination that may run afoul of constitutional imperatives. Municipalities contribute to the dismal housing picture for Latino/as by such policies as restricting construction of multifamily housing, zoning against higher-density and extended-family living arrangements, and by acting as immigration police to outlaw housing for the undocumented. Rather than exacerbating the Latino/a housing crisis, local governments should participate in its solution. Among methods to prevent discrimination in local housing enforcement, municipalities should eliminate laws against extended-family living arrangements unless based on density per bedroom or square footage. Further, enforcement of such density laws should be relaxed in times of housing shortage or economic crisis. Government should refrain from enacting any new ordinances that disproportionately impact Latino/as, and ensure that any new ordinances aren't prompted by anti-Latino/a animus. Local government should promote affordable housing projects by fast-tracking their approval and more willingly granting variances from restrictions on neighborhood density, set-back, height, and the like, especially when such projects accommodate larger families with three-bedroom apartment units. Finally, local government should leave the business of policing the undocumented to federal officials.

Combating discrimination in housing markets among private actors demands a multifaceted approach that includes statutory reform, enforcement prerogatives and funding, consumer education initiatives, and even a campaign to tackle derogatory stereotypes that portray Latino/as as undesirable neighbors and as undeserving of reform.

As with other areas of persistent discrimination such as the workplace and education, Congress enacted housing anti-discrimination legislation in the civil rights era of the 1960s and into the 1970s, including the Fair Housing Act of 1968 and the Equal Credit Opportunity Act (ECOA) of 1974, amended in 1976 to encompass race, color, national origin, and other factors. Complemented by state and local regulation, and by the federal Civil Rights Act of 1866—which was construed eventually to address housing discrimination[65]—federal law and that of most states prohibit discrimination in selling, leasing, and financing real estate. These laws, however, have proven inadequate to eradicate discrimination in housing markets. Government enforcement depends on budgetary appropriations, which are often insufficient. Most housing discrimination goes undetected or unreported—HUD estimates only 1 percent of fair housing violations are reported.[66] Few sellers, brokers, landlords, and lenders still engage in overt discrimination. For example, no lender is going to specify as the written reason for the adverse credit determination, as required by the ECOA, that the borrower was Latino/a. Nor would any landlord inform a prospective tenant that Latino/as may not apply, nor any seller or real estate broker advertise, "no offers from Latino/as please." Rather, discrimination is often masked by proxies for unlawful conduct that facially coincide with legitimate interests such as reducing mortgage risk or ensuring safety in rentals. Although some applicable statutory and administrative protections may guard against practices with discriminatory impact against Latino/as, rather than demanding proof of discriminatory intent, lawsuits often fail upon a showing of such legitimate business interests.

In the case of language discrimination, consider a landlord who refuses to rent to a monolingual Spanish-speaking tenant. As one California lawsuit against a San Jose landlord claimed, the landlord allegedly told the Latino/a applicants: "If you can't understand English, don't bother turning in an application. . . . We're not going to rent the home to Spanish-speaking people." Rejecting any claim under the federal Fair Housing Act, the jury concluded that the landlord adopted the English-fluency rule to ensure effective communication with tenants in an emergency, and did not intend to discriminate on the basis of race or national origin. Under the Fair Housing Act, proof of disparate impact may establish discrimination, even absent intent; however, the applicants failed to prove disparate impact.[67] Presumably they could have introduced statistical evidence of a large number of Spanish-speakers in the area potentially impacted, but given the absence of any statutory reference to language discrimination, they also would have needed to show that requiring English language would disproportionately impact Latino/as on the basis of race or national origin. Further, the excuse of communication in an emergency might still insulate the landlord from the disparate impact claim.[68] Legislatures might ease this burden by including ethnic traits, such as language, explicitly within the categories protected from discrimination. Moreover, the legislature could specify that any language-based discrimination adversely impacts Latino/as, thus requiring in all instances that the landlord or other actor justify the housing policy as having a legitimate business purpose.

A species of language discrimination in housing exploits the language barrier to foist unintended terms on the borrower, renter, or buyer. As explained in chapter 5, some unscrupulous mortgage lenders and brokers employed this tactic against Spanish-speaking borrowers. Although federal and some state laws require separate disclosures of the essential terms of the mortgage loan transaction, such as the federal Truth in Lending Act's disclosure statement of the interest rate, these generally are mandated only in English, even when the lender or broker is aware of a language barrier. To protect the growing population of Spanish-speakers, by far the most populous language minority in the United States, laws should require translations of real estate loan disclosures and other real estate documents such as leases, particularly when the transaction is negotiated in Spanish. Federal Truth-in-Lending law, for example, must mandate translations in these circumstances. California law already requires such translations for residential leases, and effective 2010, a translated summary of residential mortgage loans of non-federal lenders.[69] In the absence of legal mandate, community groups and Latino/a organizations should encourage lenders and other participants in real estate markets to take private initiative to supply translations from certified translators to Spanish-speaking customers.

Reinvigorated enforcement of antidiscrimination laws is needed. Some mortgage brokers and lenders steered Latino/a borrowers who would have qualified for prime loans toward subprime loans with detrimental terms.[70] And testers in the HUD study found more rampant discrimination in rental housing against Latino/a applicants than for African Americans.[71] The prevailing anti-immigrant climate may lead some to think that taking advantage of immigrants and of Latino/as, particularly those known or assumed to be undocumented, is immune from sanction. Under President Bush's leadership in the early 2000s, prosecutions of lending discrimination laws ground to a halt.[72] More federal and state fair housing testers and more enforcement actions and dollars are needed to send the message that abusing Latino/as of any citizenship or immigration status is intolerable.

Whether they are undocumented or documented, noncitizen Latino/as are excluded from protection under many fair housing laws if they experience discrimination in housing loans, purchases, or rentals. For example, although the federal Fair Housing Act prohibits discrimination on the basis of national origin, it does not explicitly address discrimination on the basis of citizenship.⁷³ ECOA regulations allow creditors to inquire about the immigration status of loan applicants, presumably on the assumption that it may affect a borrower's ability to repay or the lender's ability to collect on the loan should the immigrant leave the country. While some courts have held that the ECOA does not prohibit discrimination based on citizenship,⁷⁴ the act does not bar loans to undocumented immigrants or other noncitizens. Such lending, at present, appears to be a matter of the lender's own initiative. Therefore, community and civil rights groups might encourage lenders to pursue ITIN lending to borrowers hopeful for eventual citizenship and their own piece of the American dream.

Mistreatment by subprime lenders, language barriers, and a lack of experience of homeownership for many Latino/as all call for consumer education initiatives encompassing purchase, financing, and rental of U.S. residences. Best orchestrated locally and bilingually through trusted community networks funded either with federal dollars (perhaps delivered in partnership with HUD and other relevant government agencies) or by foundation grants, such an education and counseling program must infuse Latino/as with a healthy skepticism of the marketplace. Culturally, many Latino/as assumed lenders and mortgage brokers were looking out for their interests as customers, when the reality of the marketplace is otherwise—particularly when some brokers collect kickbacks (known as "yield spread premiums") for procuring deals on unfavorable terms.⁷⁵ The study reflected in the table below reveals the depth of misunderstandings and false trust of the marketplace among Latino/as in the home financing process.⁷⁶

Another common fallacy is to rely on the broker's representations of affordability, and the lender's approval of the loan, as validation that the borrower can afford the home and the purchase loan. The subprime crisis exposed this misunderstanding and the unpreparedness of Latino/as and other borrowers in dealing with predatory lenders. Studies have confirmed the information gap of subprime borrowers, who tend to shop around less than prime borrowers and also hold a less accurate estimate of their credit score than prime borrowers.⁷⁷ Consumer education for Latino/as, particularly for immigrants, needs to include basic concepts and terminology of the U.S. marketplace with which they may be unfamiliar, such as variable interest rates, amortization schedules, home loan impound accounts for taxes and insurance, debt-to-income ratios, prepayment premiums, credit scoring systems, and federal and state protections of buyers, borrowers, and tenants, as well as guidance on the foreclosure process and foreclosure alternatives. The HUD Report revealed that Latino/a homebuyers receive less help than

TABLE 1. *Percentage Who Know That The Following Statements Are False*

	All participants	English-Speaking Hispanics	Spanish-Speaking Hispanics
You need to have stayed in the same job for at least five years to qualify for a mortgage	65%	55%	39%
Information on home buying is only available in English	89%	93%	60%
Housing lenders are required by law to give you the best possible rates on loans	59%	42%	25%
If you want a mortgage, you have to accept a thirty-year commitment	74%	65%	27%
You need a perfect credit rating to qualify for a mortgage	73%	64%	22%

Adapted from Understanding America's Homeownership Gaps: 2003 Fannie Mae National Housing Survey, http://www.fanniemae.com/global/pdf/media/survey/survey2003.pdf

Anglos from real estate agents in procuring mortgage financing, pointing out the need for education to better equip the Latino/a buyer.[78] Bilingual websites should be developed with experiential accounts of providers in local real estate markets, and to provide a venue for reporting predatory practices. Consumer advocates have also called for bilingual "blue books" detailing the best available mortgage products as they relate to income, credit score, and down payment ability. Recipients of certain perilous mortgage loan products, such as adjustable-rate mortgages and no-documentation loans, might be compelled to undergo a program of financial training, as some states already require for high-cost loans.[79]

Many Latino/a homebuyers are first-generation purchasers, at least in the United States, and therefore do not receive advice from experienced family members that others take for granted.[80] Consumer education on credit and housing must be restored and made mandatory in high school curriculum to better equip Latino/as and other future renters, purchasers, and borrowers with marketplace rules and fruitful values such as dedication to savings and avoidance of high-cost credit such as rent-to-own and payday loans.[81]

Additionally, better-funded adult English-language education programs can help the nearly half of Latino/a immigrants (48.5 percent) who do not speak English well or at all, rendering them vulnerable to exploitation in housing transactions.[82]

Informing Latino/as of their rights is only a partial remedy for improving the state of Latino/a housing. Commentators question the effectiveness and cost benefits of such financial literacy programs for homebuyers and borrowers.[83] Even if Latino/as are armed with financial literacy, without improved financial opportunities, homeownership and uncrowded and decent housing will remain out of reach for many. The disproportionate poverty of Latino/as significantly propels discrimination against them in the housing markets and beyond. Derogatory societal impressions of Latino/as as dirty, as poor stewards of the land and their homes, and even as subhuman are reinforced by overcrowded and substandard living conditions prompted by dismal economic circumstances. As important as lowering the cost of housing, then, is raising the income of Latino/as to a level that allows them to bargain equally for their own American dream. At the same time, studies of subprime lending revealed that the disparity between Anglos and Latino/as in obtaining subprime financing increased with income, suggesting that efforts to raise the bar for Latino/a income must be accompanied by consumer education to prevent unfair advantage.[84]

15

Equity for Latino/as and the Poor

> [A] decent place for a family to live becomes a platform for dignity and self-respect and a base for hope and improvement. A decent home allows people to take advantage of opportunities in education, health and employment—the means to get ahead in our society. A decent home is the important beginning point for growth into the mainstream of American life.
> —Report of the National Housing Task Force (1988)

Speakers from savants to comedians have quipped that the real problem with poor people is they don't have enough money. Although discrimination at both the individual and the institutional level constrains housing opportunity, as does lack of consumer education and impediments such as language barriers, the overarching problem among Latino/as in the housing market is their lack of income. Dismal homeownership statistics, higher costs of home finance in the mortgage markets, overcrowded housing, and dilapidated dwellings all stem from inadequate income to sustain decent housing. Moreover, as discussed in chapter 14, many Latino/a households are severely cost burdened in the housing market because they spend too much of their income on housing expenses.

Charting a course to financial equality in the housing market is a long-range strategy. Short-term gains through wage increases, for example, fall short of instilling financial wherewithal given the need to accumulate wealth over several years for a down payment. Moreover, generational wealth plays a crucial role in housing finance, as money gifts or inheritances of residential property from family members elevate younger family members. Nothing here is a quick fix for housing market inequalities. Rather, the strategies below trigger steady gains toward homeownership, while first solving the most immediate crisis of overcrowded, substandard rental housing.

Foremost among economic reforms is the need for comprehensive immigration reform. Other writers have conveyed the urgency of a procedure for legalization and the prospect of citizenship for our substantial undocumented (and documented but noncitizen) population, most of them Latino/a, as well as a guest-worker program and similar prospects for future arrivals. These proponents ground their arguments in human rights; respect for familial relations, and the tragedy of separated families; the community disruptions of enforcement raids; the anguish of deaths during border crossings; our legacy of welcoming immigrants; and the labor, cultural, and other contributions of immigrants.[1] Here, I add to that list by articulating the ways in which immigration reform can contribute to strengthening housing markets.

Immigration reform that regularizes the status of undocumented residents and offers them citizenship might ultimately bring millions of otherwise reluctant Latino/as and other immigrants now living in overcrowded rental units into the market for home purchases, helping to erode any oversupply of homes for sale and reestablishing demand for construction of entry-level homes. Not just immigrants will benefit, as the ability to move up the housing ladder to purchase a more expensive home hinges on a vibrant market for one's existing home. As the co-founder of the National Association of Hispanic Real Estate Professionals put it, "Your client can't buy a $300,000 house if he can't sell his $150,000 house."[2] A Massachusetts demographer concurred: "What happens in California is a precursor to what will happen in the rest of the United States. There is no question that real estate in California will be shaped by immigrants and their children."[3] Immersed in the subprime crisis that began in 2007, homeowners are wondering whether their home values will rebound and whether the housing market will see growth. The key to long-term growth in the housing market is demand through immigrant growth, fueled particularly by regularizing the status of the current undocumented. Although some commentators have focused on repairing the wounded housing market through immigration reform that would offer green cards to immigrants who purchase homes in the United States and supply a substantial minimum equity investment, Latino/a immigrants tend to arrive in U.S. labor markets without significant cash reserves.[4] Rather than structuring immigration reform exclusively around homebuyers, reform that regularizes status of the current undocumented and offers future entry consistent with labor needs is more likely to confront the dynamics of Latino/a immigrants and ultimately to boost the U.S. housing market.

Immigrant growth has revitalized urban landscapes. Particularly in the Northeast, immigrant arrivals buoyed housing values in areas such as New York's Flushing that were economically distressed and sometimes derelict in the 1970s.[5] Increasing enforcement imperatives leveled against the undocumented by local, state, and federal officials, ranging from workplace raids to restrictions in housing markets such as the Hazelton ordinances (see chapter 6), will impede this renaissance. In Georgia, for example, state legislation passed in 2006 directed at undocumented immigrants in the workplace and also curtailing government benefits drove immigrants there out of the home purchase market.[6] The sooner that local communities, states, and the federal government embrace immigrant workers drawn by labor needs, the faster that housing markets will recover and grow. Those communities chasing away Latino/as and other immigrant and minority groups may wither and collapse as their Anglo homeowners age. Researchers predicted in 2009 that "the future of prosperous regions (both urban/suburban and by state) will be likely defined by their ability to attract young diverse minority home buyers."[7] As early as 2006, a *New York Times* article pointed to immigrants as the key to replacing the baby boomer generation in housing, while questioning whether immigrants, documented and not, would disburse sufficiently to rescue markets in places outside the Southwest and New York: "[E]ven though [immigrants] continue to fan out into other areas in increasing numbers, there may not be enough of them to help homeowners in places like West Virginia and Indiana."[8]

From an undocumented immigrant's perspective, immigration reform can mean freedom from treachery in the housing market. As immigration policy increasingly focused on border security and walls, the cost and risk of entering the United States from the south rose. Undocumented immigrants encumber any property they own in their home countries as collateral for their passage, thereby committing to repay the debt from earnings in the United States. Alternatively, they exhaust their financial savings on arrival. Either way, the rising costs of passage ensure that the undocumented immigrant, lacking any money for rental security deposits and needing to earn back the cost of entry and then some, will opt for housing of the cheapest variety. Usually that means coping with overcrowded conditions while renting a room—or, more likely, part of a room—in a house, apartment, garage, basement, or worse. The cost of border passage also confines the seasonal worker to a sustained presence in the United States, forcing the immigrant to rent housing year-round for work that may last a single season. As one migrant worker explained: "We have families in Mexico. Many of us have land, houses that we're building with the money we make here. Documentation would just allow people to work legally, to avoid the dangers at the border, to travel back and forth without all the expense and fear."[9] Fear of immigration enforcement officials also chills undocumented immigrants from complaining about unsafe housing or abuses in the rental market, including sexual harassment.[10] Undocumented immigrants exist on the fringes of the job market, vulnerable to workplace exploitation and to the uncertainties of migrant or day labor employment, none of which is conducive to stability or investment in the U.S. housing market.

Reform that offers undocumented immigrants a means to transform their status to lawful resident or ultimately to citizen also would deflate efforts in places such as Hazelton to persecute Latino/a residents by outlawing rentals to undocumented immigrants. Some of the neighborhood outcry over the undocumented in Hazelton and elsewhere is directly related to overcrowded housing and neighborhood externalities that immigration reform would help ease. Immigration reform also would temper the outcry against banks establishing ITIN loan programs, as presumably most undocumented immigrants would seek to regularize their status.

Comprehensive immigration reform of sorts came close to enactment in 2007, with bipartisan support to combine a tortuous path to citizenship for longstanding undocumented residents with a guest-worker program for future immigrants. But even this modest proposal floundered amid rampant anti-Latino/a and border security rhetoric. Although Republican presidential candidate John McCain tried to blame the demise of reform legislation on Barack Obama and Democrats in Spanish-language ads targeting Latino/a voters in the 2008 election, the then-head of the National Immigration Forum set the record straight: "The bill died because of intense Republican opposition fueled by anti-immigrant groups, talk radio, and talk television."[11] With the election of Obama and the strengthening of the Democratic majority in Congress, comprehensive immigration reform is once more on the table, with decent housing among the stakes for its passage. Still, the economic distress prevailing in Obama's early presidency has posed a challenge for such reform, as some workers fear competition in labor markets from immigrant workers with newfound legal status.

Whether immigrants or native-born, Latino/as earn less than Anglo workers. In 2006, the median household income for Latino/as was $37,800, compared to $52,400 for Anglos.[12] This wage gap has persisted for decades, as has the corresponding homeownership gap between Anglo and Latino/a families. Almost half (48 percent) of individual Latino/a workers earn $20,000 or less annually.[13] Migrant farm workers, mostly Latino/a, are at the bottom, earning a scant median income of $6,250 a year in 2000.[14] The Latino/a poverty rate of 22 percent compares unfavorably to an Anglo rate of only 9 percent.[15] Not surprisingly, economic stress gnaws at many Latino/a families. Even before the economic crisis fully took shape, a study released in 2007 found 31 percent of Latino/as "very worried" or "fairly worried" about their economic security, while only 18 percent of Anglos reported such worries.[16] By 2008, in a Pew Hispanic Center poll Latino/as reported their top three issues as education, the cost of living, and jobs.[17]

Latino/a employment prospects dimmed further from 2007 through 2009, as the lowest level of home construction since World War II took hold in an industry dominated by Latino/as, and second only to agriculture in its percentage of Latino/a workers. In 2006, the construction industry employed 2.9 million Latino/as, most of them (2.2 million) foreign-born, with Latino/as accounting for one in four U.S. construction workers.[18] But in 2007 alone, the United States lost 232,000 construction jobs.[19] Most of the Latino/a workers were among the last-hired and lowest-paid, many of them undocumented, and many hired as day labor by contractors. These jobs disappeared in the downturn. Overall, by April 2009 the U.S. unemployment rate for Latino/as stood at 11.3 percent—a rate eclipsed by Black unemployment (15 percent), but well in excess of the Anglo unemployment rate of 8 percent.[20]

It is in the best interest of Anglos and other groups to support reform fostering economic security for marginalized laborers. Building economic prowess for Latino/as can boost national coffers through income, property, and sales taxes; stimulate job creation through consumer spending; and ensure the longevity of Social Security funds.[21] It can also enable the United States to compete with the emerging superpowers of China and India, the world's most populous countries. Moreover, low-earning Latino/as have considerable interest convergence with most other American wage earners. Pulitzer Prize–winning journalist David Cay Johnston contended in 2008 that "one half of American workers, basically, make less than $500 a week."[22] In recent decades, average wages for all workers have fallen when controlling for inflation, and the income equality gap has grown between the rich and poor.[23] At the same time, housing costs have risen faster than incomes, making the case for meaningful wage reform.[24]

Active in the early 1970s, the Mexican American political party La Raza Unida built its platform in the Southwest around economic reform, calling for a guaranteed annual income, higher minimum wages, sharing government agricultural subsidies with farm workers, and, more broadly, a redistribution of the nation's wealth to the poor Mexican American communities.[25] Of these proposals, increasing the minimum wage has the most political traction. Still, Congress has lagged behind in fostering a minimum wage that tracks household needs—from 1997 to 2007, the minimum wage stood unchanged at $5.15 an hour. Minimum wages should be federally guaranteed, indexed for inflation, and tied to housing costs. The current rate of $7.25 per hour, effective July 2009, needs to be increased significantly to reflect skyrocketing energy, food, health, transportation, housing, and other costs of the typical American family. Both federal and state governments must grow jobs, if only to replace the millions lost in the economic downturn—almost 2.6 million jobs in 2008 alone. Senator Robert Kennedy was a visionary who emphasized job creation in landscapes of urban poverty, conjoining private enterprise and capital in partnership with government initiative. Government would supply tax incentives and subsidized loans to attract job development in ghettos and barrios.[26] Job creation and wage reform are also at the core of most proposals to confront the miserable conditions of colonia housing. One colonia reformist summarized his recommendations as implementing job-training and job-creation programs and requiring local employers of low-wage workers to grant housing bonuses and pay a livable wage.[27] As in the credit and housing markets, discrimination too plays a role in keeping otherwise qualified laborers from obtaining equal employment and wages. Invigorated anti-discrimination enforcement in the labor arena must be part of any blueprint for economic security.[28]

Wage reform and job creation have their limits if the Latino/a educational gap continues. Minimum wages address the bottom of the economic spectrum, and Latino/as who are educationally underqualified will remain at that bottom rung. Educational attainment is the key to competing equally in a U.S. job market freed from the constraints of discrimination. In fact, educational credentials are the primary currency for financial success. A college degree, for example, is strongly linked to financial security and homeownership.[29] Zapatista movement leaders in the Mexican state of Chiapas have recognized the linkage between education, fighting poverty, and acquiring ownership of land and have included demands for quality education within their agenda for land reform.[30]

In the United States, the crisis in Latino/a education rivals and complements the crisis in housing. The afflictions in the educational system are devastating for the financial future of a staggering number of Latino/as. From 1990 to 2006, the Latino/a public school population in the United States doubled. As of 2008, the ten million Latino/as in U.S. public schools amounted to about one in five students. Almost 25 percent of the U.S. Latino/a population is under the age of five, making education a crucial concern.[31] By 2050, Latino/a school-age children are expected to surpass Anglo children in number.[32] A significant majority (69 percent) of Latino/a schoolchildren in 2008 were of Mexican origin, and many (28 percent) live in poverty. In contrast, only one in ten (11 percent) Anglo students lives in a poor household.[33]

Latino/as are far less likely than Anglos to have a college degree or even a high school diploma, and are far more likely to drop out of high school and suffer huge gaps in achievement while in school. A Census Bureau survey in East Los Angeles in 2006 revealed that only 44 percent of those twenty-five and older were high school graduates, and only 4 percent held a bachelor's degree.[34] A 2003 study of East L.A.'s Roosevelt High School found that almost 70 percent of students beginning as freshmen, nearly all of them Latino/a, failed to graduate.[35] Nationally, the drop-out statistics were somewhat better, although still abysmal—one publication reported that 58 percent of Latino/a students failed to complete high school.[36] Achievement gaps between Latino/a and Anglo students remain unchanged since the early 1970s,[37] with acute disparities in key skills such as math and reading.[38] By the end of high school, Latino/a math and reading scores are virtually the same as those of Anglo eighth graders.[39] A 2004 federal report found that schools with 75 percent low-income students, many located in minority neighborhoods, had three times as many uncertified and out-of-field teachers in English and science.[40]

High school drop-outs face dismal career prospects, and their lifetime earnings reflect their lack of education. The cycle of poverty thus continues, as household poverty is a significant contributor to these dismal educational statistics of Latino/as. Several factors contribute to the high drop-out rate, but one significant cause is financial pressure to join the workforce to contribute to family income. Labor organizer César Chávez, a lifelong champion of educating the lower class, was forced to quit school after the eighth grade to become the family breadwinner in the migrant fields of California when his father was injured. As addressed below, the high costs of college play a substantial role in preventing those Latino/as who do graduate high school from continuing their studies. Throughout the formative years, poverty impedes home conditions conducive to studying and achievement. No doubt overcrowded and dilapidated housing is part of the prescription for failure. Two educational experts remarked that "[e]vidence suggests that neighborhood quality has profound effects on student outcomes," adding that "[i]nadequate heat, lack of air conditioning, inoperable plumbing, or rodent infestation—common conditions in substandard housing—can be disruptive to any learner."[41] Further, the instability of rental housing compared to homeownership contributes to the disrupted home life of young learners forced to change schools or neighborhoods when rents rise or units become too crowded with new family. Public school financing that relies on local property taxes exacerbates disparities between rich and poor neighborhoods.[42] Moreover, as Anglo families fled inner cities and placed their children in private suburban schools, pressure mounted in several states to curb property taxes and fleece educational budgets. The real estate meltdown will further curtail local school resources dependent on property taxation, particularly in neighborhoods of color devastated by mass foreclosures of subprime loans and freefalls in property values.[43] Against this background of neighborhood segregation and educational inequality, financial relief and educational imperatives will need to come from federal sources.

Reform is needed at all levels of the educational system, and from state, local, and federal initiatives. Reflecting statistics that only 43 percent of Latino/a children participated in early education programs, whereas 59 percent of Anglo children did so, three-quarters of Latino/as polled desired the federal government to spend more for preschool programs.[44] About 45 percent of Latino/a schoolchildren are learning English as a second language while going to school.[45] At all levels of education, more culturally and linguistically competent teachers are needed to reinforce the value of the Spanish language skills that these students bring to the classroom. Severely restricted by initiative in California and a few other states, bilingual education is vital in keeping English-learners afloat in their other classes while teaching them English.

While on the campaign trail in East Los Angeles in 2007, Obama outlined his plans for an educational renaissance in inner cities, and suggested what the federal government might contribute:

> Let's not pass a law called No Child Left Behind and then leave the money behind. Let's rebuild our crumbling schools, recruit an army of new teachers and get more of them to come teach right here in East L.A.—because what makes the most difference in any child's education is the person standing at the front of the classroom....
>
> ... [W]e also have to take targeted steps to improve graduation rates. That means supporting college outreach programs.... And it also means intervening much earlier in a child's education—because the downward spiral that leads a high school student to drop out often begins in elementary and middle school. That's why I've proposed a STEP UP plan to expand summer learning opportunities through partnerships between schools and community organizations. And that's why next week I'll be introducing a bill in the Senate that invests in proven strategies to support middle school students and that awards grants to states and districts that are improving graduation rates.[46]

In November 2007, Obama announced a scholarship proposal to recruit teachers by funding their undergraduate and graduate education programs in exchange for service in high-need fields or locations for at least four years.

Funding of community activity centers for youth, and of community-based organizations providing student counseling, can aid at-risk youth to stay in school and away from the alternate economies of gangs and the drug trade. As detailed in chapters 2 and 12, the federal government holds rangeland and parkland in the Southwest, particularly in New Mexico, that is arguably the property of descendants of community land grant holders from more than a century ago. In addition to the ameliorative options suggested by the U.S. General Accounting Office report discussed in chapter 12, the federal government might consider returning profits from grazing leases, hunting permits, camping permits, and the like back to surrounding communities to support schools and community centers.

Financial success depends increasingly on graduation from college rather than just high school. Four years of college boosts earnings some 65 percent.[47] Sixty-seven percent of the new jobs created in 2007 required some education or training beyond high school, as did 90 percent of the fastest-growing U.S. jobs.[48] But with financial pressures, inadequate academic preparation, and rampant attrition in high school, Latino/a enrollments in higher education are a national tragedy. Of one hundred Latino/a kindergarten students, only thirteen will ultimately obtain a bachelor's degree.[49] A survey of Latino/as revealed that 77 percent felt that tuition costs and their need to work were the greatest barriers to college.[50] Reflecting the correlation between household income and college graduation, students from families in the top U.S. income quartile are six times more likely to obtain a college degree than those from the bottom quartile.[51] Despite their disproportionate poverty, Latino/as receive the lowest average amount of college financial aid of any group. Here, the federal government can help by increasing financial aid packages as tuition skyrockets. Obama made the campaign promise to pursue a $4,000 tax credit toward college tuition conditioned on completion of 100 hours of community service—the American Recovery and Reinvestment Act of 2009 partly met this promise through a $2,500 credit for most students without requiring community service. Needed programs include loan forgiveness for low-income Latino/as and a better system to disseminate financial aid information bilingually to Latino/a families. Tuition costs particularly hamper undocumented immigrant college students, as about forty states require them to pay higher out-of-state tuition as nonresidents in their own states of residence. The Development, Relief and Education for

Alien Minors (DREAM) Act, a federal proposal debated for years by Congress, would offer a chance at citizenship to undocumented college students, render them eligible for federal financial aid, and give states the green light to treat resident undocumented students the same as other resident students.

Affirmative action programs are essential for ensuring diverse classes in top public educational institutions, but such programs were clipped by ballot initiatives in California, Michigan, Nebraska, and Washington, and by legislation in Florida. An encouraging sign is that Colorado voters in 2008 resisted the tide and retained that state's affirmative action policies.

Finally, for the substantial numbers of Latino/as in the workforce who haven't completed high school or college, federal dollars can support adult education programs that offer diplomas and English language instruction.[52]

As described previously, negative perceptions of Latino/as constrain their advancement in housing markets. Although some perceive the overrepresentation of Latino/as in overcrowded, dilapidated housing as some cultural defect or destiny, these conditions are simply the product of longstanding structural breakdowns in labor, education, immigration, and housing markets and policies. The dilemma for reformers is that negative opinions toward Latino/a immigrants, and Latino/as generally, often impede needed structural reforms, such as better funding of public education, that are the gateway to changing some of the conditions of poverty that foster these misplaced cultural assumptions. Moreover, the current sorry condition of the educational system is directly linked to segregationist efforts prompted by fears of a black or brown neighbor.[53] Today, African American and Latino/a schoolchildren are more segregated than they were in 1968 on the death of Martin Luther King, Jr.[54] With this background of hostility to opening the American dream to Latino/as, structural reforms must come through interracial and ethnic coalitions that forge antipoverty alliances among voters in lower economic classes, as well as those in higher income brackets lured by the dynamics of interest convergence articulated above.

Coalition-building is essential for Latino/as, given the political impediments they face as a youthful, often immigrant voting group, as well as their historical record of political defeats at local, state, and national levels. On the housing and land front, episodes of loss such as Chávez Ravine, freeway construction in East Los Angeles, and even congressional requirements of title certification in the Southwest after the Treaty of Guadalupe Hidalgo, together with recent examples of exclusion such as Hazelton's ordinances targeting undocumented immigrants and enforcement of zoning laws elsewhere against Latino/as, all point to the imperative of acquiring and wielding political power. Although much can be gained through mobilizing Latino/as by increasing voter registration and turnout, the impediments of youth and lack of citizenship compel coalitional efforts. These efforts must bridge the aspirations and needs of the diverse racial and ethnic groups that comprise the Latino/a population, as well as enable coalitions with African Americans, Asian Americans,[55] and other groups that lag behind in housing markets.

For all their historical differences in mistreatment in the United States, African Americans and Latino/as share common histories in housing policy and convergence on most solutions to their housing crises. The arrest in 2009 of Henry Louis Gates Jr., a prominent Black professor from Harvard, stemming from a confrontation with police who suspected him of breaking into a house—his own—was a stark reminder that the nation still sees Blacks as outsiders in the housing market. No doubt a Latino/a appearing to forcibly enter his or her own home, especially a fancy one, would draw the same presumptive suspicion from passersby and police. Restrictive covenants among homeowners primarily targeted African Americans, but in the Southwest Mexican Americans were also excluded as undesirable neighbors. Federal loan policies placed African American and Mexican American neighborhoods at the bottom of the heap for property appraisals that determined loan amounts and qualification. Local government zoning practices favored Anglo middle-class homeowners to the exclusion of poor groups composed disproportionately of racial minorities. African Americans and Latino/as have suffered housing discrimination from an array of private actors, including lenders, landlords, sellers, real estate brokers, and mortgage loan brokers. The current mortgage crisis exposed the tendencies of subprime lenders and mortgage brokers to seek out African American and Latino/a borrowers for the reverse discrimination of predatory loans. African Americans and Mexican Americans both experienced significant loss of land. In 1920, African Americans owned about fifteen million acres of farmland; today, despite significant population increases, they own less than one million acres.[56] Gentrification of Latino/a and African American neighborhoods, such as those in the Harlem area, has displaced cultural centers.

The upshot of this history of inequality is that both African Americans and Latino/as lag well behind Anglos in homeownership rates and wealth acquisition. Situated disproportionately in neighborhoods with inadequate schools and insufficient employment opportunities, African American and Latino/a communities appear to converge on policy issues of creating jobs, raising incomes, and reinvigorating public education at all levels. Immigration, however, has been a flashpoint for relations between these groups that threatens their prospects for coalition. Immigration has brought Latino/as into the jobs and geographies occupied previously by African Americans in the South, Northeast, and elsewhere. Some African Americans fear competition from immigrant laborers, whom they see as undermining wages. Therefore, African Americans may be reluctant to support comprehensive immigration reform or housing policies that boost participation by immigrant and undocumented communities. At the same time, legalization of Latino/as may empower them to pursue wage advances, and a political coalition of Latino/as and African Americans could coalesce around issues of job creation and wage reform that will inure to the benefit of both groups in their pursuit of housing equality and beyond.

Grounds for coalition on housing reforms exist with other groups, notably Native Americans, who suffered their own unique and tragic history of dispossession. Although the tools varied over time, there are many similarities in the campaigns that stripped Native Americans and Mexican Americans of their desirable lands. For example, settlers used force, intimidation, fraud, squatting, the provision of credit, and other strategies against both groups,[57] in both cases backed by prevailing stereotypes of the superiority of the Anglo as a property owner.[58] One scholar concluded that "[d]uring the Manifest Destiny era, many white Americans applied the same language they had used for centuries about Indians—inferior, savage, uncivilized, and with a hopeless future—to Mexicans."[59] As with Mexican Americans in the Southwest, under the cloak of law, rather than solely through military conquest, the federal government and the Supreme Court—the latter famously invoking imagery of "fierce savages"[60]—contributed to the demise of ancestral land for Native Americans. This sorry legal legacy suggests the benefit of an antipoverty political coalition toward structural reform between these groups that continue to share the parallels of historic land loss and current economic distress.[61]

The interests of Anglos, rich and poor, also converge with those of Latino/as on some levels. For example, wealthy and especially middle-class Anglos share with Latino/as an interest in boosting entry-level purchasing (so long as the existing mortgage interest and capital gains tax breaks are left alone), and lower- and middle-class Anglos in fostering education and boosting wages and jobs. Everyone in the United States should connect on the positive attributes of encouraging immigration and upgrading educational infrastructure to ensure that the United States remains able to compete in innovation and global influence with far more populous and burgeoning world powers such as China and India.

Although some may criticize the supposed values of Latino/as, rather than blaming the true culprit of structural inequalities for the housing crisis, a deeper value at stake in the United States is eroding. The American dream is that hard work in this nation of immigrants will bring the rewards of financial prosperity and comfortable homeownership. Although that value has held true for most past immigrant groups, more recent Latino/a immigrants, and even some native-born Latino/as, are struggling to grasp that brass ring despite undertaking some of the hardest jobs that other Americans increasingly won't do. Should policymakers fail to confront these inequalities, the American dream might fade from consciousness, replaced by an ethos of discontent that hard work leads nowhere. Immigrants who now flock to the United States for their chance at the opportunity and reward of hard work will sow their roots elsewhere, and the nation will slowly decay. Equal housing opportunities for Latino/as, then, are not just a Latino/a dream, but one beneficial for all Americans.

Writing about land reform ideals in Latin America in the 1960s, Robert Kennedy crystallized the importance of land to the working class, an ideal that holds increasing significance in the United States on the housing front as Latino/as become the face of that working class. Kennedy urged the redistribution of agricultural land from the elite to the laborers:

> [L]and reform is also the essence of human dignity and democracy in Latin America. To give land to the man who works it is to give him, for the first time, a degree of security, something more than subsistence living, a place to stand for his rights as a citizen, a share and a stake in the society around him. As our own Daniel Webster said in 1820: "The freest government, if it could exist, would not be long acceptable, if the tendency of the laws was to create a rapid accumulation of property in a few hands, and to render the great mass of the population dependent and penniless."[62]

Concurrent with land reform, Kennedy advocated for larger structural reform: "Real improvement in Latin American agriculture, and in the lives of those who till the soil, requires decades of effort—economic, educational, and social."[63] Even as the U.S. economy has evolved from one rooted in land to one driven by ideas, Kennedy's vision can still serve as the blueprint for change to preserve the American dream for current and future generations.

Conclusion

> Homeownership has been the path to security and prosperity for tens of millions of people in this country. It is the way working men and women have built up wealth for themselves and their children. It is often what people have to show for years of sweat and sacrifice. . . . I want future generations of farm workers—the people of the land—to have what too many of us were denied: the right to own a decent home, a home of our own.
> —César Chávez in *The Words of César Chávez*, ed. Richard J. Jensen and John C. Hammerback (2002), 156

Co-sponsored in the U.S. Senate by Arizona Senator John McCain, the Cesar Estrada Chavez Study Act passed in 2008 as part of the Consolidated Natural Resources Act. That act authorizes the Secretary of the Interior to undertake a resource study of sites in Arizona, California, and elsewhere to determine appropriate methods to preserve them and whether any should be designated as historic landmarks. Among the sites to be studied is the Chávez family homestead in Arizona, lost in the 1930s to the financial pressures addressed in chapter 1. Some of the potentially historic sites have already been leveled by progress that too often claims residences in communities of color. Notably, much of the Sal Si Puedes (Get Out If You Can) barrio of San Jose, California, where Chávez began work as a community organizer, was lost to freeway construction.[1] Shortly after the act's passage, the Department of the Interior designated the Forty Acres site in Delano, California, as a historic landmark. Purchased by the predecessor to the United Farm Workers union in 1966 for $2,700, this flatland property a few miles west of Delano became the union's administrative and service center. It included a meeting hall, health clinic, and even a gas station where Chávez rested in a tiny back room during his historic hunger fast for nonviolence in 1968. Although the union headquarters eventually moved to a 187-acre compound in the Tehachapi Mountains thirty miles east of Bakersfield, the union still maintains administrative offices at Forty Acres, as well as humble apartments that were built as a low-income retirement center for farm workers. As detailed in chapter 1, Chávez's father, Librado, was stripped of a forty-acre parcel he was promised in Yuma, Arizona, in exchange for his hard labor. But the Forty Acres land in Delano remains part of the collective ownership of the farm workers union and a symbol, now elevated in status as a historical embodiment of the compelling proposition that the land belongs to those who work it.

If Congress were to study and preserve landmarks of Latino/a housing and land ownership in the United States more broadly, it would confront a vast array of housing models that reflect the diversity of the Latino/a population and its historical experience battling inequality. Such sites might showcase monuments to loss in urban settings, most prominently Dodger Stadium in downtown Los Angeles, built on the ruins of the Latino/a neighborhoods of Chávez Ravine, with an elementary school buried under tons of dirt rising up to the stadium dugout. They would include the most prominent rural landmark to loss, the Carson National Forest in northern New Mexico, which marks the site of former collective land grants owned by Latino/as in the nineteenth century before the U.S. Supreme Court ruled that they belonged to the government. They might include my grandparents' second house, built in 1923 in East Los Angeles, as reflecting both the typical Spanish-style architecture of Latino/a dwellings constructed around a central open patio, with red-tiled roofs, masonry exteriors, and tiled floors, and also representing the legacy of loss through subprime financing. Landmarks of Latino/a housing might also feature testaments to the abysmal poverty in the Latino/a experience, encompassing tenements in Spanish Harlem that haven't yet given way to gentrified makeovers, makeshift farm worker shelters in the West, and campgrounds for undocumented day laborers as fictionalized in the novel *Tortilla Curtain*. They might encompass most any home built in recent years, as an homage to the role Latino/a labor likely played in its construction. Preserved sites would include colonia housing along the U.S./Mexico border, with self-built ingenuity masking the cruel absence of government services such as water, sewer, paved streets, and streetlights. Despite its legacy of ouster of Mexican residents, the Plaza area of Los Angeles surrounding Olvera Street, the Mexican birthplace of that city, is already an historic district.

As pointed out in the Introduction, family is at the core of the Latino/a experience. Although Latino/as represent diverse groups from varied origins and historical and geographical experiences, celebration of family is one characteristic that unites them as a group and with other Americans. This preeminence of family explains the avid cultural pursuit of homeownership among Latino/as. Mentioned previously, almost all Latino/as (90 percent) strongly agreed with the statement that "owning a home is better for raising a family." In the 1900s, the rallying cry for land reform of "Tierra y Libertad" swept Mexico and the Americas. Today, in our increasingly urbanized society, dreams of land and liberty are giving way to the American dream of homeownership with protection of the family at its core. Constituting the largest immigrant and minority group in the United States today, Latino/as are poised and willing to carry on this tradition that hard work should bring the reward of decent housing and stable family living. As privileged residents of the global destination for those who dream of land and liberty for themselves and their families, our duty is to help ensure these opportunities survive.

Notes

INTRODUCTION

1. See Richard Delgado and Jean Stefancic, "What If John Calmore Had a Latino/a Sibling?" *North Carolina Law Review* 86 (2008): 769, 785.

2. Fernando J. Guerra, Mara A. Marks, and Matt Barreto, "Chasing the Dream: Latinos and Housing in Los Angeles County," www.lmu.edu/Page39870.aspx (last visited September 24, 2008) (concluding that compared to non-Latino/a families, Latino/as tend to live in homes with less square footage, more persons per room, and in poorer condition).

3. Nandinee K. Kutty, "Policy Lessons from the Mexican American Experience, 1848 to the Present," http://papers.ssrn.com/sol3/papers.cfm?abstract_id=1094590 (last visited November 1, 2008) (noting that among Mexican Americans the predominant reason for not wanting to buy a home was the desire to return to Mexico, followed by insecure financial or legal citizenship status).

4. Alejandro Becerra, "Hispanic Homeownership: A Stimulus for America's Housing Renewal," http://alejandrobecerra.com/published.php?id=3 (last visited May 2, 2009).

5. Joel Kotkin, Thomas Tseng, and Erika Ozuna, *Rewarding Ambition: Latinos, Housing, and the Future of California* (Malibu, CA: Pepperdine University, School of Public Policy, Davenport Institute, September 2002), 15.

6. Mark Robert Rank, *One Nation, Underprivileged: Why American Poverty Affects Us All* (Oxford: Oxford University Press, 2004), 228 (citing U.S. Census Bureau statistics from 2001).

7. Rakesh Kochhar, *The Wealth of Hispanic Households: 1996 to 2002* (Washington, DC: Pew Hispanic Center, October 2004).

8. Ibid., 13.

9. Nikitra S. Bailey, "Predatory Lending: The New Face of Economic Injustice," www.abanet.org/irr/hr/summer05/predator.html (last visited February 7, 2008).

10. Kotkin, Tseng, and Ozuna, *Rewarding Ambition*, 11. A higher percentage of Latino/as' wealth is in home equity compared to Anglos, because Latino/as as a group lag far behind in ownership of other sources of wealth, primarily stocks.

11. Janis Bowdler, *Jeopardizing Hispanic Homeownership: Predatory Practices in the Homebuying Market*, National Council of La Raza Issue Brief (Washington, DC: National Council of La Raza, 2005), 5.

12. See A. Mechele Dickerson, "The Myth of Home Ownership and Why Home Ownership Is Not Always a Good Thing," *Indiana Law Journal* 84 (2009): 189; see also Daniel McGinn, *House Lust: America's Obsession with Our Homes* (New York: Doubleday, 2008), 241–42 (discussing Yale economist Robert Shiller's finding that since 1890 houses

have appreciated slightly faster than inflation but much slower than stock investments); Rashmi Dyal-Chand, "Exporting the Ownership Society: A Case Study on the Economic Impact of Property Rights," *Rutgers Law Journal* 39 (2007): 59 (critiquing international economist Hernando de Soto's prescription for poverty relief through property ownership, arguing that poor homeowners wind up as victims of predatory lenders and fail to translate their ownership into long-term wealth [see chapter 14 of this book for proposals to address concerns of predatory lending]).

13. See William M. Rohe, Shannon Van Zandt, and George McCarthy, *The Social Benefits and Costs of Homeownership: A Critical Assessment of the Research* (Cambridge, MA: Joint Center for Housing Studies of Harvard University, October 2001), 21 (suggesting that while these study results are intriguing, the outcome may have been determined by variables such as family assets or neighborhood conditions such as peer influences; yet homeownership itself may have a bearing on such variables).

14. William A. Fischel, *The Homeowner Hypothesis: How Home Values Influence Local Government Taxation, School Finance, and Land-Use Policies* (Cambridge, MA: Harvard University Press, 2001); Jocelyn Y. Stewart, "L.A. a City of Renters," *Los Angeles Times*, November 29, 2001, B1.

15. Ignacio M. García, *United We Win: The Rise and Fall of La Raza Unida Party* (Tucson: Mexican American Studies and Resource Center, University of Arizona, 1989).

16. Steve Wiegand, "California Latinos' Numbers Exceed Their Clout," *Sacramento Bee*, September 15, 2003, A1.

17. D. Benjamin Barros, "Home as a Legal Concept," *Santa Clara Law Review* 46 (2006): 255. Foreclosure protections in some states include rights of redemption following the foreclosure sale that allow the debtor to reclaim ownership by paying the foreclosure price and other specified sums, as well as statutes requiring expiration of a specified length of time before the foreclosure sale can be held.

18. Rohe, Van Zandt, and McCarthy, *Social Benefits and Costs of Homeownership* (pointing out methodological problems of existing research and suggesting that further study is needed).

19. Robert C. Ellickson, *The Household: Informal Order around the Hearth* (Princeton, NJ: Princeton University Press, 2008), 87 ("People who place a high value on long-term security of possession and on autonomy of control thus have good reason to own, not rent."). One of many examples of the lesser legal protection afforded to tenants is the Supreme Court's approval of a federal Department of Housing and Urban Development policy authorizing eviction of public housing tenants based on the drug activities of their household or guests, regardless of their knowledge of that activity. *Department of Housing and Urban Development v. Rucker*, 535 U.S. 125 (2002). Landlords can also oust the tenant at the lease's end should the landlord desire to rent to someone else or even to shift to owner-occupancy of the leased premises. Counterarguments for the autonomy of renters rely on the protections of rent-control jurisdictions, as well as the reality that owners in subdivisions with homeowners associations, or of condos or co-ops subject to condominium association or co-op board control, face limitations on their autonomy. See George Lefcoe, *Real Estate Transactions, Finance, and Development*, 6th ed. (Newark, NJ: Lexis/Nexis, 2009), 18–19; see also Richard Florida, "How the Crash Will Reshape America," *The Atlantic Online*, March 2009, www.theatlantic.com/doc/print/200903/meltdown-geography (last visited Apr. 27, 2009) (arguing that homeownership may limit the flexibility of

workers, as "[t]oo often, it ties people to declining or blighted locations, and forces them into work—if they can find it—that is a poor match for their interests and abilities").

20. Phillip B. Gonzales, "Struggle for Survival: The Hispanic Land Grants of New Mexico, 1848–2001," *Agricultural History* 77 (Spring 2003): 293, 322.

21. Chester Hartman, "The Case for a Right to Housing," in *A Right to Housing: Foundation for a New Social Agenda*, ed. Rachel G. Bratt, Michael E. Stone, and Chester Hartman (Philadelphia: Temple University Press, 2006), 177; McGinn, *House Lust*, 47 (discussing the research of New York University sociologist Dalton Conley, who found that residents of overcrowded homes suffer poor physical and mental health).

22. See also Dickerson, "Myth of Home Ownership," 210 (suggesting further that owners struggling to retain a home often deplete retirement funds, forgo health insurance, and defer routine home maintenance, which depletes home value).

23. National Hispanic Leadership Agenda, 2008 Hispanic Policy Agenda, http://www.maldef.org/resources/publications/NHLAPublicPolicyAgenda.pdf (last visited October 15, 2009).

24. Timothy Ready, *Hispanic Housing in the United States 2006* (South Bend, IN: University of Notre Dame Institute for Latino Studies, 2006), 5.

25. U.S. Census Bureau, "Housing Vacancies and Homeownership," http://www.census.gov/hhes/www/housing/hvs/annual07/ann07t20.html (last visited February 21, 2009) (reporting that the rate of homeownership for non-Hispanic Whites had dropped to 75.2 percent in 2007). Homeownership rates for Asian Americans and Native Americans fall between those for Anglos and Latino/as—in 2008, at 60 and 56.9 percent respectively. Higher rates for Asian Americans likely reflect their more favorable statistics in educational attainment and citizenship status.

26. Dowell Myers, *Immigrants and Boomers: Forging a New Social Contract for the Future of America* (New York: Russell Sage Foundation, 2007), 230.

27. Ibid.

28. Chris Isidore, "Homeownership in Record Plunge," http://money.cnn.com/2008/01/29/news/economy/home_ownership_vacancies/index.htm (posted January 29, 2008) (last visited November 11, 2009).

29. Rakesh Kochhar, Ana Gonzalez-Barrera, and Daniel Dockterman, *Through Boom and Bust: Minorities, Immigrants and Homeownership* (Washington, DC: Pew Hispanic Center, May 12, 2009). Another report had slightly higher figures of Latino/a homeownership: *The State of the Nation's Housing 2009* (Cambridge, MA: Joint Center for Housing Studies of Harvard University, 2009), 37 (reporting 49.1 percent rate for Hispanics in 2008).

30. Population Division, U.S. Census Bureau, "Table 4: Annual Estimates of the Hispanic Resident Population by Sex and Age for the United States: April 1, 2000 to July 1, 2008" (NC-EST2008-04-HISP), May 14, 2009, http://www.census.gov/popest/national/asrh/NC-EST2008-asrh.html (click on the penultimate excel sheet link) (last visited November 11, 2009). Homeownership data tend to be drawn from heads of household, and therefore the higher percentage of children among Latino/as does not account for the disparity in homeownership that Latino/as face relative to Anglos. Still, the relative youth of the Latino/a population matters: in 2008 when the head householder was under thirty-five, the U.S. homeownership rate for all groups was only 41 percent; in contrast, when that householder was in the next age bracket of thirty-five to forty-five, the rate jumped to 67 percent. *State of the Nation's Housing 2009* (Table A-4).

31. Ready, *Hispanic Housing.*

32. U.S. Census Bureau, "State and County QuickFacts, Los Angeles County, California," http://quickfacts.census.gov/qfd/states/06/06037.html (last visited November 20, 2008).

33. Ready, *Hispanic Housing,* 10 (New Mexico, at 69 percent, has the highest rate of Latino/a homeownership).

34. Ibid., 13. As discussed in chapter 11 of this book, Puerto Ricans living in Puerto Rico have a much higher homeownership rate (74.1 percent) that rivals that of U.S. Anglos, although housing budgets tend to be strained and homes overcrowded. Low rates of Puerto Rican homeownership in the mainland United States likely reflect their migration patterns in high-priced urban areas such as New York City and Chicago, as well as the staggering poverty rates of Puerto Ricans.

35. Although these are the dominant models, exceptions existed at both ends of the spectrum of the Latino/a experience. During the time of the rancho holdings acquired through Spanish and Mexican land grants, the hacienda workforce included poor Mexican workers such as landless sharecroppers, seasonal workers, and others. Moreover, when restrictive covenants kept Latino/as from living in certain Los Angeles neighborhoods, wealthy Latino/a actors and actresses penetrated exclusive Anglo enclaves such as Beverly Hills. See Ricardo Romo, *East Los Angeles: History of a Barrio* (Austin: University of Texas Press, 1983), 85 (observing that real estate brokers and homeowners might bend their segregationist ways if the minority had attained the "proper" class, citing as examples the Latino/a stars Ramon Novarro and Dolores del Rio, who purchased homes on the west side of Los Angeles).

36. Jim Cullen, *The American Dream: A Short History of an Idea That Shaped a Nation* (Oxford: Oxford University Press, 2003), 148 (also opining that immigrant Irish and Italians in one Massachusetts city in the 1930s made homeownership a greater priority even than educating their children).

37. Estimates predict that the U.S. non-Hispanic White population will decrease in the 2030s and 2040s, and that by 2050 the United States will be a majority-minority country, led by population increases among the youthful Latino/a demographic group, which will comprise 30 percent of the U.S. population. "Minorities Expected to Be Majority in 2050," http://www.cnn.com/2008/US/08/13/census.minorities/index.html (posted Aug. 13, 2008) (last visited July 30, 2009).

PART I

1. Steven W. Bender, *Comprende? The Significance of Spanish in English-Only Times* (Mountain View, CA: Floricanto Press, 2008), 90–93.

CHAPTER 1

1. Hernando De Soto, *The Mystery of Capital: Why Capitalism Triumphs in the West and Fails Everywhere Else* (New York: Basic Books, 2000), 125.

2. Susan Ferriss and Ricardo Sandoval, *The Fight in the Fields: Cesar Chavez and the Farmworkers Movement* (San Diego: Harcourt Brace, 1997), 13.

3. James Terzian and Kathryn Cramer, *Mighty Hard Road: The Story of Cesar Chavez* (New York: Pocket Books, 1972), 2.

4. Ferriss and Sandoval, *Fight in the Fields*, 15.

5. Daniel La Botz, *César Chávez and La Causa* (New York: Pearson Longman, 2006), 6.

6. Compare Ferriss and Sandoval, *Fight in the Fields*, 16 (specifying the debt as $3,600); and La Botz, *César Chávez*, 7 (putting it at more than $4,000).

7. La Botz, *César Chávez*, 7.

8. Interview with Dolores Huerta, co-founder of United Farm Workers, April 9, 2007.

9. Steven W. Bender, *One Night in America: Robert Kennedy, César Chávez, and the Dream of Dignity* (Boulder, CO: Paradigm Publishers, 2008), 84.

10. Terzian and Cramer, *Mighty Hard Road*, 8

11. Jacques E. Levy, *Cesar Chavez: Autobiography of La Causa* (New York: W. W. Norton, 1975), 42.

12. Ferriss and Sandoval, *Fight in the Fields*, 19.

13. Ibid., 18.

CHAPTER 2

1. Leonard Pitt, *The Decline of the Californios: A Social History of the Spanish-Speaking Californians, 1846–1890* (Berkeley: University of California Press, 1966), 252.

2. David J. Weber, ed., *Foreigners in Their Native Land: Historical Roots of the Mexican Americans*, rev. ed. (Albuquerque: University of New Mexico Press, 2003), 140.

3. Malcolm Ebright, *Land Grants and Lawsuits in Northern New Mexico* (Albuquerque: University of New Mexico Press, 1994), 25 (explaining that community grant settlers could convey their individual plots after four years).

4. Gonzales, "Struggle for Survival," 296–97.

5. Armando C. Alonzo, *Tejano Legacy: Rancheros and Settlers in South Texas, 1734–1900* (Albuquerque: University of New Mexico Press, 1998), 263 (suggesting that some rancho owners held as much as 300,000 acres). Compare Tomás Almaguer, *Racial Fault Lines: The Historical Origins of White Supremacy in California* (Berkeley: University of California Press, 1994), 47 (giving examples of Californio families in the 1840s that owned 700,000 and 488,000 acres, the latter through fourteen separate land grants).

6. Alonzo, *Tejano Legacy*, 263.

7. Almaguer, *Racial Fault Lines*, 47.

8. U.S. General Accounting Office, "Treaty of Guadalupe Hidalgo: Findings and Possible Options Regarding Longstanding Community Land Grant Claims in New Mexico" (June 2004), 14, http://www.gao.gov/new.items/d0459.pdf (last visited December 16, 2008) [hereinafter GAO Report]. But see Alonzo, *Tejano Legacy*, 260 (contending instead that "about one thousand land grants were made in New Mexico during the entire span of Spanish-Mexican rule").

9. Gonzales, "Struggle for Survival," 298.

10. When the Colorado Territory was formed in 1861, the Surveyor General of Colorado was charged with investigating Spanish/Mexican land grants there; the Surveyor General of Arizona assumed the same responsibility for the Arizona Territory in 1863. GAO Report, 43. The Court of Private Land Claims, established in 1891 for New Mexico land claims, also had jurisdiction over unsettled Arizona and Colorado claims.

11. Alonzo, *Tejano Legacy*, 260 (of the 212 land grants submitted to the Surveyor General for consideration, Congress ultimately confirmed 48).

12. Previously, Spanish land grants had been resolved in Florida pursuant to an 1819 treaty, and in Louisiana under an 1803 treaty. See generally Ebright, *Land Grants*, 30–32.

13. Guadalupe T. Luna, "Chicana/Chicano Land Tenure in the Agrarian Domain: On the Edge of a 'Naked Knife,'" *Michigan Journal of Race and Law* 4 (1998): 39, 89 (stating that "during and after the Conquest, American governmental and military officials destroyed or ordered the destruction of land grant documents").

14. Gonzales, "Struggle for Survival," 306.

15. David G. Gutiérrez, *Walls and Mirrors: Mexican Americans, Mexican Immigrants, and the Politics of Ethnicity* (Berkeley: University of California Press, 1995), 23.

16. Weber, *Foreigners in Their Native Land*, 156.

17. *Botiller v. Dominguez*, 130 U.S. 238 (1889). By contrast, the 1891 act creating the Court of Private Land Claims primarily for New Mexico land grant claims specified that holders of title "complete and perfect" when the United States acquired sovereignty had the right, but were not bound, to apply for judicial confirmation of their title. Christine A. Klein, "Treaties of Conquest: Property Rights, Indian Treaties, and the Treaty of Guadalupe Hidalgo," *New Mexico Law Review* 26 (1996): 201, 227. See also *Ainsa v. New Mexico & A.R. Co.*, 175 U.S. 76 (1899) (under 1891 act applicable to New Mexico and Arizona, the United States could elect to challenge the validity of any grant, but the holder of a "complete and perfect" grant need not initiate proceedings to establish the grant).

18. *Botiller* 130 U.S. at 250.

19. *United States v. Sandoval*, 167 U.S. 278 (1897). Community land grants, therefore, were recognized only to the extent of their individual allotments to the collective members for their homes. GAO Report, 97. In the *Sandoval* litigation, the court confirmed title to only 5,207 acres of the 315,300-acre land grant. See also Reies López Tijerina, *They Called Me "King Tiger": My Struggle for the Land and Our Rights* (Houston: Arte Público Press, 2000), 93 (calling the Supreme Court one of the instruments used by Anglos to remove Mexicans from their lands and citing the *Sandoval* decision); Laura E. Gómez, *Manifest Destinies: The Making of the Mexican American Race* (New York: New York University Press, 2007) (detailing background of *Sandoval* litigation).

20. Ebright, *Land Grants*, 48–49 (noting that the Court of Private Land Claims did not apply the *Sandoval* decision retroactively, and thus community grants confirmed before the 1897 decision remained valid). Those community land grants previously confirmed later fell victim to state laws that permitted sale of the commons by the board of trustees, resulting in sales during the Great Depression when Latino/a ranchers were financially vulnerable. Gonzales, "Struggle for Survival," 309. Today, about twenty community land grants survive. Ibid., 312.

21. GAO Report, 151.

22. See American Bar Association Model Rules of Professional Responsibility, Rule 1.5 (prohibiting unreasonable fees) and Rule 1.8(i) ("A lawyer shall not acquire a proprietary interest in the cause of action or subject matter of litigation the lawyer is conducting for a client, except that the lawyer may: [1] acquire a lien authorized by law to secure the lawyer's fee or expenses; and [2] contract with a client for a reasonable contingent fee in a civil case."), http://www.abanet.org/cpr/mrpc/mrpc_toc.html (last visited November 11, 2009). See also *Peck v. Heurich*, 167 U.S. 624 (1897) (Supreme Court strikes down agreement allowing attorney to receive one-third of recovered real estate in District of Columbia, embracing an early version of this restriction on champertous fee agreements).

23. Ebright, *Land Grants*, 42–43 (explaining how, before the Supreme Court divested community land grants, lawyers owed fees used New Mexico's partition law to subvert the Spanish and Mexican systems of community land grants). For discussion on the modern loss of land by African Americans through partition sales of land held under tenancies in common, see Thomas W. Mitchell, "From Reconstruction to Deconstruction: Undermining Black Landownership, Political Independence, and Community through Partition Sales of Tenancies in Common," *Northwestern University Law Review* 95 (2001): 505.

24. Almaguer, *Racial Fault Lines*, 67 (quoting William A. Streeter, a European American pioneer).

25. Valentina Valdez Tijerina, "La Cooperativa," in *Aztlan: An Anthology of Mexican American Literature*, ed. Luis Valdez and Stan Steiner (New York: Alfred A. Knopf, 1973), 242, 244 (quoting Clark Knowlton and Frances Swadish).

26. See Barbara Marinacci and Rudy Marinacci, *California's Spanish Place-Names: What They Are and How They Got Here* (San Rafael, CA: Presidio Press, 1980), 155.

27. Tijerina, "La Cooperativa," 245.

28. Douglas Brinkley, *American Heritage History of the United States* (New York: Viking, 1998), 151.

29. Weber, *Foreigners in Their Native Land*, 148.

30. Marinacci and Marinacci, *California's Spanish Place-Names*, 152; Antonio María Pico et al., "Compelled to Sell, Little by Little by Little," in *Foreigners in Their Native Land*, 197.

31. Richard Griswold del Castillo, *The Los Angeles Barrio, 1850–1890* (Berkeley: University of California Press, 1979), 45; Pitt, *Decline of the Californios*, 96 (detailing how squatters terrorized rancho owners).

32. Pitt, *Decline of the Californios*, 97.

33. Del Castillo, *Los Angeles Barrio*, 42 (describing the influence of squatters on the California land certification bill).

34. Pico et al., "Compelled to Sell," 198; del Castillo, *Los Angeles Barrio*, 45.

35. Kutty, "Policy Lessons," 10.

36. GAO Report, 152–53 (detailing the loss of land grant property in New Mexico to tax sales).

37. Rodolfo Acuña, *Occupied America: A History of Chicanos*, 3d ed. (New York: Harper Collins, 1988), 116 (detailing discrepancy in tax burden placed on Southern California property).

38. Robert Sandoval, "Colorado's Hispanic Heritage: The People Who Paved the Way," *Denver Post Empire Magazine*, November 25, 1979, 26, 31.

39. Almaguer, *Racial Fault Lines*, 59; Gregory Rodriguez, *Mongrels, Bastards, Orphans, and Vagabonds: Mexican Immigration and the Future of Race in America* (New York: Pantheon Books, 2007), 117 ("[N]early every wealthy Mexican family in San Antonio had a daughter who married an Anglo.").

40. Almaguer, *Racial Fault Lines*, 85; Pitt, *Decline of the Californios*, 244–46.

41. Del Castillo, *Los Angeles Barrio*, 42.

42. Marinacci and Marinacci, *California's Spanish Place-Names*, 154.

43. Weber, *Foreigners in Their Native Land*, 156.

44. See del Castillo, *Los Angeles Barrio*, 46–48 (suggesting that property disenfranchisement nonetheless was underway in the city of Los Angeles during the 1850s, and

documenting how by 1860 only one in ten Mexican landholders from 1850 continued to own property in Los Angeles).

45. Richard Griswold del Castillo, *The Treaty of Guadalupe Hidalgo: A Legacy of Conflict* (Norman: University of Oklahoma Press, 1990), 64 (revealing that the repatriation of Mexicans from New Mexico had greater success, as between 1,500 and 2,000 returned).

46. Pitt, *Decline of the Californios*, 274–75 (noting that in about two years the Los Angeles population jumped 500 percent).

47. Paul W. Gates, "Adjudication of Spanish-Mexican Land Claims in California," *Huntington Library Quarterly* 3 (May 1958): 213, 232.

48. See, for example, Klein, "Treaties of Conquest," 218 ("In California, approximately twenty-seven percent of land grant claims were rejected; in the territory of New Mexico, some seventy-six percent of such claims were rejected.").

49. GAO Report, 7–8. The Report also suggests the lower certification rate argued by some scholars includes acreage covered by claims that were withdrawn and double counts some acreage.

50. Ibid., 8.

51. Ibid., 11, 147.

52. Scholars point to staggering overall losses in the New Mexico confirmation process. One study concluded that the Court of Private Land Claims rejected some 22,718,354 acres of land, and argues that nearly 16,000,000 of those acres were rejected unfairly. Alonzo, *Tejano Legacy*, 260–61 (citing Victor Westphall, *Mercedes Reales: Hispanic Land Grants of the Upper Rio Grande Region* [Albuquerque: University of New Mexico Press, 1983]). An Associate Justice of the Court of Private Land Claims reported to the New Mexico Bar Association in 1904 that the Court of Private Land Claims confirmed only three million of the thirty-six million acres for which confirmation was sought, with thirty-three million acres "restored to the public domain." Wilbur F. Stone, *Minutes of the New Mexico Bar Association* (1904), 18. For the Arizona experience, see Alonzo, *Tejano Legacy*, 263 (reporting that confirmed grants in Arizona encompassed only 116,540 of the 837,680 acres claimed, but noting much of the disallowed land was not part of the formal grant but had been used for grazing).

53. Alonzo, *Tejano Legacy*, 152–55 (detailing that after the commission ended its work in 1851, unadjudicated land claims in Texas were resolved by suit and confirmation in district court or by legislative confirmation).

54. Ibid., 161.

55. Weber, *Foreigners in Their Native Land*, 155.

56. Gutiérrez, *Walls and Mirrors*, 25 (citing historian David Montejano).

57. Christopher David Ruiz Cameron, "One Hundred Fifty Years of Solitude: Reflections on the End of the History Academy's Dominance of Scholarship on the Treaty of Guadalupe Hidalgo," *Southwestern Journal of Law and Trade in the Americas* 5 (1998): 83, 97–98.

58. Delgado and Stefancic, "What if John Calmore Had a Latino/a Sibling?" 786.

CHAPTER 3

1. *No Refuge from the Fields: Findings from a Survey of Farmworker Housing Conditions in the United States* (Washington DC: Housing Assistance Council, September 2001), 5 (citing 1997–98 National Agricultural Workers Survey).

2. Bender, *One Night in America*, 90.

3. Marc Cooper, "Sour Grapes: California Farm Workers' Endless Struggle 40 Years Later," *L.A. Weekly*, August 11, 2005, http://www.laweekly.com/2005-08-11/news/sour-grapes (last visited November 12, 2009) (quoting economist Rick Mines).

4. Kutty, "Policy Lessons," 47.

5. Smithsonian Institution, Washington, DC, *America on the Move*, http://americanhistory.si.edu/ONTHEMOVE/collection/object_1113.html (last visited January 17, 2009).

6. Alicia Bugarin and Elias Lopez, *Farmworkers in California* (Sacramento: California Research Bureau, July 1998), 23–24; *Migrant Farmworker Housing in California: A Study Pursuant to AB 3628* (Sacramento: California Department of Housing and Community Development, 1988).

7. Jorge Casuso, "Migrants Suffer in Fetid Camps," *Chicago Tribune*, September 15, 1991, C3.

8. Steven W. Bender, *Greasers and Gringos: Latinos, Law, and the American Imagination* (New York: New York University Press, 2003), 140.

9. Mario Obledo, "On the Braceros' Backs," *Seattle Post-Intelligencer*, January 30, 2000, G1.

10. Carla Marinucci, "Treated Like an Animal for Years," *San Francisco Examiner*, September 26, 1993, B1.

11. Steven Greenhouse, "As Economy Booms, Migrant Workers' Housing Worsens," *New York Times*, May 31, 1998, I1.

12. Arturo Rodriguez, president of United Farm Workers, "Should Anyone Live Like This?," posted at lared-l@listserv.cyberlatina.net, June 13, 2006.

13. Mike Anton, "In the Coachella Valley, Hope Withers on the Vine," *Los Angeles Times*, June 23, 2009, 1.

14. Glen Martin, "Napa Valley Celebrates the Good Life," *San Francisco Gate*, December 19, 2004, CM6.

15. *No Refuge from the Fields*, 9, 17, 24, 28 (also finding that among cost-burdened farm worker households, defined as those paying more than 30 percent of their monthly income on housing, 86 percent had children present in the home).

16. Ibid, 17.

17. Martin, "Napa Valley."

18. *No Refuge from the Fields*.

19. Ibid., 22.

20. *De Bruyn Produce Co. v. Romero*, 508 N.W.2d 150 (Mich. Ct. App. 1993) (Michigan landlord–tenant protections held inapplicable to farm workers who had no obligation to pay rent and were provided housing by employer in mobile home). But see *Vasquez v. Glassboro Service Ass'n*, 415 A.2d 1156 (N.J. 1980) (upon termination of employment Puerto Rican migratory worker was ordered to leave his employer-supplied barracks immediately; New Jersey Supreme Court held that although the migrant worker did not qualify as a tenant, he nonetheless could be evicted only by judicial proceedings as a tenant would).

21. See *Muniz v. Kravis*, 757 A.2d 1207 (Conn. App. Ct. 2000) (occupancy incidental to employment is a mere license that ceases when the employment terminates); but see S.C. Code Ann. § 27-35-130 (domestic servants entitled to twenty days' written notice before they must vacate the premises). See generally Mary Romero, *Maid in the U.S.A.* (New York: Routledge, 1992), 117 (detailing the subordination of live-in maids who, apart from their room, which may double as a storage room, are expected to avoid rest or leisure in other comfortable parts of the house except for the kitchen).

22. Ilene J. Jacobs, "Farmworker Housing in California," *La Raza Law Journal* 9 (1996): 177, 180.

23. Karen Gutierrez and Janice Morse, "New Immigrants: Safe, Decent Housing Hard to Come By," *Cincinnati Enquirer*, January 14, 2004, 1A.

24. Michelle Wilde Anderson, "Cities Inside Out: Race, Poverty, and Exclusion at the Urban Fringe," *UCLA Law Review* 55 (2008): 1095, 1102–6 (describing colonia communities in California's San Joaquin Valley and elsewhere in the United States).

25. Jane E. Larson, "Free Markets Deep in the Heart of Texas," *Georgetown Law Journal* 84 (1995): 179, 191–92.

26. See Kristen Rees, "Texas Colonias: A Paternalistic Depiction of Unconscionability at the Bottom of the Market," *Temple Political and Civil Rights Law Review* 16 (2006): 167, 181.

27. Peter M. Ward, *Colonias and Public Policy in Texas and Mexico: Urbanization by Stealth* (Austin: University of Texas Press, 1999), 3.

28. Nancy L. Simmons, "Memories and Miracles—Housing the Rural Poor along the United States–Mexico Border: A Comparative Discussion of Colonia Formation and Remediation in El Paso County, Texas, and Doña Ana County, New Mexico," *New Mexico Law Review* 27 (1997): 33, 64.

29. Consider the following example of the supposed cost-prohibitive economics of barracks regulation: "My company provided a dormitory for 25 single men. The housing was always inspected and found to be in compliance. A new federal regulation now says the housing is not in compliance based on a change in the square footage required per employee housed. The square footage change permitted us to accommodate only 14. Result: the cost is prohibitive for 14, so we eliminated the dormitory." *Migrant Farmworker Housing in California*, 30. A related strain on farmer-provided housing is the short harvest season. Housing away from the farm may allow more opportunities for alternative employment during the down-months, or at least for replacement tenants, whereas employer-provided property is situated only for farm worker tenants: "[T]he migrants are there only 3–4 months and what does the farmer do the rest of the year with those assets that are tied up in housing . . . ?" Ibid., 31.

30. Guadalupe T. Luna, "*Chasing Rural Democracy and 'Food Glorious Food': Farmers of Color and Anti-Trust Legislation*," forthcoming in *UCLA Chicana/o Latina/o Law Review* 28 (2010).

31. U.S. Department of Agriculture, *Counting Diversity in American Agriculture*, http://www.agcensus.usda.gov/Publications/2002/FINAL_Counting_Diversity_in_American_Ag.pdf (last visited September 2, 2008).

32. *Robledo Family Winery*, http://www.robledofamilywinery.com/the_robledo_story_vineyards.html (last visited August 17, 2008).

33. Marc Ramirez, "From Farmhand to Farm Owner," *Seattle Times*, July 2, 2006, A1.

CHAPTER 4

1. Ann Aurelia López, *The Farmworkers' Journey* (Berkeley: University of California Press, 2007), 152.

2. Alina Tugend, "The Least Affordable Place to Live? Try Salinas," *New York Times*, May 7, 2006, sec. 11, p. 1.

3. Miriam Jordan, "In Tony Monterey County, Slums and a Land War," *Wall Street Journal*, August 26, 2006, A1.

4. *Farmworker Housing and Health Needs Assessment Study of the Salinas and Pajaro Valleys* (Salinas, CA: Applied Survey Research and the Center for Community Advocacy, June 2001).

5. Ibid.

6. López, *Farmworkers' Journey*, 148.

7. Latino/as evoke many negative constructions in the American imagination. Elsewhere I have documented how many Americans regard Latino/as as criminally inclined, hot-tempered, lazy, welfare-minded, of lesser intelligence, thirsty for booze, sexually driven, and unwilling or unable to assimilate. Bender, *Greasers and Gringos*.

8. Mario T. García, "Americanization and the Mexican Immigrant, 1880–1930," in *From Different Shores: Perspectives on Race and Ethnicity in America*, ed. Ronald T. Takaki (New York: Oxford University Press, 1987), 73 (quoting *The Survey*).

9. Arnoldo De León, *They Called Them Greasers: Anglo Attitudes toward Mexicans in Texas, 1821–1900* (Austin: University of Texas Press, 1983), 21.

10. Richard Delgado, "Rodrigo's Corrido: Race, Postcolonial Theory, and U.S. Civil Rights," *Vanderbilt Law Review* 60 (2007): 1691, 1721. See also Daniel D. Arreola, "The Picture Postcard Mexican Housescape: Visual Culture and Domestic Identity," in *Landscape and Race in the United States*, ed. Richard H. Schein (New York: Routledge, 2006), 113 (describing how stereotypical images on popular postcards of Mexicans residing in primitive housing helped influence a pejorative view of Mexicans as homeowners).

11. See, generally, William Julius Wilson, *More Than Just Race: Being Black and Poor in the Inner City* (New York: W. W. Norton, 2009) (suggesting the interrelationships of structural and cultural explanations for racial inequalities).

12. John Steinbeck, *Tortilla Flat* (1935; reprint, New York: Penguin Books, 1997), 2.

13. Ibid., 5.

14. Ibid., 129.

15. Ibid., 142.

16. T. C. Boyle, *Tortilla Curtain* (New York: Penguin Books, 1995), 29.

17. Ibid., 127.

18. Ibid., 348.

19. John Nichols's *The Milagro Beanfield War* (New York: Holt, Rinehart and Winston, 1974), brought to film by Robert Redford, depicts a southwestern Latino who husbands a bean field in a tribute to enterprise. Still, he procures the necessary water supply illegally by tapping into an irrigation channel, avoiding one stereotype but invoking the familiar media image of the Latino/a as a trespasser and a thief.

20. Sandra Cisneros, *The House on Mango Street* (New York: Vintage Books, 1984), 108.

21. John Steinbeck, foreword to *Tortilla Flat* (New York: Modern Library, Random House, 1937), n.p.

22. See *City of Monterey v. Jacks*, 73 P. 436 (Cal. 1903).

23. See, generally, Peter L. Reich, "Dismantling the Pueblo: Hispanic Municipal Land Rights in California Since 1850," *American Journal of Legal History* 45 (October 2001): 353. The irony of the Monterey outcome is that the municipality might have retained most of its land had it bargained with the lawyer at the outset to pay the legal fee with a portion of the land being confirmed. Instead, it suffered loss of the whole land grant to pay the legal bill.

24. Bruce Ariss, *Inside Cannery Row: Sketches from the Steinbeck Era* (San Francisco: Lexikos, 1988), 9.

25. Steinbeck, *Tortilla Flat* (1997), 2.

26. For example, two tiny homes in the hills above Monterey Bay were listed for sale in summer 2007 at $599,000 (676 square feet, built in 1919) and $575,000 (600 square feet, built in 1941); Multiple Listing Numbers 729741, 720279.

27. "Latino Homeowners Claim Discrimination in Loans—Salinas, California," *Monterey County Herald*, November 30, 2007, http://www.hispanictips.com/2007/11/30/latino-home-owners-claim-discrimination-loans-salinas-california/ (last visited December 9, 2008).

CHAPTER 5

1. Richard Metcalf, "American Nightmare," *Albuquerque Journal*, December 16, 2007, C1.

2. Bowdler, *Jeopardizing Hispanic Homeownership*, 3 (2003 statistic).

3. Douglas S. Massey, "Origins of Economic Disparities: The Historical Role of Housing Segregation," in *Segregation: The Rising Costs for America*, ed. James H. Carr and Nandinee K. Kutty (New York: Routledge, 2008), 71.

4. Benjamin Howell, "Exploiting Race and Space: Concentrated Subprime Lending as Housing Discrimination," *California Law Review* 94 (2006): 101, 107–8; Becky M. Nicolaides, *My Blue Heaven: Life and Politics in the Working-Class Suburbs of Los Angeles, 1920–1965* (Chicago: University of Chicago Press, 2002), 179, 189, 192.

5. Nicolaides, *My Blue Heaven*, 192.

6. Ibid., 193.

7. Ibid., 72.

8. Rodney Hero, *Latinos and the U.S. Political System: Two-Tiered Pluralism* (Philadelphia: Temple University Press, 1992), 169.

9. Ronald Brownstein, "A Crisis within a Crisis," *Los Angeles Times*, February 1, 2008, A27.

10. Richard Williams, Reynold Nesiba, and Eileen Diaz McConnell, "The Changing Face of Inequality in Home Mortgage Lending," *Social Problems* 52 (2005): 181, 189 (providing this example of subprime lending economics).

11. Dickerson, "Myth of Home Ownership," 203.

12. See *Martinez v. Freedom Mortgage Team, Inc.*, 527 F. Supp. 2d 827 (N.D. Ill. 2007) (Latino borrower states cause of action under federal Fair Housing Act and Equal Credit Opportunity Act by alleging that lender knew its payment of yield spread premiums to mortgage brokers was causing brokers to target racial minorities for excessive rate loans).

13. "One Street's Subprime Struggle," *Orange County Register*, August 12, 2007, Marketplace-1.

14. Dickerson, "Myth of Home Ownership," 204.

15. William C. Apgar and Allegra Calder, "The Dual Mortgage Market: The Persistence of Discrimination in Mortgage Lending," in *The Geography of Opportunity: Race and Housing Choice in Metropolitan America*, ed. Xavier de Souza Briggs (Washington, DC: Brookings Institution Press, 2005), 101, 104 (noting that in 1980, almost half of mortgage loans were made by thrift institutions such as savings and loans, and commercial banks accounted for another 22 percent of mortgage loans).

16. Ibid. (nearly 70 percent of home loans are securitized and sold on the secondary mortgage market).

17. Vicki Been, Ingrid Ellen, and Josiah Madar, "The High Cost of Segregation: Exploring Racial Disparities in High-Cost Lending," *Fordham Urban Law Journal* 36 (2009): 361.

18. Manny Fernandez, "Racial Disparity Found among New Yorkers with High-Rate Mortgages," *New York Times*, October 15, 2007, B1.

19. Hortense Leon, "High Hopes for Immigrant Homeownership," *Mortgage Banking* (October 1999): 29.

20. Sue Kirchhoff, "Higher Subprime Rates for Blacks, Hispanics Baffling," *USA Today*, September 13, 2007, 9A.

21. "One Street's Subprime Struggle."

22. Fernandez, "Racial Disparity" (the subprime rate for Black borrowers of this income level was a staggering 62 percent).

23. Kochhar, Gonzalez-Barrera, and Dockterman, *Through Boom and Bust*, v (providing these statistics for so-called higher-priced home purchase loans, defined as loans with interest rates that exceed the rate on U.S. Treasury securities of similar maturity by at least 3 percent, in the case of a first lien).

24. Binyamin Appelbaum, "Fed Report Shows Racial Gap in Home Loan Rates," *Charlotte Observer*, September 13, 2007, 1D.

25. Bowdler, *Jeopardizing Hispanic Homeownership*, 3.

26. Ibid., 14; Calvin Bradford, *Risk or Race? Racial Disparities and the Subprime Refinance Market* (Washington, DC: Center for Community Change, May 2002) (stating Freddie Mac estimated in 1997 that some 10 to 30 percent of subprime mortgage borrowers could have qualified for conventional loans).

27. Stuart T. Rossman, "Selected Hot Topics in Auto, Mortgage, and Subprime Lending," *Practicing Law Institute*, no. 11165 (March–May 2007).

28. Congressional Testimony of David Berenbaum, Executive Vice President, National Community Reinvestment Coalition, June 27, 2007, Committee on Senate Banking, Housing and Urban Affairs Subcommittee on Housing, Transportation and Community Development.

29. Jennifer Delson and Christopher Goffard, "Mortgages Written in English Can Be Misleading," *Press of Atlantic City*, November 25, 2007, D1.

30. *Vasquez-Lopez v. Beneficial Oregon, Inc.*, 152 P.3d 940 (Or. Ct. App. 2007). A lawsuit filed in California in 2007 on behalf of four Latino/a families claimed they were assured in Spanish by a developer's sales representative that the homes they were buying were guaranteed with a money-back promise, an assurance at odds with the untranslated documents written in English. Larry Parsons, "Latino Homeowners Claim Discrimination in Loans," *Monterey County Herald*, November 29, 2007, B1.

31. Steven W. Bender, "Consumer Protection for Latinos: Overcoming Language Fraud and English-Only in the Marketplace," *American University Law Review* 45 (1996): 1027, 1044–45. The act permits Spanish disclosures in the Commonwealth of Puerto Rico if English disclosures are available on request.

32. Leon, "High Hopes," 30.

33. Bowdler, *Jeopardizing Hispanic Homeownership*, 11.

34. Tim Iglesias, "State and Local Regulation of Particular Types of Affordable Housing," in *The Legal Guide to Affordable Housing Development*, ed. Tim Iglesias and Rochelle E. Lento (Chicago: American Bar Association, 2006), 113, 118.

35. Apgar and Calder, "Dual Mortgage Market," 108.

36. Ibid.

37. John Emmeus Davis, "Between Devolution and the Deep Blue Sea: What's a City or State to Do?" in *A Right to Housing: Foundation for a New Social Agenda*, ed. Rachel G. Bratt, Michael E. Stone, and Chester Hartman (Philadelphia: Temple University Press, 2006), 364, 375.

38. Viji Sundaram, "New Legislation Targets Sub-Prime Loans, But Is It Too Late for Black, Latino Families," *Athens News*, January 7, 2008, 30.

39. Juan Gonzalez, "Set Up for a Fall," *New York Daily News*, March 28, 2007, 13 (statistics from report by Center for Responsible Lending).

40. Dickerson, "Myth of Home Ownership," 207.

41. Mark Hugo Lopez, Gretchen Livingston, and Rakesh Kochhar, *Hispanics and the Economic Downturn: Housing Woes and Remittance Cuts* (Washington, DC: Pew Hispanic Center, January 8, 2009), http://pewhispanic.org/files/reports/100.pdf.

42. Jerry Kronenberg, "Study: Minorities' 'Dream' Foreclosed," *Boston Herald*, January 15, 2008, 22.

43. Raul Hinojosa-Ojeda, Albert Jacquez, and Paule Cruz Takash, *The End of the American Dream for Blacks and Latinos: How the Home Mortgage Crisis Is Destroying Black and Latino Wealth, Jeopardizing America's Future Prosperity, and How to Fix It*, William C. Velasquez Institute White Paper (San Antonio: William C. Velasquez Institute, June 2009).

44. *State of the Nation's Housing 2009*, 9.

45. Apgar and Calder, "Dual Mortgage Market," 118.

46. See Dickerson, "Myth of Home Ownership," 209–10 (remarking on the effect of foreclosure on one's credit rating and the need to replenish monies lost in the foreclosed investment as constraining re-entering the purchase market for a decade).

47. Kathleen C. Engel and Patricia A. McCoy, "From Credit Denial to Predatory Lending: The Challenge of Sustaining Minority Homeownership," in *Segregation: The Rising Costs for America*, ed. James H. Carr and Nandinee K. Kutty (New York: Routledge, 2008), 99.

48. Ibid.

PART II

1. Robert G. Schwemm, "Cox, Halprin, and Discriminatory Municipal Services under the Fair Housing Act," *Indiana Law Review* 41 (2008): 717 (discussing cases brought as equal protection challenges, as well as recent case law rejecting most claims against municipalities under federal Fair Housing Act for discriminatory services).

2. David B. Bryson, "The Role of Courts and a Right to Housing," in *A Right to Housing: Foundation for a New Social Agenda*, ed. Rachel G. Bratt, Michael E. Stone, and Chester Hartman (Philadelphia: Temple University Press, 2006), 193, 203.

CHAPTER 6

1. Cenia Alvarado-Beltre and Patricia Pedraza, "Recession Lands Immigrants in 'Devil's Cave,'" www.cnn.com/2009/US/01/29/porch.cave/ (posted January 29, 2009; last visited January 29, 2009).

2. J. W. Ehrlich, *Ehrlich's Blackstone* (San Carlos, CA: Nourse Publishing Co., 1959), 576. But see John G. Sprankling, "The Antiwilderness Bias in American Property Law," *University of Chicago Law Review* 63 (1996), 519 (noting that in contrast to the English doctrine, which considered entry by neighboring animals to graze as a trespass, an American "free range" view emerged that allowed public grazing on unenclosed private wilderness property).

3. *Keziah v. Seaboard Air Line R. Co.*, 158 S.E.2d 539, 548 (N.C. 1968).

4. Ehrlich, *Ehrlich's Blackstone*, 578.

5. See, generally, Jerry L. Anderson, "Britain's Right to Roam: Redefining the Landowner's Bundle of Sticks," *Georgetown International Environmental Law Review* 19 (2007): 375 (describing the Countryside and Rights of Way Act 2000 that gives Britain's public the right to walk over private land containing mountains, moors, heath, or downland). This statutory right goes well beyond the rights established by the common law doctrine of custom that required a showing of customary use of the actual trail. In other countries such as Sweden, Finland, and Norway, the public enjoys rights of *allemansrätten*—a right of access over private land that does not interfere with privacy (such as near dwellings) or crops, and which is steeped in the doctrine of custom. Ibid., 391, 404. The custom doctrine has been recognized by some U.S. jurisdictions, such as in Oregon, where the Oregon Supreme Court employed the custom doctrine to impose the equivalent of a public easement on the dry sand area of its coastline. *State ex rel. Thornton v. Hay*, 462 P.2d 671 (Or. 1969). See also *McKee v. Gratz*, 260 U.S. 127 (1922) (acknowledging the custom in many parts of the country of hunting and fishing on large expanses of unenclosed and uncultivated land); *Public Access Shoreline Hawaii v. Hawai'i County Planning Comm'n*, 903 P.2d 1246 (Haw. 1995) (protecting customary access rights of Native Hawaiians in issuance of property development permits). Query whether the doctrine of custom supports a right of Mexican residents to cross onto privately held property in the United States as a retracing of indigenous routes and wanderings in the borderlands.

6. Tom I. Romero II, "The 'Tri-Ethnic' Dilemma: Race, Equality, and the Fourteenth Amendment in the American West," *Temple Political and Civil Rights Law Review* 13 (2004): 817; Cullen, *The American Dream*, 141 (at the time of the Homestead Act's passage eighty-three million acres were included, and another fifteen million were added later from California, Colorado, Washington, and Wisconsin—perhaps in California and Colorado the added acreage came from land failing certification by Latino/as, addressed in chapter 2).

7. Marc Stimpert, "Counterpoint: Opportunities Lost and Opportunities Gained: Separating Truth from Myth in the Western Ranching Debate," *Environmental Law* 36 (2006): 481, 489–94.

8. Away from the borderlands, Victor Davis Hanson wrote of his encounters with undocumented immigrants trespassing on his central California farm: "But increasingly, keeping illegal aliens and Mexican gang members off the property is a hopeless task; in the banter that follows my requests, some trespassers seem piqued that anyone in California should dare to insist on the archaic notion of property rights. One especially smart teenager told me in broken English, 'Hey, it's our land anyway—not yours.'" Victor Davis Hanson, *Mexifornia: A State of Becoming* (San Francisco: Encounter Books, 2003), 64.

9. *In re Hartman*, 210 P.2d 53 (Cal. Dist. Ct. App. 1949) (upholding the trial court order making the boys wards of the state and requiring them to pay restitution to the parents of the dead Mexican boy for funeral and medical bills).

10. Peter Laufer, *Wetback Nation: The Case for Opening the Mexican-American Border* (Chicago: Ivan R. Dee, 2004), 96.

11. Jerry Seper, "16 Illegals Sue Arizona Rancher," *Washington Times*, February 9, 2009, A03; "Arizona Jury Finds Vigilante Rancher Liable for Attack on Immigrants," http://www.maldef.org/news/releases/vicente_barnett_2_18_09/index.html (posted February 18, 2009; last visited February 21, 2009).

12. The Arizona Supreme Court refused to hear Barnett's appeal in 2008, effectively ending the case.

13. Andrew Pollack, "2 Illegal Immigrants Win Arizona Ranch in Court," *New York Times*, August 19, 2005, A16.

14. See Susy Buchanan, "Will Gun-Toting Vigilante Get the Justice He Deserves?" www.alternet.com/rights/51084/will_gun-toting_vigilante_get_the_justice_he_deserves/ (posted April 30, 2007; last visited September 14, 2007).

15. Tom Tancredo, *In Mortal Danger: The Battle for America's Border and Security* (Nashville: Cumberland House Publishing, 2006), 177. Fear of Latino/a interlopers is not limited to undocumented immigrants. When the United Farm Workers proposed an initiative to California voters in 1976 that authorized union organizers to enter the fields to talk with workers, opponents tapped into stereotypes of the criminally depraved Mexican to help defeat the proposal. Presenting the initiative as a threat to property rights and the safety of the farmer's family, one advertisement opposing the measure featured a woman peering nervously out her farmhouse window, conveying the implicit message, "Do you want a Mexican on your property attacking your daughter?" See Bender, *Greasers and Gringos*, 139.

16. Restatement (Second) of Torts § 197 (1965).

17. Robert F. Castro, "Exorcising Tombstone's Evil Spirits: Eradicating Vigilante Ranch Enterprises through Public Interest Litigation," *Law and Inequality: A Journal of Theory and Practice* 20 (2002): 203, 234 (noting the migrants are in transit rather than invading the land, thus obviating concerns of adverse possession). See also *Nome 2000 v. Fagerstrom*, 799 P.2d 304 (Alaska 1990) (use of trails insufficient for adverse possession). But query whether the threat of the legal doctrine of prescriptive easement or the doctrine of custom exists where crossings are sustained on a specific trail over the ranchland. See, for example, *State* ex rel. *Thornton v. Hay*, 462 P.2d 671 (Or. 1969) (conferring easement rights to public in beach dry sand area by custom based on ancient, uninterrupted use of property so long "the memory of man runneth not to the contrary").

18. The most famous of these decisions, *State v. Shack*, 277 A.2d 369 (N.J. 1971), reversed the trespass convictions of a legal aid lawyer and a health services worker who insisted on visiting farm workers residing in the employer's camp in the privacy of their living quarters rather than in the employer's office with the employer present; holding the "employer may not deny the worker his privacy or interfere with his opportunity to live with dignity and to enjoy associations customary among our citizens."). See also *People v. Medrano*, 144 Cal. Rptr. 217 (Ct. App. 1978) (free speech rights of union organizers visiting farm worker tenants on employer's property outweighed the property interest and thus trespass law could not be constitutionally applied); *Franceschina v. Morgan*, 346 F. Supp. 833 (S.D. Ind. 1972) (enjoining employer from interfering with free speech right of union organizers to visit migrant labor camps on employer's property). The *Shack* case may be distinguishable on the ground that it focused on the right of the worker, already residing on the property with permission from the owner, to receive visitors, as opposed to the rights to entry of the

visiting social worker and lawyer. In the case of a border crosser, the ranch owner has not given permission to anyone to enter or remain on his ranch property.

19. Yvonne Abraham, "N.H. Police Chief's Tactics Stir a Storm on Immigration," *Boston Globe*, May 22, 2005, A1.

20. Ibid.

21. N.H. Rev. Stat. § 635:2. A violation of this provision is typically punishable by a fine of up to $1,000, without jail time.

22. Abraham, "N.H. Police Chief's Tactics."

23. Pam Belluck, "Town Uses Trespass Law to Fight Illegal Immigrants," http://www.virginiacops.org/News-Resources/articles/News2005/July05/Illegals.htm (last visited December 18, 2008) (remarks of law professor Kris Kobach); see generally Kris W. Kobach, "The Quintessential Force Multiplier: The Inherent Authority of Local Police to Make Immigration Arrests," *Albany Law Review* 69 (2005): 179.

24. Pam Belluck, "Towns Lose Tool against Illegal Immigrants," *New York Times*, August 13, 2005, A7. See also Michael R. Boland, Jr., "Comment, No Trespassing: The States, the Supremacy Clause, and the Use of Criminal Trespass Laws to Fight Illegal Immigration," *Penn State Law Review* 111 (2006): 481, 501–2 (agreeing that, given the wide variation among these laws, trespass prosecution by states would frustrate the federal objective of uniformity in immigration enforcement; some such laws [for example, New Hampshire's] seem to encompass undocumented immigrants, while others [such as Indiana's] are written more narrowly and do not appear amenable to a construction to encompass undocumented immigrants).

25. Mari Lolli, "Cracking Down on Illegal Aliens," *Cincinnati Post*, October 22, 2005, A10.

26. Corey Dolgon, *The End of the Hamptons: Scenes from the Class Struggle in America's Paradise* (New York: New York University Press, 2005), 81.

27. See the documentary film *Farmingville*, dir. Carlos Sandoval and Catherine Tambini (Camino Bluff Productions, 2004).

28. Jon Ward, "Arrests Not Linked to Illegals Crackdown," *Washington Times*, October 29, 2004, B1.

29. *City of Chicago v. Morales*, 527 U.S. 41 (1999).

30. *Comite de Jornaleros de Redondo Beach v. City of Redondo Beach*, 475 F. Supp. 2d 952 (C.D. Cal. 2006); see also Nicholas Shields, "Ruling Aids Day Laborers," *Los Angeles Times*, May 19, 2005, B3 (federal judge strikes down Glendale, California, ordinance against curbside solicitation by day laborers). Some cities have also sought to outlaw or heavily regulate so-called taco trucks operated mostly by Latino/a immigrants. See Miguel Bustillo, "Hold the Tacos, New Orleans Says," *Los Angeles Times*, July 14, 2007, A1.

31. *Lopez v. Town of Cave Creek, Arizona*, 559 F. Supp. 2d 1030 (D. Ariz. 2008) (relying on First Amendment as applicable to local government under the Fourteenth Amendment).

32. Randal C. Archibold, "Immigrants Work on as Bill Dies and Views Divide," *New York Times*, June 30, 2007, A1. See also the documentary film *The Invisible Mexicans of Deer Canyon*, dir. John Carlos Frey (Gatekeeper Productions LLC, 2006) (showing the handmade sleeping shacks of these Latino/a day laborers made from scrap lumber and plastic tarping, as well as the constant push from local officials who demolish the shacks and force the residents deeper into the rugged countryside; disdaining the expense of a

$700 per month furnished room in Escondido, one laborer revealed, "If I live this kind of [simple] life here [my family in Mexico] will benefit").

33. Marisa Bono, "Don't You Be My Neighbor: Restrictive Housing Ordinances as the New Jim Crow," *Modern American* (Summer–Fall 2007): 29, 31.

34. Rigel C. Oliveri, "Between Rock and Hard Place: Landlords, Latinos, Anti-Illegal Immigrant Ordinances, and Housing Discrimination," *Vanderbilt Law Review* 62 (2009): 80.

35. *Garrett v. City of Escondido*, 465 F. Supp. 2d 1043 (S.D. Cal. 2006) (issuing temporary restraining order).

36. *Villas at Parkside Partners v. City of Farmers Branch*, 496 F. Supp. 2d 757 (N.D. Tex. 2007).

37. Virginia Martinez, Jazmin Garcia, and Jasmine Vasquez, "A Community under Siege: The Impact of Anti-Immigrant Hysteria on Latinos," *DePaul Journal for Social Justice* 2 (2008): 101, 129. The City of Valley Park eventually repealed the housing ordinance, but a challenge to the complementary ordinance barring employment of the undocumented failed after the city removed the litigation to federal court. See *Gray v. City of Valley Park, Mo.*, 567 F.3d 976 (8th Cir. 2009).

38. *Lozano v. City of Hazleton*, 496 F. Supp. 2d 477 (M.D. Pa. 2007). Query the enforceability of a restrictive covenant among neighbors denying sales or rentals to undocumented immigrants or even to noncitizens regardless of their legal status. Although such a covenant is private rather than public, arguably its judicial enforcement would offend the supremacy clause through state action running contrary to federal immigration law, as the *Lozano* case found in denying enforcement of the Hazelton ordinance. As discussed in chapter 7, such a covenant could also offend the Equal Protection Clause if there was evidence of anti-Latino/a animus in its adoption. Alternatively, the *Lozano* case concluded the Hazelton ordinance violated 42 U.S.C. § 1981, which ensures that all persons have the same ability to make contracts as White persons. Because that statute encompasses nongovernmental discrimination, this lower court holding could invalidate private restrictive covenants as well. Still, the Supreme Court has not resolved the application of this federal statute to protect aliens generally or undocumented immigrants specifically. Finally, such restrictive covenants might also run afoul of constraints on private contracts sourced in public policy. For example, a covenant against sale or rental to the undocumented would invite racial profiling that could even violate the federal Fair Housing Act. Moreover, the presence of such a covenant might chill occupancy by Latino/a families of U.S. citizens or documented immigrants who, while not violating the covenant, would not want to face the prospect of scrutiny by neighbors as to their documentation. See Oliveri, "Between Rock and Hard Place" (arguing Hazelton-type ordinances violate the Fair Housing Act based on likely racial profiling in which a landlord might request documentation from someone with Latino/a appearance but not from individuals who appear to be Anglo).

39. Oliveri, "Between Rock and Hard Place," 117 (observing the difference between current federal databases on work-authorized individuals and a hypothetical database of every legally present noncitizen).

40. Cal. Civ. Code § 1940.3.

41. A website was created by one boycott organizer. See http://www.bankofamericaboycott.com (last visited September 19, 2008).

42. Nancy Mullane, "Politics Undercut Mortgages for Illegal Workers," http://www.npr.org/templates/story/story.php?storyId=96557544 (posted November 4, 2008; last visited November 11, 2008).

43. Miriam Jordan, "Mortgage Prospects Dim for Illegal Immigrants," *Wall Street Journal*, October 22, 2008, A3.

44. See 48 U.S.C. §§ 1501, 1502 (no alien or noncitizen shall own any land in the Territories of the United States, but exempting bona fide resident aliens).

45. See *Fujii v. State*, 242 P.2d 617 (Cal. 1952).

46. *Terrace v. Thompson*, 263 U.S. 197 (1923); see generally Keith Aoki, "No Right to Own? The Early Twentieth-Century 'Alien Land Laws' as a Prelude to Internment," *Boston College Law Review* 40 (1998): 37.

47. *Namba v. McCourt*, 204 P.2d 569 (Or. 1949), *Fujii v. State*, 242 P.2d 617 (Cal. 1952).

48. 242 P.2d at 630. Congress eventually lifted the naturalization restrictions on Asians, and thus would have nullified most of the effect of those Alien Land Laws directed at persons ineligible for naturalization.

49. See generally James A. Frechter, "Note, Alien Landownership in the United States: A Matter of State Control," *Brooklyn Journal of International Law* 4 (1988): 147.

50. States that restrict ownership of property by nonresident aliens include Kentucky (Ky. Rev. Stat. Ann. § 381.320), Mississippi (Miss. Code Ann. § 89-1-23; but allowing nonresident aliens to hold up to five acres of land for residential purposes and 320 acres for purposes of industrial development), Oklahoma (Okla. Stat. Ann. tit. 60, §§ 121, 122), and Wisconsin (Wis. Stat. Ann. § 710.02; prohibiting aliens not resident of a state of the United States from owning more than 640 acres of land in Wisconsin; upheld against equal protection and treaty power challenges in *Lehndorff Geneva, Inc. v. Warren*, 246 N.W.2d 815 [Wis. 1976]). States that restrict the ownership by aliens of farmland include Minnesota (Minn. Stat. Ann. § 500.221) (only resident aliens and citizens allowed to purchase) and Missouri (Mo. Ann. Stat. § 442.571).

51. Jill Esbenshade, *Division and Dislocation: Regulating Immigration through Local Housing Ordinances* (Washington, DC: Immigration Policy Center, Summer 2007), 12–13 (remarks of president of Hispanic Bar Association).

CHAPTER 7

1. *Philosophy and Mission Statement of the Sachem Quality of Life Organization*, http://www.cir-usa.org/articles/perez_SQL_mission_stmt.htm (last visited September 29, 2008).

2. Michael Rothfield, Theresa Vargas, and Denise M. Bonilla, "A Street Divided," *Newsday*, July 18, 2005, A8.

3. See Norman Williams, Jr., and Thomas Norman, "Exclusionary Land Use Controls: The Case of North-Eastern New Jersey," *Syracuse Law Review* 22 (1971): 475 (identifying exclusionary techniques in northern New Jersey counties before the *Mount Laurel* litigation to include minimum floor space and lot size, and exclusion of multifamily dwellings).

4. *NAACP v. City of Kyle*, No. A-05-CA-979-LY (W.D. Tex. Mar. 30, 2009) (judge ruled plaintiffs failed to show that the amended ordinances made housing unavailable to minorities in disproportionate numbers).

5. Rolf Pendall et al., "Connecting Smart Growth, Housing Affordability, and Racial Equity" in *The Geography of Opportunity: Race and Housing Choice in Metropolitan America*, ed. Xavier de Souza Briggs (Washington, DC: Brookings Institution Press, 2005), 230.

6. John A. Powell, "Reflections on the Past, Looking to the Future: The Fair Housing Act at 40," *Indiana Law Review* 41 (2008): 605, 614.

7. Wilson, *More Than Just Race*, 33.

8. Chris Kirkham, "Parish's Housing Ban Gets Tossed," *Times-Picayune*, March 27, 2009, B1.

9. Charisse Jones, "Crowded Houses Gaining Attention in Suburbs," *USA Today*, January 31, 2006, 5A.

10. Leo R. Chávez and Rebecca G. Martínez, "Mexican Immigration in the 1980s and Beyond: Implications for Chicanas/os," in *Chicanas/Chicanos at the Crossroads: Social, Economic, and Political Change*, ed. David R. Maciel and Isidro D. Ortiz (Tucson: University of Arizona Press, 1996), 25, 38.

11. See Iglesias, "State and Local Regulation of Particular Types of Affordable Housing," 126–30 (discussing local regulation of accessory dwelling units).

12. Alternatively, the Manassas ordinance did permit up to three unrelated people in a single household unit. Thus, for example, a group of three friends might share a house, but if one were to marry, the spouse joining the household would exceed the legal limit.

13. Stephanie McCrummen, "Manassas Defends New Rule on Who Can Live Together," *Washington Post*, December 30, 2005, B1.

14. Bender, *Greasers and Gringos*, 114–17 (detailing stereotypical visions of Latino/as as unclean).

15. Stephanie McCrummen, "Anti-Crowding Law Repealed," *Washington Post*, January 12, 2006, A1.

16. See, for example, William M. Randle, "Professors, Reformers, Bureaucrats, and Cronies: The Players in *Euclid v. Ambler*," in *Zoning and the American Dream: Promises Still to Keep*, ed. Charles M. Haar and Jerold S. Kayden (Chicago: Planners Press, 1989), 31, 40–41.

17. Rachel D. Godsil, "Race Nuisance: The Politics of Law in the Jim Crow Era," *Michigan Law Review* 105 (2006): 505, 539 (detailing ordinances in the days of separate-but-equal jurisprudence to include those that "sought to keep each block either all white or all black by prohibiting anyone of a different race from entering, others divided the municipality into distinct racial districts, some limited new entrants to a particular block to the race of the majority of current residents, and one, New Orleans, required new residents of a particular race to obtain the consent of the current residents if of a different race").

18. Ivan Light, *Deflecting Immigration: Networks, Markets, and Regulation in Los Angeles* (New York: Russell Sage Foundation, 2006), 75.

19. Ibid., 76.

20. See, for example, Christopher Caldwell, "The Way We Live Now: A Family or a Crowd?" *New York Times*, February 26, 2006, sec. 6, p. 9. See also Susan Blank and Ramon S. Torrecilha, "Understanding the Living Arrangements of Latino Immigrants: A Life Course Approach," *International Migration Review* 32 (1998): 3, 10–11 ("Mexican immigrants, for example, are often young men who are either single or who migrate without their spouses and children. For these reasons, Mexican men are more likely to share a household with extended kin, and it is not until marriage or family reunification that an independent household becomes preferable.").

21. Ellen J. Pader, "Space of Hate: Ethnicity, Architecture and Housing Discrimination," *Rutgers Law Review* 54 (2002): 881, 887.

22. Ready, *Hispanic Housing*.

23. Eileen Diaz McConnell and Timothy J. Ready, *The Roof over Our Heads: Hispanic Housing in the United States* (South Bend, IN: University of Notre Dame Institute for Latino Studies, June 2005), 14.

24. Charisse Jones, "Communities Crack Down on Overcrowded Homes," *USA Today*, January 31, 2006, 1A.

25. Hugo Martin, "War on Illegal Garage Units Softened," *Los Angeles Times*, June 5, 1997, B1 (reporting the mid-1990s estimate of 200,000 people in Los Angeles living in more than 42,000 garage residences). See also Light, *Deflecting Immigration*, 77 ("Occupied garages emerged in [Los Angeles] as colorful, regional solutions to high housing costs. Lacking plumbing, heating, ventilation, and windows, and lit only by one dangling light bulb, unconverted garages could not legally serve as residences. However, facing high housing costs, poor immigrant families sublet the detached garage to even poorer families. Mornings and evenings, garage dwellers emptied their slop bucket into the toilet in the main house and showered.").

26. Dolores Hayden, *Building Suburbia: Green Fields and Urban Growth, 1820–2000* (New York: Vintage Books, 2003), 13.

27. Jones, "Communities Crack Down."

28. Jones, "Crowded Houses Gaining."

29. *Yick Wo v. Hopkins*, 118 U.S. 356 (1886); see generally Lisa C. Young, "Breaking the Color Line: Zoning and Opportunity in America's Metropolitan Areas," *Journal of Gender, Race and Justice* 8 (2005): 667.

30. Frank S. Alexander, "The Housing of America's Families: Control, Exclusion, and Privilege," *Emory Law Journal* 54 (2005): 1231, 1251.

31. *Buchanan v. Warley*, 245 U.S. 60, 70 (1917) (taken from text of ordinance).

32. Carol Rose, "Property Stories: *Shelley v. Kraemer*," in *Property Stories*, ed. Gerald Korngold and Andrew P. Morriss (New York: Foundation Press, 2004), 169, 174 (suggesting that the race-neutral terms of the Louisville ordinance presumably were drafted in line with the then-prevailing separate-but-equal segregationist protocol of *Plessy v. Ferguson*).

33. *Buchanan v. Warley*, 245 U.S. 60, 70 (1917), 81. The Court concluded that this ordinance was "in direct violation of the fundamental laws enacted by the Fourteenth Amendment of the Constitution preventing state interference with property rights except by due process of law." Ironically, then, the decision striking down the discriminatory ordinance was grounded in protection of the substantive rights of property owners to sell their property to a person of their choosing, rather than in the antidiscrimination guarantees of the Equal Protection Clause. See generally Jon C. Dubin, "From Junkyards to Gentrification: Explicating a Right to Protective Zoning in Low-Income Communities of Color," *Minnesota Law Review* 77 (1993): 739, 744–46. See also *Harmon v. Tyler*, 273 U.S. 668 (1927) (striking down a similar ordinance forbidding Blacks from establishing residence in a White community "except on the written consent of a majority of the persons of the opposite race inhabiting such community or portion of the City to be affected"). See generally Godsil, "Race Nuisance," 539–42.

34. Jones, "Crowded Houses Gaining."

35. Bruce Lambert, "L.I. Home Held up to 64 Men, Authorities Say," *New York Times*, June 21, 2005, B1.

36. Jones, "Communities Crack Down."

37. Anna Gorman, "Escondido Is Using a Wave of Policies to Try to Drive Away Illegal Immigrants," *Los Angeles Times*, July 13, 2008, B1.

38. Anabelle Garay, "Hispanics See Red over Proposal," *Eagle* (Bryan-College Station, TX), October 11, 2007, A9. Author Sandra Cisneros sparked a similar controversy when she painted her home in a San Antonio historical district a periwinkle purple, http://www.accd.edu/sac/english/mcquien/htmlfils/kingwill.htm (last visited January 4, 2010). When the sun faded the house paint to blue, Cisneros repainted her home pink, http://www.sandracisneros.com/bio.php (last visited January 4, 2010).

39. *United States v. Fawley*, 137 F.3d 458 (7th Cir. 1998).

40. To establish race-based challenges to official action under the Equal Protection Clause requires proof of racially discriminatory intent or purpose, rather than a mere showing of racially disproportionate impact. *Washington v. Davis*, 426 U.S. 229 (1976). In the context of a later dispute involving zoning, the Supreme Court clarified that the *Davis* decision "does not require a plaintiff to prove that the challenged action rested solely on racially discriminatory purposes." Rather, a discriminatory purpose is impermissible if it is the "motivating factor" in the government decision. *Village of Arlington Heights v. Metropolitan Housing Development Corp.*, 429 U.S. 252, 265–66 (1977).

41. J. R. Kemper, "Exclusionary Zoning," *American Law Reports Third* 48 (1973): 1210.

42. See *Warth v. Seldin*, 422 U.S. 490 (1975) (denying standing to various organizations and individuals seeking to challenge Rochester, New York's lot size, floor space, and related requirements as effectively excluding residents of low and moderate income).

43. *Ybarra v. City of the Town of Los Altos Hills*, 503 F.2d 250 (9th Cir. 1974). The standing requirement to pursue the lawsuit, found fatal in the *Warth* case, was no doubt supplied here by the contractual option the Mexican American group had obtained to purchase lots in Los Altos contingent on a rezoning of the land for multifamily dwellings.

44. This glimmer of hope for invoking the strict scrutiny standard as a protected class of the impoverished came from a Supreme Court decision in 1973, but no subsequent Supreme Court decision has pursued this avenue. *San Antonio Indep. Sch. Dist. v. Rodriguez*, 411 U.S. 1 (1973). Rather, meaningful equal protection for the impoverished probably hinges on the presence of some independent constitutional right, particularly a fundamental right. See generally Gilbert Paul Carrasco and Congressman Peter W. Rodino, Jr., "'Unalienable Rights,' The Preamble, and the Ninth Amendment: The Spirit of the Constitution," *Seton Hall Law Review* 20 (1990): 498 (arguing despite the absence of protection of housing as a fundamental right under the Equal Protection Clause that those government policies keeping people in abject poverty, such as subsidies to agribusiness, may be vulnerable to challenge under the Ninth Amendment's protection of such retained fundamental rights as a minimum quality of life).

45. See also *Confederacion de la Raza Unida v. City of Morgan Hill*, 324 F. Supp. 895 (N.D. Cal. 1971) (dismissing similar claims against city density ordinance).

46. *Southern Burlington County N.A.A.C.P. v. Township of Mount Laurel*, 336 A.2d 713 (N.J. 1975) (known as Mount Laurel I) (rejecting among other arguments that the absence of municipal sewer or water utilities required larger lots for individual well and septic systems, and reasoning that the township could readily require installation of such utilities by developers or impose them by special assessment). See generally Charles M. Haar, *Suburbs under Siege: Race, Space, and Audacious Judges* (Princeton, NJ: Princeton University Press, 1996), 131, 166–67 (remarking that some 15,400 affordable housing units

had been built as a result of the *Mount Laurel* precedent, but discussing how the judicial emphasis in that litigation on remedies to spur affordable home ownership rather than rental housing left many behind as even low-cost housing was beyond the reach of inner-city minorities unable to obtain purchase loans).

47. Ken Zimmerman and Arielle Cohen, "Exclusionary Zoning: Constitutional and Federal Statutory Responses," in *The Legal Guide to Affordable Housing Development*, ed. Tim Iglesias and Rochelle E. Lento (Chicago: American Bar Association, 2006), 39, 63–67; Haar, *Suburbs under Siege*, 93–94 (discussing how the new law in fact somewhat muted the judicial rulings).

48. *Mt. Holly Citizens in Action, Inc. v. Township of Mount Holly*, 2009 WL 387753 (D. N.J. 2009).

49. *Village of Belle Terre v. Boraas*, 416 U.S. 1 (1974).

50. *Moore v. City of East Cleveland, Ohio*, 431 U.S. 494, 498–99 (1977). See generally Oliveri, "Between Rock and Hard Place," 101 (explaining the *Moore* plurality applied a strict scrutiny standard based on the fundamental rights implicated of privacy and familial association).

51. *Moore*, at 500 (also noting that East Cleveland has an occupancy ordinance that ties the maximum permissible occupancy to the habitable floor area, and noting this living arrangement fell within those limits).

52. Nevertheless, the courts of most states to consider the issue have followed the federal constitutional approach that enforces family-based zoning restrictions unless they purport to exclude traditional family members. See generally Adam Lubow, "'. . . Not Related by Blood, Marriage, or Adoption': A History of the Definition of 'Family' in Zoning Law," *Journal of Affordable Housing and Community Development Law* 16 (2007): 144.

53. *City of Santa Barbara v. Adamson*, 610 P.2d 436 (Cal. 1980).

54. *State v. Baker*, 405 A.2d 368, 371 (N.J. 1979).

55. The New Jersey Supreme Court also looked to whether the household unit was the functional equivalent of a family, asking whether the group living arrangement bore the "genetic character of a family unit as a relatively permanent household." Ibid., 372. Housing arrangements of immigrant workers, by contrast, might be seen as too transient to constitute the functional equivalent of a family unit.

56. See Pader, "Space of Hate," 889 (describing federal litigation against a Chicago suburb brought under the federal Fair Housing Act that alleged an occupancy restriction was designed to prevent Latino/a families from residing there; among the allegations were that the restrictive occupancy standard was enforced only against newcomers, who were primarily Latino/as, not predominantly White existing homeowners).

CHAPTER 8

1. *Austin v. Richardson*, 278 S.W. 513 (Tex. Ct. Civ. App. 1925).

2. *Matthews v. Andrade*, 198 P.2d 66 (Cal. 1948).

3. See, for example, *Los Angeles Investment Co. v. Gary*, 186 P. 596 (Cal. 1919); *Porter v. Barrett*, 206 N.W. 532 (Mich. 1925); see generally Rose, "Property Stories: *Shelley v. Kraemer*," 169, 179.

4. Christopher Ramos, "Comment, The Educational Legacy of Racially Restrictive Covenants: Their Long Term Impact on Mexican Americans," *Scholar: St. Mary's Law Review of Minority Issues* 4 (2001): 149, 158.

5. See generally Robert G. Schwemm, *Housing Discrimination: Law and Litigation* (St. Paul, MN: West Group, 2007) § 3.3 (noting that the FHA changed its policy after the *Shelley* case discussed below, announcing it would no longer insure loans on property with racially restrictive covenants created after 1950).

6. Dennis R. Judd, "Symbolic Politics and Urban Policies," in *Without Justice for All: The New Liberalism and Our Retreat from Racial Equality*, ed. Adolph Reed, Jr. (Boulder, CO: Westview Press, 1999), 129.

7. Ibid.

8. Ian F. Haney López, *Racism on Trial: The Chicano Fight for Justice* (Cambridge, MA: Belknap Press, 2003), 70.

9. Howell, "Exploiting Race," 112–13. For example, the FHA's 1938 *Underwriting Manual* specified that "recorded restrictive covenants should strengthen and supplement zoning ordinances and to be really effective should include the provisions listed below . . . [including] g. prohibition of the occupancy of properties except by the race for which they are intended." Evan McKenzie, *Privatopia: Homeowner Associations and the Rise of Residential Private Government* (New Haven, CT: Yale University Press, 1994), 65.

10. Charles Abrams, *Forbidden Neighbors: A Study of Prejudice in Housing* (New York: Harper, 1955), 162.

11. Rodriguez, *Mongrels, Bastards*, 189.

12. *Shelley v. Kraemer*, 334 U.S. 1 (1948). See also *Barrows v. Jackson*, 346 U.S. 249 (1953) (complementing *Shelley* by holding that a property owner who breached a racial covenant by selling to Black buyers was not liable for damages). It wasn't until the enactment of the federal Fair Housing Act that the inclusion of such covenants in property deeds, as opposed to their attempted enforcement, was treated as legally impermissible. See, for example, *Mayers v. Ridley*, 465 F.2d 630 (D.C. Cir. 1972).

13. *Shelley*, 334 U.S. at 21 n. 26.

14. *Clifton v. Puente*, 218 S.W.2d 272 (Tex. Ct. Civ. App. 1948).

15. Amy Taxin, "Calif. Bill Aims to Strike Racist Housing Language," *San Jose Mercury News* (wire), http://www.mercurynews.com/nationworld/ci_11913739?source=email (posted March 14, 2009; last visited May 22, 2009). California's Assembly passed the bill unanimously in May 2009, and it awaits approval by the state Senate.

16. Bender, *Greasers and Gringos*, 143–45.

17. *Hernandez v. Texas*, 347 U.S. 475 (1954). See generally Michael A. Olivas, ed., *"Colored Men" and "Hombres Aquí": Hernandez v. Texas and the Emergence of Mexican-American Lawyering* (Houston: Arte Público Press, 2006).

18. Stephen Grant Meyer, *As Long As They Don't Move Next Door: Segregation and Racial Conflict in American Neighborhoods* (Lanham, MD: Rowman and Littlefield, 2000), 95.

19. Nicolaides, *My Blue Heaven*, 211.

20. Alexander, "Housing of America's Families."

21. Ibid.

22. José Miguel Flores, "Globalization and Urban Opportunities in the Immigrant Cityscape," *Florida Journal of International Law* 17 (2005): 719, 739.

23. McKenzie, *Privatopia*, 78.

24. Lior Jacob Strahilevitz, "Exclusionary Amenities in Residential Communities," *Virginia Law Review* 92 (2006): 437.

25. See generally Schwemm, *Housing Discrimination*, § 11E:3; see also *Pfaff v. U.S. Department of Housing and Urban Development*, 88 F.3d 739 (9th Cir. 1996) (landlord of 1,200-square-foot house with master bedroom, small second bedroom, and den opening to main living area acted reasonably in denying rental to couple with three young children).

26. Godsil, "Race Nuisance" (explaining why courts generally refused to apply nuisance law to exclude Black families from White neighborhoods at the same time courts would enforce racially restrictive covenants).

27. Ibid., 515.

28. *Worm v. Wood*, 223 S.W. 1016, 1019 (Tex. Ct. Civ. App. 1920).

29. *Harty v. Guerra*, 269 S.W. 1064 (Tex. Ct. Civ. App. 1925).

30. See also *People* ex. rel. *Gallo v. Acuna*, 929 P.2d 596 (Cal. 1997) (wielding public nuisance theory against Latino gang members terrorizing neighborhood).

31. Judd, "Symbolic Politics."

32. Anna M. Santiago, "The Spatial Dimensions of Ethnic and Racial Stratification," in *Race and Ethnicity in the United States: An Institutional Approach*, ed. William Velez (Dix Hills, NY: General Hall, 1998).

33. Ramos, "Educational Legacy," 166.

34. Ibid., 166–67.

PART III

1. Kutty, "Policy Lessons," 23.

2. Nancy A. Denton, "Segregation and Discrimination in Housing," in *A Right to Housing: Foundation for a New Social Agenda*, ed. Rachel G. Bratt, Michael E. Stone, and Chester Hartman (Philadelphia: Temple University Press, 2006), 62, 65.

3. Michael E. Martin, *Residential Segregation Patterns of Latinos in the United States, 1990–2000: Testing the Ethnic Enclave and Inequality Theories* (New York: Routledge, 2007), 8.

4. John A. Powell and Jason Reece, "The Future of Fair Housing and Fair Credit: From Crisis to Opportunity," *Cleveland State Law Review* 57 (2009): 209, 224.

5. Richard Fry, *Latino Settlement in the New Century* (Washington, DC: Pew Hispanic Center, October 23, 2008), iv (supplying statistic that 59 percent of the Black population lived in the nation's 100 largest Black non-Latino/a counties).

CHAPTER 9

1. Del Castillo, *Los Angeles Barrio*, 46–47.

2. Ibid., 48.

3. Romo, *East Los Angeles*, 114.

4. Gilbert Paul Carrasco, "Latinos in the United States: Invitation and Exile," in *Immigrants Out! The New Nativism and the Anti-Immigrant Impulse in the United States*, ed. Juan F. Perea (New York: New York University Press, 1977), 190.

5. Ibid.

6. Douglas Monroy, *Rebirth: Mexican Los Angeles from the Great Migration to the Great Depression* (Berkeley: University of California Press, 1999), 29.

7. Rodolfo F. Acuña, *A Community under Siege: A Chronicle of Chicanos East of the Los Angeles River 1945–1975* (Los Angeles: Chicano Studies Research Center Publications, UCLA, 1984), 9.

8. Monroy, *Rebirth*, 29.

9. Romo, *East Los Angeles*, 72–73.

10. George J. Sánchez, *Becoming Mexican American: Ethnicity, Culture and Identity in Chicano Los Angeles, 1900–1945* (New York: Oxford University Press, 1993), 226; see also William Deverell, *Whitewashed Adobe: The Rise of Los Angeles and the Remaking of Its Mexican Past* (Berkeley: University of California Press, 2004); Steven W. Bender, "Knocked Down Again: An East L.A. Story on the Geography of Color and Colors," *Harvard Latino Law Review* 12 (2009): 109 (detailing the history of loss and exclusion for Mexican Americans in East L.A. and Los Angeles generally); Richard Delgado and Jean Stefancic, "California's Racial History and Constitutional Rationales for Race-Conscious Decision Making in Higher Education," *UCLA Law Review* 47 (2000): 1521 (authors' research suggests the possibility of a mid-twentieth-century campaign to purge Mexican American residents to allow for eventual expansion of the University of California campus in the budding university town of Davis, California).

11. Romo, *East Los Angeles*, 85.

12. Flores, "Globalization," 729.

13. Acuña, *Community under Siege*, 15.

14. Ronald William López II, *The Battle for Chavez Ravine: Public Policy and Chicano Community Resistance in Post War Los Angeles, 1945–1962* (Ann Arbor, MI: UMI Dissertation Services, 1999), 9.

15. Ibid., 74.

16. Ibid., 13.

17. Thomas S. Hines, *Richard Neutra and the Search for Modern Architecture* (New York: Rizzoli, 2005), 249 (biography of the project's famous architect).

18. López, *Battle for Chavez Ravine*, 74; Don Normark, *Chávez Ravine, 1949: A Los Angeles Story* (San Francisco: Chronicle Books, 1999), 18 (excerpting letter from Housing Authority to local residents informing them that "a public housing development will be built on this location for families of low income. . . . You will be visited by representatives of the Housing Authority who will . . . inspect your house in order to estimate its value. . . . Later you will have the first chance to move back into the new Elysian Park Heights development.").

19. Thomas S. Hines, "Housing, Baseball, and Creeping Socialism: The Battle of Chavez Ravine, 1949–1959," *Journal of Urban History* 8 (February 1982): 123, 141.

20. *City of Los Angeles v. Superior Court of the County of Los Angeles*, 333 P.2d 745 (Cal. 1959) (finding immaterial that some of the provisions might benefit only the baseball club, as the transfer of the small stadium and the promise to construct public recreational facilities had an obvious public purpose; unnecessary to consider the various indirect public benefits such as bringing to the city a major league team or the tax revenues from the stadium). A current member of the California Supreme Court, the Latino justice Carlos Moreno, grew up in Chávez Ravine.

21. Normark, *Chávez Ravine*, 33.

22. Ibid., 127 (letter of Natalie Ramirez, dated July 15, 1988).

23. Romo, *East Los Angeles*, 170. See also Gerald Paul Rosen, *Political Ideology and the Chicano Movement: A Study of the Political Ideology of Activists in the Chicano Movement*

(San Francisco: R and E Research Associates, 1975), 25 (suggesting that East Los Angeles is crossed by more freeways than anywhere else in Los Angeles and perhaps the world); Mary Pat Brady, *Extinct Lands, Temporal Geographies: Chicana Literature and the Urgency of Space* (Durham, NC: Duke University Press, 2002), 15 (describing the deleterious effect of freeway construction in Tucson, Arizona, cutting through a Latino/a neighborhood); David R. Diaz, *Barrio Urbanism: Chicanos, Planning, and American Cities* (New York: Routledge, 2005), 99 (describing the destruction of Latino/a neighborhoods in the expansion of Sky Harbor Airport in Phoenix, Arizona); Eric R. Avila, "The Folklore of the Freeway: Space, Culture, and Identity in Postwar Los Angeles," *Aztlán* 23 (Spring 1998): 15 (discussing protests in East Los Angeles against freeway construction and the portrayal in Chicano/a culture of the resulting devastation).

24. Diaz, *Barrio Urbanism*, 217.

25. Richard Anthony Eribes, "A Microanalysis of the Housing System within East Los Angeles: The Dynamics of Housing within a Mexican American Community" (Ph.D. diss., University of Southern California, February 1977), 158.

26. Anderson, "Cities Inside Out," 1152.

27. Robert Fishman, *Bourgeois Utopias: The Rise and Fall of Suburbia* (New York: Basic Books, 1987), 161–66 (detailing how the automobile eventually displaced the streetcar system in early Los Angeles).

28. Ibid., 177.

29. Listed at http://www.zillow.com/HomeDetails.htm?zprop=21081832 (last visited July 29, 2008).

30. The subprime mortgage crisis and attendant decline in property values ignited the foreclosure option of the so-called short sale for properties with mortgage balances below the property's worth. Under the short-sale procedure, the borrower secures the agreement of the mortgage lender to release the mortgage upon a bona fide sale to a third party for an agreed-upon price below the mortgage loan balance. The broker's listing of my grandparents' former home stated: "Please don't let the price discourage you from sending any offers. Sellers price subject to lenders approval of short pay and commissions to selling and listing agents. House is 2 Bed. 1 Ba. [V]ery well tak[en] care of." http://www.prudentialcal.com/Listing/ListingDetail.aspx?Listing=29635708 (last visited April 21, 2008).

31. *Housing That Works 2008–2013: A 5 Year, $5 Billion Housing Plan for LA's Families,* http://www.ci.la.ca.us/mayor/stellent/groups/electedofficials/@myr_ch_contributor/documents/contributor_web_content/lacity_004903.pdf (last visited December 16, 2008) [hereinafter *Housing That Works*].

32. Stewart, "City of Renters" (using 2000 Census figures).

33. Diaz, *Barrio Urbanism*, 83.

34. Eribes, "Microanalysis of the Housing System," 163 (finding between 1960 and 1970 that 85 percent of the housing units removed for freeway construction in East Los Angeles were single-family homes, reflecting both the single-family nature of that community and the cheaper cost of removal when compared to multifamily housing, which no doubt influenced the placement of freeway routes).

35. Lara Farrar, "Is America's Suburban Dream Collapsing into a Nightmare?" www.cnn.com/2008/TECH/06/16/suburb.city/index.html (posted June 16, 2008) (last visited June 17, 2008); Christopher B. Leinberger, *The Option of Urbanism: Investing in a New*

American Dream (Washington, DC: Island Press, 2008) (discussing demand for walkable urbanism as opposed to the drivable suburban model of real estate development).

36. Ibid.

37. Bender, *Comprende?*, 79.

38. John F. Wasik, *The Cul-De-Sac Syndrome: Turning Around the Unsustainable American Dream* (New York: Bloomberg Press, 2009), 144–45 (estimate from Arthur Nelson of Virginia Tech's Metropolitan Institute).

CHAPTER 10

1. U.S. Census Bureau, http://factfinder.census.gov/servlet/ADPTable?_bm=y&-qr_name=ACS_2005_EST_G00_DP1&-geo_id=16000US1245000&-ds_name=ACS_2005_EST_G00_&-_lang=en (last visited January 4, 2010) (estimate for Blacks or African Americans who are not Hispanic or Latino; these Census figures should be used cautiously given the difficulties under the Census of categorizing Miami's significant Afro-Latino/a population, such as Haitians).

2. Alejandro Portes and Alex Stepick, *City on the Edge: The Transformation of Miami* (Berkeley: University of California Press, 1993).

3. Ibid., 104 (but noting the proportion of Blacks and mulattoes was much lower than in Cuba, and that the exiles were disproportionately urban dwellers).

4. Morton D. Winsberg, "Housing Segregation of a Predominantly Middle Class Population: Residential Patterns Developed by the Cuban Immigration into Miami 1950–74," *American Journal of Economics and Sociology* 38 (October 1979): 403.

5. Winsberg, "Housing Segregation," 410.

6. Paul S. George, *Images of America: Little Havana* (Charleston, SC: Arcadia Publishing, 2006), 7.

7. "Cuban Ancestry," http://www.epodunk.com/ancestry/Cuban.html (last visited January 4, 2010) (using 2000 Census figures).

8. Timothy Ashby, "Cuban Real Property—Current Laws and Future Prospects," *Real Estate Law Journal* 33 (2004): 126.

9. Steven E. Hendrix, "Tensions in Cuban Property Law," *Hastings International and Comparative Law Review* 20 (1996): 31.

10. Nicolas J. Gutierrez, Jr., "The De-Constitutionalization of Property Rights: Castro's Systematic Assault on Private Ownership in Cuba," *University of Miami Yearbook of International Law* 5 (1996–97): 51, 55.

11. Hendrix, "Tensions in Cuban Property Law," 1; Kern Alexander and Jon Mills, "Resolving Property Claims in a Post-Socialist Cuba," *Law and Policy in International Business* 27 (1995): 137, 142.

12. Hendrix, "Tensions in Cuban Property Law," 91.

13. Ashby, "Cuban Real Property," 123, 147 (suggesting that personal and real property assets seized from Cuban residents had an estimated worth in the early 2000s of $20 billion).

14. Ibid.; Stephen J. Kimmerling, "Rights and Remedies Concerning Cuban Residential Property," *Cuba in Transition, Association for the Study of the Cuban Economy* 11 (2001): 258, http://lanic.utexas.edu/project/asce/pdfs/volume11/kimmerling.pdf (last visited Dec. 20, 2008) (offering approaches to resolve these disputes over expropriated residential properties).

15. Ashby, "Cuban Real Property," 129.
16. Ibid., 131; Kimmerling, "Rights and Remedies."
17. Marc Lacey, "With a Whisper, Cuba's Housing Market Booms," *New York Times*, January 28, 2008, A1.
18. Hendrix, "Tensions in Cuban Property Law," 69.
19. Lacey, "With a Whisper."
20. Kimmerling, "Rights and Remedies."
21. Ashby, "Cuban Real Property," 132.
22. Ibid., 137–38.
23. Frank Hamilton, "Spanish Land Grants in Florida," *Florida Historical Quarterly* (1941): 77.
24. "Florida Homes Have International Appeal, Says Florida Association of Realtors' Study," http://media.living.net/releases/InternationalStudy.htm (posted July 14, 2005; last visited November 25, 2008).

CHAPTER 11

1. See Pedro A. Malavet, *America's Colony: The Political and Cultural Conflict between the United States and Puerto Rico* (New York: New York University Press, 2004).
2. Virginia E. Sánchez Korrol, *From Colonia to Community: The History of Puerto Ricans in New York City* (Berkeley: University of California Press, 1994), 46.
3. Inés M. Miyares, "Changing Latinization of New York City," in *Hispanic Spaces, Latino Places: Community and Cultural Diversity in Contemporary America*, ed. Daniel D. Arreola (Austin: University of Texas Press, 2004), 145, 149.
4. *Puerto Rican Migration to New York*, http://en.wikipedia.org/wiki/Puerto_Rican_migration_to_New_York (last visited December 17, 2008).
5. Victor Manuel Ramos, "More Puerto Ricans on Mainland than Island," *Orlando Sentinel*, July 14, 2009, B2.
6. Joseph Rodriguez, *Spanish Harlem* (New York: Distributed Art Publishers, 1994).
7. "Puerto Rico Has Higher Homeownership, Larger Households," *U.S. Census Bureau News*, http://www.census.gov/Press-Release/www/releases/archives/american_community_survey_acs/011755.html (posted April 2, 2008; last visited February 9, 2009).
8. Arlene Dávila, *Barrio Dreams: Puerto Ricans, Latinos, and the Neoliberal City* (Berkeley: University of California Press, 2004), 7–8.
9. Ibid., 28.
10. See generally Lance Freeman, *There Goes the 'Hood: Views of Gentrification from the Ground Up* (Philadelphia: Temple University Press, 2006) (detailing both benefits and negatives to indigenous residents associated with gentrification, and studying gentrification in Harlem and Brooklyn's Clinton Hill).
11. Patricia Cayo Sexton, *Spanish Harlem* (New York: Harper and Row, 1965).
12. Abrams, *Forbidden Neighbors*, 61.
13. Dávila, *Barrio Dreams*, 31.
14. Ibid., 32.
15. Francisco L. Rivera-Batiz and Carlos E. Santiago, *Island Paradox: Puerto Rico in the 1990s* (New York: Russell Sage Foundation, 1996), 148 (quoting a Puerto Rican transplant

from New York City to Florida who explained, "[W]e wanted to own our home and New York was too expensive.").

16. S. Jhoanna Robledo, "Harlem's Other Half," http://nymag.com/realestate/realestate-column/42759/ (posted January 13, 2008; last visited January 27, 2008).

17. Russell Leigh Sharman, *The Tenants of East Harlem* (Berkeley: University of California Press, 2006), 205.

18. Timothy Williams and Tanzina Vega, "As East Harlem Develops, Its Accent Starts to Change," *New York Times*, January 21, 2007, sec. 1, p. 29.

19. *Hell's Kitchen, Manhattan*, http://en.wikipedia.org/wiki/Hell's_Kitchen,_Manhattan (last visited September 14, 2008).

20. Sharman, *Tenants of East Harlem*, 121.

21. A study by the NYU Law School's Furman Center for Real Estate and Urban Policy revealed that the subprime crisis also impacted New York City renters, as some 60 percent of the properties entering foreclosure there in 2007 were multifamily properties, imperiling more than 15,000 renter households, most of them in two- to four-family dwellings in Brooklyn and Queens. Testimony of Vicki Been before New York City Council Committee on Community Development, Foreclosure Activity in New York City, and the Neighborhood Impacts of Foreclosures (January 22, 2009), http://furmancenter.org/files/testimonies/Been_Foreclosures_City_Council_Testimony_January_22_2009.pdf (last visited December 27, 2009).

22. Timothy Williams, "Mixed Feelings as Change Overtakes 125th St.," *New York Times*, June 13, 2008, B1.

23. Christine Haughney, "On a Harlem Block, Boarded-Up Buildings and a Changing Mood," *New York Times*, July 8, 2009, A1 (detailing the woes of investors in Harlem real estate as the economic crisis in 2009 derailed their renovation plans). The higher prices fetched by Harlem town homes before the crash, in relation to new condominium units, no doubt was due to their higher square-footage.

CHAPTER 12

1. Donald A. Krueckeberg, "The Grapes of Rent: A History of Renting in a Country of Owners," *Housing Policy Debate* 10 (1999): 9, 22.

2. Monte Burke and William P. Barrett, "This Land Is My Land," *Forbes*, October 6, 2003, http://www.forbes.com/free_forbes/2003/1006/050.html (last visited November 19, 2008).

3. López, *Battle for Chavez Ravine*, 178. The Arechiga family battled in court as well. See *Arechiga v. Housing Authority of City of Los Angeles*, 324 P.2d 973 (Cal. Ct. App. 1958) (concluding that even though the housing project was abandoned, the family was not able to have the judgment condemning their home set aside). Public opinion shifted against the Arechigas when local newspapers reported that the family owned other homes in the area they presumably could move to. But see Ernesto Chávez, *"¡Mi Raza Primero!": Nationalism, Identity, and Insurgency in the Chicano Movement in Los Angeles, 1966–1978* (Berkeley: University of California Press, 2002), 29 (revealing that one of their other homes was condemned in construction of the Golden State Freeway).

4. Miguel Melendez, *We Took the Streets: Fighting for Latino Rights with the Young Lords* (New York: St. Martin's Press, 2003).

5. Ibid., 234–36.
6. Treaty of Guadalupe Hidalgo, art. V.
7. The director of the Catalina Island Museum summarizes the history of the island's ownership as follows:

> Mexican Governor Pio Pico awarded Santa Catalina Island to Thomas Robbins as a land grant in 1846, just four days before the United States invaded California. Robbins was a naturalized Mexican citizen who had been living in California for about 20 years and had performed various services for the government, mainly as a ship captain. . . . Robbins established a small rancho on the Island, but sold it in 1850 to Jose Maria Covarrubias, just two years after California became a part of the United States as the result of the Treaty of Guadeloupe [sic] Hidalgo.
>
> . . . The landowners in the former Mexican province had been promised that under the new American government they would retain title to their land grants, but they had to prove ownership. Cases often took years to resolve before the Land Commission. With title in doubt, squatters often moved onto land and laid claim by virtue of possession. On Santa Catalina Island, various squatters laid claim to different areas and began running sheep and cattle. . . . At the same time, in Santa Barbara on the mainland, men were buying and selling portions of the Island. The various sections were eventually purchased by James Lick of San Francisco and his title was confirmed by patent in 1867 (when it was finally decided that Robbins' grant was legal).

Archived at http://www.catalina.com/history.html (last visited August 22, 2008). If Santa Catalina Island had remained part of Mexico's territory, then the requirements of establishing title under U.S. law would not have applied. Presumably, though, the Mexican government would have honored any individual land grant by the Spanish or Mexican government, as well as any subsequent conveyances thereof. The Brown Berets apparently were not bothered by such subtleties, as they assumed the island was Mexican territory and not properly in private ownership. Still, the Brown Berets were faced with the complications of the standing of a substantial Mexican presence in the United States, and resolved the dilemma by declaring the islands as belonging to "people of Mexican decent living in the United States, as well as the people of Mexican citizenship, and the people of Indian descent." David Sanchez, *Expedition through Aztlán* (La Puente, CA: Perspective Publications, 1978), 185. An argument does exist that the land grant for Catalina Island was invalid because it was made after the declaration of the Mexican-American War (see del Castillo, *Treaty of Guadalupe Hidalgo*, 141), but the timeline detailed above is contrary. Regardless, as discussed below, the U.S. courts have concluded the Channel Islands passed into U.S. control, and thus the certification of land grant title by the United States in the 1800s would control now.

8. Sanchez, *Expedition through Aztlán*, 175.
9. Ibid., 181.
10. See *United States v. Ringrose*, 788 F.2d 638 (9th Cir. 1986) (land grants from Mexican government to the Santa Rosa and Santa Cruz Islands were encompassed within the Treaty of Guadalupe Hidalgo territory and thus the failure of the predecessor in title to timely seek confirmation of title with the California Land Claims Commission established in 1851 meant that title passed to the public domain of the United States; the court felt the question of whether the Channel Islands were part of the territory acquired by the United States

had been resolved affirmatively as part of Supreme Court litigation on dominion over submerged waters in the Channel Islands National Monument). See *United States v. California*, 436 U.S. 32, 34 n.3 (1978) (in deciding whether the federal government or the State of California had such dominion, the court stated that "[f]ederal title to the islands can be traced to the 1848 Treaty of Guadalupe Hidalgo . . . by which Mexico ceded to the United States the islands lying off the coast of California, along with the adjacent mainland.").

11. Tijerina argues that if the communal lands belonged to the sovereignty, then why didn't Mexico claim title to them when Spain's control over Mexico ended? Tijerina, *King Tiger*, 44. There is some dispute over the disposition of communal land grant property in New Mexico, with one scholar contending that two-thirds of the common lands under one land grant were distributed by the federal government under homestead laws and thus mostly restored to local residents. But the San Joaquín grant that Tijerina targeted, for example, became national forestland and thus was not subject to homesteading. See Ebright, *Land Grants* (finding that the scholar's conclusions are limited to the specific land grant known as San Miguel del Vado).

12. Alianza Federal de Mercedes, *Spanish Land Grant Question Examined* (Albuquerque, NM: Alianza Federal, 1966), 8–9.

13. See Ebright, *Land Grants*, 106–8 (describing both some confusion over the name of this land grant and the delivery of possession of the land to the grantees in 1808).

14. Peter Nabokov, *Tijerina and the Courthouse Raid* (Berkeley, CA: Ramparts Press, 1969), 52.

15. Tijerina was found guilty of two assault charges, and a couple of other Alianza members were convicted of conversion for impounding two government trucks during their detention of the rangers, but a mistrial was ordered on the conspiracy charge. See *U.S. v. Tijerina*, 407 F.2d 349 (10th Cir. 1969). See generally Tony Hillerman, "The U.S. Stole Our Land," *True: The Man's Magazine* (January 1968): 49, 84 (detailing how Tijerina was unswayed and traveled to Washington, DC, to seek diplomatic recognition of the sovereign Republica de San Joaquín, before his involvement in a notorious New Mexico courthouse raid).

16. Marco Anguiano, "The Battle of Chicano Park: A Brief History of the Takeover," http://www.calacapress.com/cpsc/cpscbattleof.html (last visited December 16, 2008).

17. Today, homes just across the Coronado Bridge sell for roughly five times the price for similar square footage as those in Barrio Logan.

18. A more hostile approach to developing recreational space for Latino/as comes from Springfield, Tennessee, where a town alderman in 2006 proposed banning undocumented immigrants from public parks, and suggested for profiling purposes that he assumed those speaking Spanish to be illegal.

19. Diaz, *Barrio Urbanism*, 152–53.

20. See *Arechiga v. Housing Authority of City of Los Angeles*, 324 P.2d 973 (Cal. Ct. App. 1958) (concluding that even though the housing project was abandoned, the family was not able to have the judgment condemning their home set aside).

21. *South Central Farm*, http://en.wikipedia.org/wiki/South_Central_Farm (last visited December 17, 2008) (noting as part of the repurchase that the buyer agreed to donate 2.6 acres for a public soccer field).

22. *Made in L.A.: Hecho en Los Angeles* (Semilla Verde Productions, Inc., 2007).

23. Archived at http://latimesblogs.latimes.com/greenspace/2008/08/celebrated-sout.html (last visited August 21, 2008).

24. Richard Delgado, "Rodrigo's Twelfth Chronicle: The Problem of the Shanty," *Georgetown Law Journal* 85 (1997): 687 (suggesting a strategy of resistance to contest inadequacy of basic government services in *colonia* housing: "Resistance, sit-ins, and various forms of civil disobedience will get the attention of the developers, factory owners, and lazy bureaucrats who benefit from the current arrangement.").

25. See Marc Ballon, "A Harvest of Conflict: Did Anti-Semitism Take Root at the South Central Farm?" http://www.cai-la.org/230606.html (June 23, 2006; last visited August 23, 2008).

26. This may be due in part to the disparate views among Puerto Ricans on their desired status for the islands of Puerto Rico, with the choices including independence, statehood, a commonwealth, and other variations in terms of autonomy or colonialism. See generally Malavet, *America's Colony*.

27. Diaz, *Barrio Urbanism*, 303-4.

28. Archived at http://www.costilla-county.com/ (last visited September 5, 2008).

29. *Lobato v. Taylor*, 71 P.3d 938 (Colo. 2002).

30. *Lobato v. Taylor*, 70 P.3d 1152 (Colo. 2003).

31. Sam Howe Verhovek, "Cattle Barons of Texas Yore Accused of Epic Land Grab," *New York Times*, July 14, 1997, A1.

32. Ibid.

33. *Aguillera v. John G. and Marie Stella Kenedy Memorial Foundation*, 162 S.W.3d 689 (Tex. Ct. App. 2005).

34. Archived at http://www.balli.org/07142008.htm (last visited September 5, 2008).

35. Ibid.

36. Archived at http://www.balli.org/ (last visited September 5, 2008).

37. *Kerlin v. Sauceda*, 263 S.W.3d 920 (Tex. 2008).

38. Alianza Federal, *Spanish Land Grant*, 19-20.

39. Ben Neary, "Clinging to Claims," *The New Mexican*, June 9, 2004, B1.

40. GAO Report, 144-45.

41. Ibid., 13.

42. *Statement of Administration Policy*, September 10, 1998, http://clinton2.nara.gov/OMB/legislative/sap/105-2/HR2538-h.html (last visited September 5, 2008).

43. Rodolfo F. Acuña, "The Treaty of Guadalupe Hidalgo: My Take on the Possible Implications for Today," *Southwestern Journal of Law and Trade in the Americas* 5 (1998): 109, 115.

44. María Teresa Vázquez Castillo, *Land Privatization in Mexico: Urbanization, Formation of Regions, and Globalization in Ejidos* (New York: Routledge, 2004), 22-23.

45. Ibid., 25; see also James J. Kelly, Jr., "Article 27 and Mexico Land Reform: The Legacy of Zapata's Dream," *Columbia Human Rights Law Review* 25 (1994): 541, 549.

46. Mark Wasserman, *Everyday Life and Politics in Nineteenth-Century Mexico: Men, Women, and War* (Albuquerque: University of New Mexico Press, 2000), 177.

47. Castillo, *Land Privatization*, 25.

48. Ibid., 26. Another source states a slightly higher percentage of landless. Monroy, *Rebirth*, 78 ("By 1910, no less than 90 percent of rural Mexicans did not possess land, and in some states that figure reached 99 percent."). Also, on the number of hacienda owners, another source provides that fewer than 11,000 haciendas controlled 57 percent of Mexican territory. John J. Dwyer, *The Agrarian Dispute: The Expropriation of American-Owned Rural Land in Postrevolutionary Mexico* (Durham, NC: Duke University Press, 2008), 18.

However, the figures of hacienda control might be reconciled if the same family controlled more than one hacienda.

49. See generally Friedrich Katz, "The Agrarian Policies and Ideas of the Revolutionary Mexican Factions Led by Emiliano Zapata, Pancho Villa, and Venustiano Carranza," in *Reforming Mexico's Agrarian Economy*, ed. Laura Randall (Armonk, NY: M. E. Sharpe, 1996), 21 (examining the contradictions of the Mexican Revolution on the issue of whether it was centered on agrarian reform on all fronts, particularly given the civil war between factions in the north that each advocated land reform).

50. See Castillo, *Land Privatization*, 29 (suggesting a distinction between Villa and Zapata in their mutual desire to reform the hacienda landholdings, as "Villa supported small private ownership of property, while for Zapata, redistribution respected the communal aspect of Indigenous lands"); Katz, "Agrarian Policies," 28 (articulating that the greatest difference between the policies of Villa and Zapata was that Zapata distributed land seized from hacienda owners to villages, but under Villa the largest estates seized remained under state administration). The Ayala Plan that Zapata helped formulate in 1911 later became the basis for constitutional reform, specifying as part of its mandates that

> we declare that the land, woodlands, and waters usurped by the plantation-owners . . . under the cover of tyranny and venal justice shall become forthwith the property of the villages or citizens who have the appropriate deeds and have been dispossessed through the trickery of our oppressors. . . .
>
> . . . Hence, the powerful landowners will be expropriated, and compensation paid for a third of these monopolies, so that the villages and citizens of Mexico may acquire common land and new settlements . . . [to] overcome their lack of prosperity and well-being.

Adolfo Gilly, *The Mexican Revolution: A New Press People's History* (New York: The New Press, 2005).

51. Ron Chernow, *The House of Morgan: An American Banking Dynasty and the Rise of Modern Finance* (New York: Grove, 2001), 239.

52. Kelly, "Article 27," 542–43; Carlota Botey, "Introduction to Panel I," in *Reforming Mexico's Agrarian Economy*, ed. Laura Randall (Armonk, NY: M. E. Sharpe, 1996), 15, 18 (noting that land reform delivered 103 million hectares to the *ejido* farmers; each hectare is 2.47 acres); Dwyer, *The Agrarian Dispute*, 26 (describing laws in the Mexican state of Sonora pursuant to the Constitution that placed legal limits on land ownership, such as 25 acres of grazing land and 250 acres of irrigable land, and distributing the rest to landless peasants).

53. Dwyer, *The Agrarian Dispute*, 1, 159, 161, 258–59 (also discussing how some of the land was expropriated without compensation).

54. Kelly, "Article 27," 553.

55. Dwyer, *The Agrarian Dispute*, 53, 154 (noting how living standards rose for Mexican peasants as landowners under the *ejido* system).

56. Kelly, "Article 27," 562; Wayne A. Cornelius and David Myhre, eds. *The Transformation of Rural Mexico: Reforming the Ejido Sector* (San Diego: Center for U.S.-Mexican Studies, University of California, 1998). Foreign private investors who enter into production associations or joint ventures with the *ejido* owners are subject to a limit of 49 percent of the equity capital in the venture.

57. Wenonah Hauter, "The Limits of International Human Rights Law and the Role of Food Sovereignty in Protecting People from Further Trade Liberalization under the Doha Round Negotiations," *Vanderbilt Journal of Transnational Law* 40 (2007): 1071, 1075; Joseph M. Whitmeyer and Rosemary L. Hopcroft, "Community, Capitalism, and Rebellion in Chiapas," *Sociological Perspectives* 39 (Spring 1996): 517, 524.

58. Don M. Mitchell, "The Geography of Injustice: Borders and the Continuing Immiseration of California Agricultural Labor in Era of 'Free Trade,'" *Richmond Journal of Global Law and Business* 2 (2001): 145, 163.

59. Marco Palau, Note, "The Struggle for Dignity, Land, and Autonomy: The Rights of Mexico's Indigenous People a Decade after the Zapatista Revolt," *Columbia Human Rights Law Review* 36 (2005): 427, 433.

60. George A. Collier and Elizabeth Lowery Quaratiello, *Basta! Land and the Zapatista Rebellion in Chiapas*, rev. ed. (Oakland: Food First Books, 1999), 64.

61. Ibid., 152.

62. *Current Housing Situation in Mexico 2005* (Mexico City: Centro de Investigación y Documentación de la Casa and Sociedad Hipotecaria Federal), 22.

63. *The State of Mexico's Housing 2004* (Cambridge, MA: Joint Center for Housing Studies at Harvard University, June 9, 2004). For comparative discussion of the extralegal housing settlements in Peru, see Hernando de Soto, *The Other Path: The Economic Answer to Terrorism* (New York: Basic Books, 1989).

64. *State of Mexico's Housing 2004*. For other factors curtailing mortgage financing in Mexico, see Michael T. Madison, Jeffry R. Dwyer, and Steven W. Bender, *The Law of Real Estate Financing* (St. Paul, MN: Thomson/West, 2007), § 2.81 (discussing the undeveloped title insurance market, uncertainties of mortgage lien priority, foreclosure delays, and other factors).

65. Ward, *Colonias*, 70.

66. Soula Proxenos, *Homeownership Rates: A Global Perspective*, http://findarticles.com/p/articles/mi_qa5441/is_/ai_n21323317 (last visited December 17, 2008).

67. *State of Mexico's Housing 2004*.

68. NAFTA art. 1110.

69. "Real Estate," *Alaska Airlines and Horizon Air Magazine* (July 2007): R11.

70. Archived at http://www.loretobay.com/ (last visited September 12, 2008).

71. "Trump Baja Venture Leaves Buyers High and Dry," *Los Angeles Times*, March 7, 2009, 5 (also blaming the battered real estate market south of the border on Mexico's drug violence, and noting Trump, who had licensed his name for the project, was already targeted in litigation along with the developer by one disappointed buyer, with more lawsuits expected).

72. Mike Davis, "The Baby Boomer Border Invasion," http://www.alternet.org/story/42133/ (posted September 26, 2006; last visited September 12, 2008).

73. Ibid.

CHAPTER 13

1. Kotkin, Tseng, and Ozuna, *Rewarding Ambition*, 36.
2. *State of the Nation's Housing 2009*, 5.
3. Myers, *Immigrants and Boomers*, 245.

4. Hinojosa-Ojeda, Jacquez, and Takash, *End of the American Dream*, 27

5. Bender, *One Night in America*, 175.

6. Alcee L. Hastings and Maria Foscarinis, "End Racial Disparities in Housing," *Miami Herald*, March 14, 2008, A21.

7. Delgado, "Rodrigo's Twelfth Chronicle," 682 (suggesting that reformers of colonia housing conditions place too little blame on the racism and conquest that produced the colonias and thereby overlook the "proper role of the government in redressing historical wrongs").

8. See Kevin R. Johnson, "A Handicapped, Not 'Sleeping,' Giant: The Devastating Impact of the Initiative Process on Latina/o and Immigrant Communities," *California Law Review* 96 (2008): 1259, 1280 (discussing a Harvard sociologist who flatly contends affirmative action must exclude immigrants).

9. Ramos, "Educational Legacy." See also Gabriel J. Chin, "Segregation's Last Stronghold: Race Discrimination and the Constitutional Law of Immigration," *UCLA Law Review* 46 (1998): 1 (cataloging the lingering deleterious impacts on Asian Americans of our legacy of de jure exclusion of Chinese and other Asian immigrants).

10. *Grutter v. Bollinger*, 539 U.S. 306 (2003); *Gratz v. Bollinger*, 539 U.S. 244 (2003).

11. See Richard D. Kahlenberg, *The Remedy: Class, Race, and Affirmative Action* (New York: Basic Books, 1996), 117–20.

12. Hanson, *Mexifornia*.

13. Ibid., 51.

14. Although I suggest that for colonia housing arrangements the government should tolerate and authorize self-help building, nonetheless minimum standards of health and safety, such as sewer systems and clean water, must be established. Arguments that Mexican and other Latino/a immigrants would have faced challenges in securing these minimum standards in their home countries should be irrelevant in setting the bar for decent housing in the United States.

15. Powell, "Reflections on the Past," 609.

16. Delgado, "Rodrigo's Twelfth Chronicle," 680.

17. Light, *Deflecting Immigration*, 140 (discussing that the Southern California Association of Governments recommended that member cities permit self-help labor on homes, and modify local laws requiring electricians, plumbers, and carpenters to be certified).

18. *National Low Income Housing Coalition 2008 Advocates' Guide to Housing and Community Development Policy* (Self-Help Homeownership Opportunity Program) [hereinafter *2008 Advocates' Guide*] (noting the program has been repeatedly underfunded). See also Deborah Kenn, "Paradise Unfound: The American Dream of Housing Justice for All," *Boston University Public Interest Law Journal* 5 (1995): 69, 81–83 (describing the limited equity cooperative program in New York City funded by public and private sources that staves off gentrification by awarding ownership in cooperative apartment buildings to homesteaders who rehabilitate the property).

19. Larson, "Free Markets," 195, 196.

20. Ibid., 194.

21. See, e.g., Lauren E. Willis, "Against Financial-Literacy Education," *Iowa Law Review* 94 (2008): 197; Dickerson, "Myth of Home Ownership."

22. "Pre-K and Latinos," *Reading Rockets*, http://www.readingrockets.org/article/26098 (last visited November 21, 2008).

23. Jim Gilchrist, "An Essay by Jim Gilchrist," *Georgetown Immigration Law Journal* 22 (2008): 415.

24. Bender, *Greasers and Gringos*, 81.

25. Diaz, *Barrio Urbanism*, 300–301.

26. Krueckeberg, "Grapes of Rent," 23. Still, state laws tend to provide greater protection to property owners facing mortgage foreclosure than to renters facing eviction, leading some commentators to urge greater safeguards for tenants. See, e.g., Margaret Jane Radin, "Residential Rent Control," *Philosophy and Public Affairs* 15 (1986): 350; Kenneth Salzberg and Audrey A. Zibelman, "Good Cause Eviction," *Willamette Law Review* 21 (1985): 61 (arguing for implication of just-cause eviction standard for leases).

27. See generally Haar, *Suburbs under Siege*, 175–85 (examining the activist role of courts in the *Mount Laurel* litigation and arguing the legitimacy of judicial intervention in pressing social issues such as housing); David L. Kirp, John P. Dwyer, and Larry A. Rosenthal, *Our Town: Race, Housing, and the Soul of Suburbia* (New Brunswick, NJ: Rutgers University Press, 1995), 112–14 (applauding the ability of the New Jersey Supreme Court to transcend the paralysis of the legislature and craft "broad remedies for systemic social problems").

28. See, e.g., *Lindsey v. Normet*, 405 U.S. 56, 74 (1972) (refusing to find a constitutional imperative for adequate housing and suggesting that the assurance of adequate housing is a legislative function).

29. *United States v. Sandoval*, 167 U.S. 278 (1897), discussed in chapter 2.

CHAPTER 14

1. Kotkin, Tseng, and Ozuna, *Rewarding Ambition*, 17.
2. Ibid., 19.
3. Ready, *Hispanic Housing*, 7.
4. *Housing That Works*, 5.
5. Tim Padgett, "Despite the Crash in Prices, Affordable Housing Still Lacking," http://www.time.com/time/nation/article/0,8599,1881482,00.html (posted February 25, 2009; last visited May 22, 2009).
6. *The State of the Nation's Housing 2008* (Cambridge, MA: Joint Center for Housing Studies of Harvard University, 2008), 25.
7. Nicholas P. Retsinas, "The Endangered Land of Renter-World," *Boston Globe*, May 5, 2006, A19.
8. *2008 Advocates' Guide*.
9. *State of the Nation's Housing 2008*, 30.
10. Ibid., 30–31.
11. Ibid.
12. Rodolfo F. Acuña, *Anything But Mexican: Chicanos in Contemporary Los Angeles* (New York: Verso, 1996), 93.
13. Eugene L. Grant, "Workplace Housing: New Tools for Solving the Affordable Housing Dilemma," *PSU Center for Real Estate Quarterly & Urban Development Journal* (1st Quarter, 2009): 24.
14. *Housing That Works*.

15. Peter Salsich, "State and Local Regulation Promoting Affordable Housing," in *The Legal Guide to Affordable Housing Development*, ed. Tim Iglesias and Rochelle E. Lento (Chicago: American Bar Association, 2006), 107.

16. Kenn, "Paradise Unfound," 77–81.

17. Salsich, "State and Local Regulation Promoting Affordable Housing," 92 (describing density bonus programs).

18. Rick Judd and Barbara E. Kautz, "Local Government Financing Powers and Sources of Funding," in *The Legal Guide to Affordable Housing Development*, ed. Tim Iglesias and Rochelle E. Lento (Chicago: American Bar Association, 2006), 295, 312 (describing Seattle's transferable development rights program, which benefits developers who produce or preserve affordable housing, and Monterey County's inclusionary zoning to spur affordable housing in new developments). See also http://www.bouldercounty.org/openspace/ces.htm (last visited July 30, 2009) (describing program of conservation easement transferable development rights saleable to developers in Boulder County, Colorado).

19. *Housing That Works*.

20. Davis, "Between Devolution," 368. For legal issues of inclusionary zoning, see Salsich, "State and Local Regulation Promoting Affordable Housing"; Michelle DaRosa, Comment, "When Are Affordable Housing Exactions an Unconstitutional Taking?" *Willamette Law Review* 43 (2007): 453 (confronting potential constitutional infirmities of these inclusionary development requirements); Laura M. Padilla, "Reflections on Inclusionary Housing and a Renewed Look at Its Viability," *Hofstra Law Review* 23 (1995): 539; *Home Builders Association of Northern California v. City of Napa*, 108 Cal. Rptr. 2d 60 (2001) (upholding city's inclusionary zoning ordinance requiring 10 percent of new units to be affordable housing based on local median income). Colorado's Supreme Court struck down the ski resort town of Telluride's inclusionary zoning law requiring developers to create affordable housing for 40 percent of the employees generated by new development. Because developers could satisfy the requirement by constructing housing with fixed below-market rental rates, the town ordinance violated state law prohibiting local rent control. *Town of Telluride v. Lot Thirty-Four Venture, LLC*, 3 P.3d 30 (Colo. 2000).

21. Roberta F. Mann, "The (Not So) Little House on the Prairie: The Hidden Costs of the Home Mortgage Interest Deduction," *Arizona State Law Journal* 32 (2000): 1347, 1393–96 (proposing a federal shelter tax credit with a location efficiency premium designed to reduce sprawl).

22. See 8 U.S.C. § 1188(c)(4) (addressing housing as condition to importing a temporary H-2A worker).

23. See Lise Nelson, "Racialized Landscapes: Whiteness and the Struggle over Farmworker Housing in Woodburn, Oregon," *Cultural Geographies* 15 (January 2008): 41 (detailing the struggle for approval of farm worker housing projects in Oregon's fertile Willamette Valley).

24. Delgado, "Rodrigo's Twelfth Chronicle," 675 (suggesting the dangers of settlements outside the city, away from public educational facilities and quality health care).

25. Michael Grunwald, "Why Our Farm Policy Is Failing," *Time*, http://www.time.com/time/magazine/article/0,9171,1680139,00.html (posted November 2, 2007; last visited July 29, 2009).

26. The federal Housing and Economic Recovery Act of 2008 permits nonitemizers to claim some or all of their real property tax obligation, at least for 2008 tax returns. A

majority (more than 70 percent in 2007) of Americans take only the standard deduction and thus cannot participate in the mortgage interest deduction.

27. Peter Dreier, "Federal Housing Subsidies: Who Benefits and Why?" in *A Right to Housing: Foundation for a New Social Agenda*, ed. Rachel G. Bratt, Michael E. Stone, and Chester Hartman (Philadelphia: Temple University Press, 2006), 105, 106 (2000 figures). See also Dorothy A. Brown, "Shades of the American Dream," *Washington University Law Review* 87 (forthcoming): 3, 12 (emphasizing that higher-income taxpayers in the 35 percent bracket receive greater benefits from the mortgage interest deduction than those in the 15 percent bracket, and estimating the mortgage interest deduction will amount to $94.5 billion lost revenue in fiscal year 2009).

28. Dreier, "Federal Housing," 107.

29. Ibid.

30. Alexander, "The Housing of America's Families," 1269.

31. Dreier, "Federal Housing." But see Brown, "Shades of the American Dream," 51 (rejecting a tax deduction for rent on the assumption that landlords would respond by increasing rents and thus defeat the goal of making housing more affordable).

32. Mann, "Little House," 1368 (suggesting that eliminating the home mortgage interest deduction would likely reduce home prices, citing estimates varying from 34 percent to minimal).

33. Brown, "Shades of the American Dream," 11.

34. See ibid., 41 (arguing for conversion of the mortgage interest deduction into a refundable credit, and citing then Senator Obama's tax plan in the 2008 presidential campaign as providing for a refundable credit).

35. Ibid., 44.

36. One of the ironies of segregation is the valuable community identity forged in ethnic or racial communities, such as Little Havana, Spanish Harlem, or East Los Angeles, that can serve as a cultural anchor for the particular group. Although neighborhood segregation has overwhelmingly negative effects on areas such as education, nevertheless the disbursal of a minority population through gentrification may destroy this cultural grounding, which is particularly vital when structural and societal inequalities persist against the group.

37. Protecting unspecified groups of underrepresented homeowners, of course, raises the complexity of how such groups would be defined—by race, national origin, age, or some other measure? Using racial/ethnic categories, Asian Americans would fall just outside this proposed standard, as their rate of homeownership as of 2008 stands at 59.1 percent, in contrast to the overall rate of 67.8 percent that year. Kochhar, Gonzalez-Barrera, and Dockterman, *Through Boom and Bust*, iv.

38. The 2009 credit allows the homebuyer to claim up to 10 percent of the purchase price as a credit, with a maximum of $8,000. As extended by Congress into mid-2010, the first-time homebuyer credit must be repaid if the home is sold within three years. The credit extension provisions also added new limits on the sale price of the home ($800,000) and taxpayer income, in addition to offering a lesser credit ($6,500) for qualified repeat homebuyers.

39. Although taxpayers eligible for the $8,000 credit might amend their previously filed tax return to claim the credit sooner, nevertheless those monies won't come before the home closing.

40. For example, assuming a $10,000 credit, if the purchase price is $100,000 with a 20 percent down payment, the lender would advance $90,000 at closing, requiring only $10,000 from the purchaser. The lender would receive $90,000 on the loan resale, thus making it whole, whereas the loan documents would reflect only the $80,000 repayment obligation.

41. Hinojosa-Ojeda, Jacquez, and Takash, *End of the American Dream*, 35 (proposing a 10 percent tax credit, capped at 3.5 percent of FHA loan limits, which in 2008 ranged between $271,050 and $729,750 depending on location, thus ranging between $10,000 and the mid-$20,000s).

42. See generally *2008 Advocates' Guide*.

43. Wendy Koch, "In Recession, Home Builders Reduce Square Footage," *USA Today*, January 9, 2009, 1A (reporting the downward turn of average square footage in the third quarter of 2008 to 2,438 square feet); Alex Wilson and Jessica Boehland, "Small Is Beautiful: U.S. House Size, Resource Use, and the Environment," http://www.greenerbuildings.com/feature/2005/07/13/small-beautiful-us-house-size-resource-use-and-environment (posted July 13, 2005; last visited December 14, 2008) (1940s and 1950s statistics); McGinn, *House Lust*, 23 (contrasting the robber baron mansions of the past that featured dozens of bedrooms with today's megahome that instead takes the same number of rooms found in a smaller home and supersizes them).

44. Wilson and Boehland, "Small Is Beautiful" (using statistics from 2002 of average new home size and 2003 for average family size).

45. McGinn, *House Lust*, 43.

46. Although undocumented Latino/as who suffer the most crowded living conditions might not submit tax returns for fear of interdiction, the possibility of immigration reform with a means of acquiring citizenship could alter that practice.

47. See Dickerson, "Myth of Home Ownership," 221 (listing states requiring subprime lenders to consider a borrower's ability to repay the loan). Also slated for reform is the yield spread premium that some lenders pay to mortgage brokers for delivering a loan that exceeds the interest rate the lender otherwise required. See generally Howell E. Jackson and Laurie Burlingame, "Kickbacks or Compensation: The Case of Yield Spread Premiums," *Stanford Journal of Law, Business and Finance* 12 (Spring 2007): 289. Now on the legislative radar screen, efforts in Congress to curtail the yield spread premium, such as in the proposed Mortgage Reform and Anti-Predatory Lending Act (H.R. 1728), thus far have not been enacted.

48. Vikas Bajaj and Ford Fessenden, "What's behind the Race Gap," *New York Times*, Week in Review, November 4, 2007, p. 16.

49. Peter Dreier and John Atlas, "The GOP's Blame-ACORN Game," *The Nation*, November 10, 2008.

50. Ibid.

51. *2008 Advocates' Guide*.

52. Dreier and Atlas, "GOP's Blame-ACORN Game."

53. See, e.g., *Vasquez-Lopez v. Beneficial Oregon, Inc.*, 152 P.3d 940 (Or. Ct. App. 2007).

54. Martha Argelia Martinez, *Promoting and Maintaining Household Ownership among Latino Immigrants* (South Bend, IN: University of Notre Dame Institute for Latino Studies, June 2007).

55. Jo Carrillo, "In Translation for the Latino Market Today: Acknowledging the Rights of Consumers in a Multilingual Housing Market," *Harvard Latino Law Review* 11 (2008): 5.

56. Ibid., 10–11 (discussing such alternate underwriting).

57. 122 Stat. 2654, Pub. L. 110-289, § 2124.

58. Carrillo, "Translation for the Latino Market," 13–16 (suggesting that another reform to boost the ITIN loan markets is the creation of partnerships among government agencies, banks, and community organizations, but pointing out the experience of political troubles with government subsidies of such loan programs).

59. Resolution 2.02, National Latino Congreso (adopted September 7, 2006), http://www.latinocongreso.org/resolutionsapproved.php?id=153 (last visited December 16, 2008).

60. *Discrimination in Metropolitan Housing Markets: National Results from Phase I HDS 2000* (Washington, DC: U.S. Department of Housing and Urban Development, November 2002) [hereinafter HUD Discrimination Report].

61. Raul Yzaguirre, Laura Arce, and Charles Kamasaki, "The Fair Housing Act: A Latino Perspective," *Cityscape: A Journal of Policy Development and Research* 4 (1999): 161, 163.

62. HUD Discrimination Report, 3–17.

63. Margery Austin Turner et al., *All Other Things Being Equal: A Paired Testing Study of Mortgage Lending Institutions* (Washington, DC: U.S. Department of Housing and Urban Development, 2002), 26.

64. Yzaguirre, Arce, and Kamasaki, "Fair Housing Act," 164. See also Apgar and Calder, "Dual Mortgage" (detailing other studies that attempt to account for credit history in answering the "risk or race" question and that conclude race and ethnicity are key in explaining the lack of access to prime financing by Latino/a and African American borrowers).

65. Steven W. Bender et al., *Everyday Law for Latino/as* (Boulder, CO: Paradigm Publishers, 2008), 38.

66. *2008 Advocates' Guide*

67. *Veles v. Lindow*, 243 F.3d 552 (9th Cir. 2000).

68. Bender et al., *Everyday Law*, 45 (noting that the tenant applicant nevertheless might prevail on demonstrating a less discriminatory alternative to the English-ability rule, such as requiring the tenant to obtain a translation and submit any housing complaint in English). In the case of mortgage loans, the federal Office of Thrift Supervision has warned banks that "requiring fluency in the English language as a prerequisite for obtaining a loan may be a discriminatory practice based on national origin" under federal housing antidiscrimination law. 12 C.F.R. § 528.9(c)(2). The landlord context does supply a potentially curative dynamic, however, as lenders would be hard-pressed to identify a sufficient business justification for English-fluency, whereas landlords might hide behind the pretext of a safety justification.

69. Cal. Civ. Code §§ 1632, 1632.5; see generally Carrillo, "Translation for the Latino Market," 1. At least one state (Arizona) requires lenders to translate their Truth in Lending Act disclosures into Spanish on request. Ariz. Rev. Stat. Ann. § 6-631.

70. An example of litigation claiming such discriminatory steering in violation of the federal Fair Housing Act and the Equal Credit Opportunity Act is *Ramirez v. GreenPoint Mortgage Funding, Inc.*, 2008 WL 2051018 (N.D. Cal. 2008).

71. Apgar and Calder, "Dual Mortgage," 121.

72. Engel and McCoy, "Credit Denial," 87 (noting the Department of Justice prosecuted no new lending discrimination cases after Bush took office).

73. See generally Charu A. Chandrasekhar, Note, "Can New Americans Achieve the American Dream? Promoting Homeownership in Immigrant Communities," *Harvard Civil Rights–Civil Liberties Law Review* 39 (2004): 169 (suggesting a violation might be shown if the discrimination is tantamount to discrimination on the basis of national origin, but recognizing the difficulties of proving such discrimination; also suggesting the potential for redress by noncitizens under the Civil Rights Act of 1870, 42 U.S.C. § 1981).

74. See, e.g., *Nguyen v. Montgomery Ward & Co.*, 513 F. Supp. 1039 (D.C. Tex. 1981) (ECOA doesn't proscribe credit denial based on lack of citizenship).

75. Mercedes Olivera, "Latinos Feel the Sting of Subprime Mortgage," *Dallas Morning News*, January 12, 2008, 6B.

76. *Understanding America's Homeownership Gaps: 2003 Fannie Mae National Housing Survey*, http://www.fanniemae.com/global/pdf/media/survey/survey2003.pdf (last visited December 18, 2009).

77. Been et al., "The High Cost of Segregation," 368–69.

78. HUD Discrimination Report, 3–17.

79. States such as Arkansas (Ark. Code Ann. § 23-53-104), Georgia (Ga. Code Ann. § 7-6A-5), Maine (9-A Me. Rev. Stat. Ann. § 8-206-C), Massachusetts (Mass. Gen. Laws Ann. ch. 184, § 17B 1/2), New Mexico (N.M. Stat. Ann. § 58-21A-5), New York (McKinney's Banking Law § 6-1), North Carolina (N.C. Gen. Stat. Ann. § 24-1.1E), Rhode Island (R.I. Gen. Laws § 34-25.2-6), and South Carolina (S.C. Code § 37-23-40) require borrowers of high-cost home loans to receive counseling on the advisability of the loan. One challenge is that financial products evolve so quickly that legal imperatives and financial literacy programs can hardly keep up. Financial literacy, then, must be regarded more as one potential safety net, rather than as a fix-all for injustice in the mortgage industry.

80. Bowdler, *Jeopardizing Hispanic Homeownership*, 8.

81. Willis, "Against Financial-Literacy Education," 261–62 (discussing high-school financial literacy courses mandatory in some states and elective in others). Some might argue that renting personal property at extravagant prices is superior to purchasing given the flexibility to terminate the contract. Similar arguments praise the freedom renters of real estate enjoy to relocate, but in both instances renters are vulnerable to exploitation.

82. Martinez, *Promoting and Maintaining Household Ownership*, 12.

83. See, e.g., Willis, "Against Financial-Literacy Education;" Dickerson, "Myth of Home Ownership."

84. Bradford, *Risk or Race?* 5.

CHAPTER 15

1. See, e.g., Kevin R. Johnson, *Opening the Floodgates: Why America Needs to Rethink Its Borders and Immigration Laws* (New York: New York University Press, 2007).

2. Jenny Jarvie, "Georgia Law Chills Its Latino Housing Market," *Los Angeles Times*, June 19, 2006, A4.

3. Damon Darlin, "By the Numbers: The Immigration Equation," *New York Times*, September 10, 2006, sec. 6, p. 32.

4. See, e.g., Gregory Scott Crespi, "Green Cards for Foreign House Buyers: A Way to Help Stabilize Housing Prices," *Tulsa Law Review* (forthcoming) (advocating a $40,000 minimum equity investment).

5. Julia Vitullo-Martin, "Save Our Cities," *Wall Street Journal*, March 30, 2007, W13.
6. Jarvie, "Georgia Law Chills."
7. Hinojosa-Ojeda, Jacquez, and Takash, *End of the American Dream*, 30.
8. Darlin, "By the Numbers."
9. Martin, "Napa Valley."
10. Cf. Haddad v. Gonzalez, 576 N.E.2d 658 (Mass. 1991) (landlord renting "deplorable" apartment to Puerto Rican woman suggested if she were cold, he would "come over at night and give her heat" himself. Apparently assuming Puerto Rico was a foreign country, he also threatened to have her deported).
11. Frank Sharry, "Bienvenidos a Election 2008: The Truth on McCain's Immigration Ad," http://www.huffingtonpost.com/frank-sharry/bienvenidos-a-election-20_b_127544.html (posted September 18, 2008; last visited October 26, 2008).
12. Becerra, *Hispanic Homeownership*, 10.
13. National Hispanic Leadership Agenda, *2008 Hispanic Policy Agenda*, 21.
14. Bender, *One Night in America*, 90.
15. National Hispanic Leadership Agenda, *2008 Hispanic Policy Agenda*, 21.
16. Agenda Latina, *The State of Latinos 2008: Defining an Agenda for the Future* (Denver: University of Denver Latino Center for Community Engagement and Scholarship, 2008), http://www.du.edu/newsroom/releases/media/agendalatina.pdf (last visited October 27, 2008), 37.
17. Ibid., 13.
18. *Construction Jobs Expand for Latinos Despite Slump in Housing Market* (Washington, DC: Pew Hispanic Center, March 7, 2007) (study released before the construction industry meltdown in 2007 and 2008).
19. *State of the Nation's Housing 2008*, 7.
20. *State of the Nation's Housing 2009*, 3.
21. Agenda Latina, *State of Latinos 2008*, 37.
22. Aired October 26, 2008; archived at http://www.edition.cnn.com/TRANSCRIPTS/0810/26/ldtw.01.html.
23. Chris Tilly, "The Economic Environment of Housing: Income Inequality and Insecurity," in *A Right to Housing: Foundation for a New Social Agenda*, ed. Rachel G. Bratt, Michael E. Stone, and Chester Hartman (Philadelphia: Temple University Press, 2006), 20.
24. Rachel G. Bratt, Michael E. Stone, and Chester Hartman, "Why a Right to Housing Is Needed and Makes Sense: Editors' Introduction," in *A Right to Housing: Foundation for a New Social Agenda*, ed. Rachel G. Bratt, Michael E. Stone, and Chester Hartman (Philadelphia: Temple University Press, 2006), 7.
25. Martin Waldron, "Chicanos Reject 2 Old Parties, Then Formally Found a 3d One," *New York Times*, September 5, 1972, 17 (La Raza Unida's platform also called for honoring the Mexican and Spanish land grants as well as for an end to real estate taxes).
26. Bender, *One Night in America*, 86–87.
27. Ward, *Colonias*, 129.
28. See, e.g., Mike Davis, *Magical Urbanism: Latinos Reinvent the U.S. City* (London: Verso, 2000), 101 (discussing an investigation by the *San Francisco Chronicle* that revealed the digital divide in Silicon Valley employment was fueled by rampant job discrimination against Latino/as). See also Hope Yen, "Pay Gap Wider for Minorities with Degrees," *Oregonian*, April 28, 2009, B7 (discussing census data released in April 2009 showing that

Latino/as with bachelor degrees earned only 75 percent of wages earned by similarly situated Anglos, the lowest ratio in more than a decade).

29. Myers, *Immigrants and Boomers*, 240–43 (demonstrating that for all ethnic groups successively higher educational attainment correlates with higher home values and earnings).

30. Collier and Quaratiello, *Land and the Zapatista Rebellion*, 64 (excerpting the Zapatistas' thirty-four-point agenda for negotiation in 1994 to include, "We demand an end to illiteracy among the indigenous communities, and for this we need better primary and secondary schools with free textbooks and university-trained teachers who are ready to serve the people, and not just the rich.").

31. Agenda Latina, *State of Latinos 2008*.

32. Richard Fry and Felisa Gonzales, *One-in-Five and Growing Fast: A Profile of Hispanic Public School Students* (Washington, DC: Pew Hispanic Center, August 26, 2008).

33. Ibid. (noting that foreign-born Latino/a students are more likely [35 percent] to live in poverty than U.S.-born Latino/a students [27 percent]).

34. *U.S. Census Bureau American FactFinder*, http://factfinder.census.gov/servlet/NPTable?_bm=y&-geo_id=16000US0620802&-qr_name=ACS_2006_EST_G00_NP01&-ds_name=&-redoLog=false (last visited July 30, 2008). Older Latino/a immigrants coming to the United States without high school degrees constitute a portion of this figure, but that doesn't alter the conditions for educational despair in East Los Angeles.

35. Patrisia Gonzales and Roberto Rodriguez, "Leave No School Behind," *Commondreams.org*, July 30, 2004, http://www.commondreams.org/cgi-bin/print.cgi?file=/views04/0730-08.htm (last visited August 20, 2008).

36. Agenda Latina, *State of Latinos 2008*, 23 (citing *Education Week* statistic). The Latino/a drop-out rate is 3.5 times higher than for Anglo students. Ibid.

37. Ibid., 22.

38. Fry and Gonzales, *One-in-Five and Growing Fast*, 9.

39. Agenda Latina, *State of Latinos 2008*, 24.

40. Deborah L. McKoy and Jeffrey M. Vincent, "Housing and Education: The Inextricable Link," in *Segregation: The Rising Costs for America*, ed. James H. Carr and Nandinee K. Kutty (New York: Routledge, 2008), 131.

41. Ibid., 130.

42. The Supreme Court ruled against a challenge in Texas by Mexican American students to this property tax approach to funding schools, rejecting the contention that the system violated the constitutional guarantee of equal protection. *San Antonio Indep. Sch. Dist. v. Rodriguez*, 411 U.S. 1 (1973). In contrast, California's Supreme Court relied on its state constitution to strike down the local control of school funding through property taxes, *Serrano v. Priest*, 487 P.2d 1241 (Cal. 1971), but poor communities there have seen little change for the better under the reformed system of finance. Jon Sonstelie, Eric Brunner, and Kenneth Ardon, *For Better or For Worse? School Finance Reform in California* (2000), http://www.ppic.org/content/pubs/report/R_200JSR.pdf (last visited July 30, 2008) (concluding that the shift from a localized to a state allocation of educational resources led more to a reduction in high-spending school districts than a raising of low-spending ones, and that the pinch caused by dramatic revenue drops after adoption of California's property tax reduction measure, Proposition 13, led to per pupil spending reductions from 1970 to 1997, a dramatic rise in student-teacher ratios, and to declining

student achievement, all relative to the rest of the United States. In turn, private school enrollment increased, particularly among higher-income families.).

43. Raymond H. Brescia, "Beyond Balls and Strikes: Towards a Problem-Solving Ethic in Foreclosure Proceedings," *Case Western Law Review* 59 (2009): 305, 325 (citing estimates of declines between $356 billion and $1.2 trillion).

44. Agenda Latina, *State of Latinos 2008*, 27.

45. Ibid., 22.

46. Sam Graham-Felsen, "Barack in East LA," *Organizing for America*, October 20, 2007, http://my.barackobama.com/page/community/post_group/ObamaHQ/CnYq (last visited May 10, 2008); see also Patricia Gándara and Frances Contreras, *The Latino Education Crisis: The Consequences of Failed Social Policies* (Cambridge, MA: Harvard University Press, 2009) (articulating a policy agenda for educational reform).

47. Agenda Latina, *State of Latinos 2008*, 39.

48. Ibid., 26.

49. Ibid., 25.

50. Ibid., 31.

51. "Middle of the Class," *The Economist*, July 14, 2005, 9.

52. National Hispanic Leadership Agenda, *2008 Hispanic Policy Agenda*, 7.

53. Ramos, "Educational Legacy."

54. Gary Orfield, *Reviving the Goal of an Integrated Society: A 21st Century Challenge* (Los Angeles: The Civil Rights Project/Proyecto Derechos Civiles at UCLA), 6.

55. Kochhar, Gonzalez-Barrera, and Dockterman, *Through Boom and Bust*, i (reporting 2008 statistics that 74.9 percent of Whites owned homes, in contrast to only 59.1 percent of Asians, 48.9 percent of Latino/as, and 47.5 percent of African Americans).

56. James H. Carr and Nandinee K. Kutty, "The New Imperative for Equality," in *Segregation: The Rising Costs for America*, ed. James H. Carr and Nandinee K. Kutty (New York: Routledge, 2008), 14.

57. See generally Stuart Banner, *How the Indians Lost Their Land: Law and Power on the Frontier* (Cambridge, MA: Belknap Press, 2005) (detailing the phases of deprivation that entailed government treaties, forced removal, the establishment of reservations, and mandatory allocations, as well as private action toward the same end of extracting desirable land from Native Americans, sometimes with compensation, but often accompanied by coercion, trickery, or violence. Some of the strategies perhaps unique to the Native American dispossession included the practice of purchasing tribal land from a dissenting faction without authority to bind the tribe. Sales of *ejido*-owned community property in the Southwest, however, have drawn the same complaint of an absence of legal authority to convey the common land. As in the Southwest, greedy lawyers also played a role in the dispossession of native lands. Ibid., 284–85 (discussing predatory lawyers exploiting unfamiliarity with the American legal system).

58. Ibid., 151–52 (debunking a book on land titles by a Massachusetts attorney general that belittled the agricultural prowess of Native Americans with descriptions such as the "carelessly tilled" fields of natives).

59. Robert J. Miller, *Native America, Discovered and Conquered: Thomas Jefferson, Lewis & Clark, and Manifest Destiny* (Westport, CT: Praeger, 2006), 120.

60. See, e.g., *Johnson v. M'Intosh*, 21 U.S. (8 Wheat.) 543 (1823) (embracing the discovery doctrine that consigns indigenous landowners to the status of occupants, with title

and the exclusive right to purchase those occupancy rights resting in the discovering sovereign; describing Indian tribes as "fierce savages, whose occupation was war, and whose subsistence was drawn chiefly from the forest. To leave them in possession of their country, was to leave the country a wilderness." Ibid., 590); *Lone Wolf v. Hitchcock*, 187 U.S. 553 (1903) (upholding the mandatory allotment system distributing individual parcels of reservation land and purporting to compensate the tribes for surplus land not allotted). See generally Banner, *How the Indians Lost Their Land*; Miller, *Native America*, 27–29, 56 (describing the vacant lands component of the discovery doctrine, known as terra nullius, by which the colonies could appropriate apparently unused land, and citing the Supreme Court's use of the concept); Lindsay G. Robertson, *Conquest by Law: How the Discovery of America Dispossessed Indigenous Peoples of Their Lands* (Oxford: Oxford University Press, 2005). Of course, the confluence of interest between Latino/as and Native Americans is complicated by the legacy of dispossession and subjugation of native tribes in what is now the southwestern United States, as well as those in Mexico, at the hands of Spanish colonists and missionaries who adhered to the same discovery doctrine and ideals of superiority.

61. "Life Is Bare Bones on the Lakota Reservation," http://edition.cnn.com/2009/POLITICS/08/13/king.sotu.economy/ (posted August 14, 2009; last visited August 17, 2009) (revealing 80 percent or more unemployment rates on a South Dakota reservation, and describing the housing of a tribal member in a tiny one-room shack with no utilities save for a rusted wood stove).

62. Robert F. Kennedy, *To Seek a Newer World* (Garden City, NY: Doubleday, 1967), 77 (acknowledging that compensation for redistributed lands will present serious difficulties).

63. Ibid., 79.

CHAPTER 16

1. Joe Rodriguez, "Despite Sign, Chavez Home No Longer Where It Once Was," Contra Costa Times, March 29, 2007, F4 (revealing that the one-bedroom wooden home in the Sal Si Puedes neighborhood that Chávez bought in 1952 was replaced with a duplex built by his brother in 1989).

Index

Acuña, Rodolfo, 132
Affirmative action, 144–45, 184
African Americans: discrimination against, similarities with Latino/as, 46, 49–51, 54, 100, 107, 162, 169, 184–85; gentrification of Harlem and, 114–16; political influence of, 119; potential tensions with Latino/a workers, 186; promoting homeownership by, 161; property covenants targeting, 85–88, 91; redress for past wrongs, 143; subprime mortgage lending and, 165; unemployment and, 179
Alianza Federal de Mercedes, 124, 131
Alien Land Laws, 71
American Family, 2
American Recovery and Reinvestment Act, 162, 183
Arechiga family, protest by, 121–22
Association of Community Organizations for Reform Now (ACORN), 165
Atrisco Land Grant, 26

Baja Boom, 138–39
Ballí Villarreal, Jose Manuel, and family's land grant battle, 130
Barnett, Roger, 62
Barrio Logan, 125
Bourland-Miller Commission, 25
Boyle Heights, 86, 88, 98; freeway displacement within, 103
Bracero labor, 30, 61
Brown Berets, 123
Brown v. Board of Education, 88
Bruce Church, Inc., 13, 15

California Land Claims Commission, 19–22, 25
Californios, 17–18, 24
Carson National Forest, 123–24, 127, 129, 190
Castro, Fidel, 107–8
Catron, Thomas, 23
Cesar Estrada Chávez Study Act, 189
Chávez, César, 8, 13–15, 181; and Forty Acres site, 189–90
Chávez, Librado, 14–15, 190
Chávez Ravine, 100–102, 104, 184, 190
Champaign, Illinois, zoning laws, 80
Chicano Movement, 123
Chicano Park, occupation of, 125
Chinese immigrants: discrimination faced by, 71, 76, 78; housing covenants against, 87
Cisneros, Sandra, 41
Clinton administration, 83, 132
Coachella Valley, 30–31
Cobb County, Georgia, zoning laws, 75
Colonia housing, 33–34, 148, 180; in Mexico, 137
Colorado, current land dispute, 129–30
Communal land grants: divestment of, 18–26; continued fight for, 123–35, 183, 190
Community land trusts, 157, 160
Community Reinvestment Act, 160, 165–67
Construction industry, 179
Consumer education, 172–4
Countrywide, 49
Court of Private Land Claims, 19–20
Covenants, restrictive, role in discrimination, 85–93

| 239

Credit scoring systems, 166–67
Crystal City, Texas, 4
Cuban Americans, 107–9
Cuban revolution: cause of Cuban immigration, 107; housing laws following, 108–10

Day laborers, 65–66, 190
Divestment of land grants, 18–26
Dobbs, Lou, 69
Dodger Stadium, 101–2, 121
Doolittle, John, 70
DREAM Act, 183–84

Eastern European immigrants, discrimination faced by, 76
East Los Angeles, 97–105
Education gap, 5, 180–84
Ejidos. *See* Communal land grants
El Barrio. *See* Spanish Harlem
Environmentalism, 163–64; and resistance to affordable housing, 37, 158
Equal Credit Opportunity Act (ECOA), 46, 169–70, 172
Equal Protection Clause, 68, 78, 80; and covenants, 88
Escondido, California, 67, 79
Exclusionary amenities, 90

Fairfax County, discriminatory ordinances, 77
Fair Housing Act, 46, 81, 83, 88–90, 169–71
Farmingville, Long Island, 77–80, 82–83
Farmers Branch, Texas, 67–68, 79
Farm workers: housing, 29–35, 37–38, 145–46, 159–60
Federal Housing Administration (FHA): covenants and, 86; creation of, 46
Federal Housing Finance Reform Act, 70
Fideicomiso, 138
Foreclosures, 54–56
Forever 21, 126
Fourteenth Amendment, Due Process Clause and, 82
Fraternity houses, zoning of, 82

Gates, Henry Louis, Jr., 185
Gentrification, 185; in East Los Angeles, 105; in Spanish Harlem and Harlem, 114–16
Gingrich, Newt, 132
Great Depression, 14

Hannah, Daryl, 126
Hanson, Victor Davis, 145
Hazelton, Pennsylvania: English language law, 66, 69; housing ordinances, 66–68, 72, 77, 177–78, 184
Hearst, William Randolph, 134
Hell's Kitchen, 116
Home Owners Loan Corporation (HOLC), 46
Homeownership: benefits and detriments of, 3–5; impediments to Latino/a ownership, 5–6; statistics for Latino/as, 2, 5
Homestead Act of 1862, 60
Housing and Economic Recovery Act of 2008, 157, 162, 166
Huerta, Dolores, 13–14
Hurricane Katrina, 74

Immigration and Nationality Act of 1965, 61
Immigration, undocumented: effects on housing reform, 145–46, 171–72, 175–78
ITIN loans, 69–70, 172

Kenedy Memorial Foundation, 130
Kennedy, Robert, 180, 187
Kobach, Kris, 65

Language barrier: education and, 182, 184; housing discrimination due to, 170–71; and mortgage lending, 52, 167; policies regarding, 173
La Raza Unida, 179–80
Large-lot ordinances, 80–81
Lawyers, role in dispossession, 21
Little Havana, 95–96
Loitering, 65–66
Long Island ordinance, 82

240 | *Index*

Lopez, Javier, 35
Los Altos Hills, California, zoning law in, 80
Los Angeles Affordable Housing Plan, 157–59

Manassas, Virginia, zoning laws, 75
Manufactured housing, restrictions on, 53
McCain, John, 178, 189
McKenzie, Evan, 89–90
Mexican Constitution of 1917, 134–38; Article 27, 134–36; "modernization" of, 135
Mexican revolution: and 1917 Constitution, 134–35; roots of 133–34
Mexifornia, 145
Minimum wage, 179–80
Minutemen, 62
Monterey, California, lost municipal land, 42
Monterey County, California, 42
Montoya, Joseph, 124
Mount Laurel, New Jersey: litigation surrounding, 154, 158; zoning in, 81

Napa Valley, 30–31
Napolitano, Janet, 65
National Fair Housing Alliance, 79
Native Americans, and discrimination against, 186
Nethercott, Casey, 62
New Hampshire, criminal trespass statute, 64–65
New Jersey Fair Housing Act, 81
New Jersey Supreme Court, 83
New Mexico, and land grants, 18–21, 23–5
North American Free Trade Agreement, 135–36, 138
Nuisance: criminal laws, 65; legal doctrine, 90; use for exclusion, 90–93

Obama, Barack, 178, 182–83
Operation Gatekeeper, 61, 70

Padre Island, 130
Pajaro Valley, 37
Protest: Arechiga family and, 121–22; as strategy in land disputes, 121; land occupation as, 121–26
Puerto Rican Legal Defense and Education Fund, 78
Puerto Ricans, housing, 113–17

Ranch Rescue, 62
Real property taxes, role in dispossession, 23
Redlining, 46
Restrictive covenants. *See* Covenants
Robledo Family Winery, 35

Salinas, California: agricultural significance, 37; farm worker housing in, 38; subprime lending in, 42–43
Salinas Valley, 37
San Diego County, 34
San Francisco, zoning laws, 78
San Miguel del Vado land grant, 20–21
Santa Barbara, zoning ordinance, 83
Santa Catalina Island, 123, 127
Santa Cruz County: agricultural significance, 37; farm worker housing in, 38
Santa Fe Ring, 23
Santa Cruz County, 37
Segregation, 49, 54–55, 87–88
Self-Help Ownership Opportunity Program, 148
Shelley v. Kraemer, 86, 92
South Central Farm, 125–28
Spanish-American War, 113
Spanish Harlem, 95, 114–17, 190
Statue of Liberty, seizure of, 122
Steinbeck, John, 39–43; reaction to criticism of *Tortilla Flat*, 41
Stereotypes: derogatory of Latino/as, 38, 167, 169, 174, 186; and literature, 39–43
Subcomandante Marcos, 136
Supreme Court, U.S., 20, 124, 186, 190; and housing discrimination law, 71, 77, 81–82; zoning laws, 85
Subprime loans, 47–56, 165–67
Sutter County, farm worker housing in, 32

Index | 241

Tancredo, Tom, 62–63, 69
Taxation: mortgage interest deduction, 160; housing tax credit, 161–63
Taylor Grazing Act of 1934, 61
Taylor Ranch, legal battle over, 129–30
Territorial Land Act of 1887, 71
Tierra y Libertad, origin of slogan, 1
Tijerina, Reies, 123–24, 131–33
Tortilla Curtain, 39–41, 190
Tortilla Flat, 39–43
Town of Paradise Valley, Arizona, zoning, 74
Treaty of Guadalupe Hidalgo, 18, 20, 98, 139, 184; Article VIII, 19; Article X, 18–19; GAO report, 131–32; occupations after, 123
Trespass, 60–65; in Arizona, 65–66
Trump Ocean Resort, 138–139
Truth in Lending Act, 52, 171
Tulare County, California, 4

United Nations Committee on the Elimination of Racial Discrimination, 142
United States v. Sandoval, 20–21, 25, 131

Valley Park, Missouri, 67–68
Vieques, Puerto Rico, 127
Villa, Pancho, 134

Wage gap, 5, 178–80
Waukegan, Illinois, zoning ordinance in, 83
Worm v. Wood, 91

Young Lords, 122

Zapata, Emiliano, 1, 134; and Zapatista movement, 1
Zapatista movement, 1, 136–37, 180
Zoning laws: exclusionary, 74–75, 80; occupancy restrictions, 75–83

About the Author

STEVEN W. BENDER is James and Ilene Hershner Professor of Law at the University of Oregon School of Law. He is the author of *Greasers and Gringos: Latinos, Law, and the American Imagination* (NYU Press, 2003) and *One Night in America: Robert Kennedy, César Chávez, and the Dream of Dignity*.